Chouinard

V

Alain Lipietz

Mirages and Miracles

The Crises of Global Fordism

Translated by David Macey

VERSO
The Imprint of New Left Books

British Library Cataloguing in Publication Data

Lipietz, Alain
    Mirages and Miracles: the Crises of Global
    Fordism.
    1. Economic history — 1971-
    I. Title   II. Mirages et miracles. *English*
    330.9′048   HC59

First Published 1987
© Alain Lipietz 1987

Verso
15 Greek Street, London W1V 5LF

Typeset in 10pt Garamond Book by
Leaper & Gard Ltd, Bristol, England

Printed by The Thetford Press
Thetford, Norfolk

ISBN 0-86091-152-7
ISBN 0-86091-865-3 Pbk

Contents

Tables and Graphs

Translator's Note

Earlier versions of sections of this book have previously appeared in English translation as 'Towards Global Fordism' and 'Marx of Rostow?', *New Left Review* 132, March-April 1982; 'Imperialism or The Beast of the Apocalypse', *Capital and Class* 22, Spring 1984; 'How Monetarism Choked Third World Industrialization', *New Left Review* 145, May-June 1984. Existing translations have been modified.

David Macey.

Introduction

'In science it is self-evident that concepts are going to change; that is to say that, you hope to learn something. This is not theology, after all. You do not make declarations which you must preserve unchanged for the rest of your life. By contrast, in the social sciences or in humanistic studies, positions are often personalized. Once you have taken a position, you are supposed to defend it, no matter what happens. It becomes a question of honour not to change or revise an opinion, (that is, to learn something). Instead you are accused of refuting yourself if you modify your position.'[1]

This is a time for doubts and for questions, a time when schemas fall apart and when every apostasy can be justified. New industrial powers rise up from the depths of extreme poverty. In the Third World, socialism is ravaged by war and famine. Guerrillas become ministers and run countries that were modernized by *gorillas*. Lepers and *flagellados* ('scourged ones') beg on the spotless steps of the banks. Those who once practiced self-reliance are opening their doors to transnational companies. Interest rates provoke hunger riots. Everything has become confused. The enemy has become an abstraction. This is a time for curses to be lifted and for miracles to turn sour.

And yet, twenty years ago, everything seemed so clear-cut, even if not every judge handed down the same verdict. The international division of labour divided the industrialized nations from the rest of the world. The industrialized countries exported manufactured goods; the under-developed countries exported mineral or agricultural raw materials, or migrant labour. According to the dominant liberal view of economics, it was all a matter of 'stages of economic growth';[2] the underdeveloped countries were simply

1

'behind' the industrialized countries in the same way that children are 'behind' adults. It would not be long before they reached adolescence ('take-off'), the 'industrial age' and then the 'post-industrial age', with integration into the world market speeding up the process.

In contrast, the heterodox currents – the Marxists, the 'dependency theorists' and the 'third worldists' –[3] argued that it was precisely those relations between the 'centre' and the 'periphery' – or, to use another image, between 'North' and 'South' – which precluded even the possibility of 'normal' capitalist development in the South. The dependency argument went roughly as follows. The North needed the South so that it could export its surplus. Moreover, most of the wealth produced in the primary sector in the South was transferred to the North via a process of unequal exchange. The industrial emancipation of the South would therefore be a form of aggression against the North, which, in turn, had the military capacity to ensure that it would never take place.

This thesis – and we will see later to what extent it was correct – had one great advantage over the liberal argument. It concentrated upon studying the links that bound economic spaces into international relations, and it saw the world economy as a system. Its weakness was that it paid little attention to the concrete conditions of capitalist accumulation either in the centre or on the periphery. It therefore could not visualize that transformations in the logic of accumulation in the centre would modify the nature of centre–periphery relations. Nor could it see, in consequence, that transformations in the basis of that logic within the peripheral countries would lead to nothing less than the fragmentation of the 'Third World' into a series of distinct developmental tiers.

The supporters of the dogma of the inevitable 'development of underdevelopment' were therefore caught off balance when, in the seventies, real capitalist industrialization began in certain 'peripheral' countries and when, during the same period, there was a marked downturn in the North. When this happened, some Marxists rallied body and soul to Rostow's arguments, and even went so far as to sing the praises of 'imperialism, pioneer of capitalism' because it promoted the development of the productive forces and 'the unification of mankind'.[4]

Others, like Palloix[5] and Frank, simply denied that anything new was happening. Frank responded to growth in the 'Newly Industrializing Countries' (NICs) by reasserting dogma: 'As the analysis of imperialism, dependence and the world system has emphasized, the very growth pattern of the leaders has been based upon, indeed has generated, the inability of the rest of the world to follow. The underlying reason is that this development or ascent has been misperceived as taking place in particular countries, whereas it has really been one of the processes of the world system itself. The recent export-led growth of the NICs is also part and parcel of capital accumulation on a world scale.'[6] According to Frank, the emergence of the NICs simply meant that emigrant workers were now being employed in their own countries. It did not alter the workings of the 'world economy'. Concrete reality – the class struggle, class alliances, and the specific dynamics of different social formations – was explicitly ignored.

Despite the undeniable formal superiority of the imperialism–dependency approach, it seems that, like the rival liberal approach (the 'stages of development'), it had degenerated into an ahistorical dogmatism by the end of the sixties. It is as though two theorists were contemplating the development of history, each of them wearing a watch that had stopped. If the South was stagnating, one theorist could tell you precisely what time it was: if 'new industrialization' was taking place, another would say it was time for 'take-off'. If the NICs were in crisis, the other would reply, 'I told you so.'

In order to get beyond this stalemate,[7] we obviously have to take into account the historical and national diversity of capital accumulation in each of the nation-states under consideration, beginning with the countries of the centre, but not forgetting those of the so-called periphery.

My ambition here is not, however, to outline 'The Correct Theory' of tendencies at work within the international division of labour, from the origins of imperialism until the present crisis. On the contrary, I would like first of all to put forward a few modest methodological points and to warn against the misuse of certain terms and concepts that we all use ('all' meaning, of course, those women and men who refer to Marxist theory, or, more generally to analyses using the concepts of dependency and domination). Their misuse explains the stalemate to some extent.

All too often, we reacted against the optimism (or cynicism) of liberal thought – and no doubt we will go on doing so – by presenting concrete history as the inevitable unfolding of a concept such as imperialism: thus indulging in what Bourdieu calls 'pessimistic functionalism'[8] by arguing that the world is as it is because it was designed to serve 'the interests of the powerful' or 'the interests of the system'. The very notion of an 'international division of labour' (not to mention an International Economic Order) suggests that there is some Great Engineer or Supreme Entrepreneur who organizes labour in terms of a pre-conceived world plan. Depending on one's tastes and style, this watchmaker's activity is the outcome of the efforts of readily identifiable subjects such as Multinational Companies or the Trilateral Commission, or the expression of the immanent needs of an ectoplasm which is as protean as it is Machiavellian: World Capitalism, the World Economy ....

Such tendencies can only lead, again depending upon one's style or upon the way experience affects one's personality, to either a banal pessimism of the intellect ('We can't do anything about it; the system is against us') or a new opium of the people ('It will soon collapse under the weight of its own contradictions'). And so we deny the living soul of Marxism and the basis for optimism of the will: the concrete analysis of concrete situations.

When researchers, or worse militants, adopt such attitudes, they abdicate their intellectual responsibilities. Every aspect of a real social formation is seen as resulting from the evils of 'dependency'. Every concrete situation is forced into the Procrustean bed of a schema established by some Great Author of the past, while anything that won't fit is simply lopped off.

In the following pages I will attempt to present, succinctly and in schematic form, the results of my work on how the present crisis is transforming the international division of labour.[9] I will not venture so far as to make a concrete analysis of the one hundred and fifty countries that make up the world or of their irreducible specificities. I leave that task to more competent specialists. The so-called 'socialist' countries have simply been omitted from this study in international relations. Their workings are so specific as to require a separate study.[10] Besides, it so happens that, from a strictly economic point of view, they played a fairly minor and even a diminishing role in the transformations that occurred on the periphery in the 1960-84 period. The only socialist countries that will be discussed here are those, which, like Poland or Yugoslavia, are articulated with the developed capitalism of the West in a similar way to the NICS.

And, naturally enough, I will cast caution to the winds. I will talk about old and new divisions of labour, the centre, the periphery, Fordism, 'bloody Taylorism', peripheral Fordism and other bold conceptualizations. I hope to show that these constructs can in some sense help us to understand the real world, while remembering that in other respects (or levels of abstraction) they are fit for the fire. A character who will have a certain role to play later puts it very clearly: 'The order that our mind imagines is like a net, or like a ladder, built to attain something. But afterward you must throw the ladder away, because you discover that, even if it was useful, it was meaningless. ... The only truths that are useful are instruments to be thrown away.'[11]

The reader has been warned. She would do better to burn this book without reading it, if all she is going to get out of it is a new collection of labels to stick on real nations and actual existing international relations without first analysing them carefully. Hopefully the first chapter will be an antidote to that.

The second chapter will review the methodological contribution made by recent work on regimes of accumulation and modes of regulation. This work helps us to grasp the various solutions which capitalism has found for its internal contradictions during the course of its history: the most recent being Fordism, the dominant form of the postwar period. It is only on this basis, which takes us beyond national diversities, that we can begin to identify, albeit in tentative form given the current state of research, the logic governing changes in relations between the central economies themselves, and relations between those economies and what, in a bow to a conceptualization which must be overturned, I will continue to describe as the 'periphery'.

The third chapter re-examines the historical development of centre–periphery relations in this light. Classical theories of imperialism and dependency will be shown to be misleading in that they give a timeless picture of a configuration which in fact belongs to a vanished period in the history of central capitalism, namely the period of extensive accumulation and competitive regulation.

The fourth chapter brings us to the heart of our subject: the novel phenomenon of the partial industrialization of the Third World, which will be shown to be the result of the various ways in which elements of the logic of Fordism have been extended to the periphery. In the fifth chapter, these developments will be related to political events in Southern Europe during the seventies and to what Nicos Poulantzas has termed the 'crisis of the dictatorships'. Finally, we will see in Chapter Six how the crisis in central Fordism combined with internal factors to destroy many of the 'miracles' of the seventies.

We will end by looking at what might be meant by a struggle against a world order which is in fact a monstrous disorder, even if it is less rigid than it might once have seemed. For this book would never have been written were it not for the outburst of indignation which in the sixties led the young people of the West to share the hopes of those fighting in the Third World against a system which enriched a minority while allowing the majority to sink into unremitting poverty. Even if we do now know that the relationship between wealth and poverty is not as mechanical as we once thought; even if the 'workings of the system' do not mean that oppressed peoples are irredeemably damned; and even if the most 'successful' roads to development are not the ones we wanted to see; the fact remains that even when 'growth' is achieved it is by brutal methods that, all too often, do nothing to alter the gross inequalities which make it impossible to speak seriously of the 'unity of the human race'. In terms of democracy the struggle has scarcely begun.

This book is therefore dedicated to my comrades, to my

friends, and to the women and men who continue to fight for a more just world order; especially to those in the Third World who taught me something about their countries, their problems, and their hopes.

1
Questions of Method

(this = a revised version of an NLR paper)

I would like, then, to begin with a warning against two common errors. The first consists of deducing concrete reality from immanent laws which are themselves deduced from a universal concept (Imperialism, Dependency). The second is simply the other side of the same coin: analysing every concrete development in terms of the needs of the said concept, or, to be more specific, analysing the internal evolution of national socio-economic formations as though they were merely parts of a musical score conducted by a world maestro, even if we do admit that the maestro is not himself a (bad) subject.

Imperialism, or The Beast of the Apocalypse

A few years ago, Umberto Eco, an Italian intellectual who has seen it all before but who is not totally disillusioned, published a remarkable detective novel entitled *The Name of the Rose*. It tells how William de Baskerville, a Franciscan Sherlock Holmes, solves a mysterious series of murders that take place in a medieval abbey. The murders seem to follow on from one another like the curses of the Apocalypse. By pursuing this line of investigation, William discovers both the murderer and the motive, and realizes that there is a specific reason for each murder. Each has its immediate

9

causes, and they have nothing to do with the Apocalypse. But (and this is the final twist) the murderer himself is convinced that he is acting out the scenario of the Apocalypse. At least one of the murders was staged accordingly. In the final analysis, he did play the role of the Antichrist – in a very specific sense.

William (who is of course primarily a mouthpiece for William of Ockham, the great English Franciscan philosopher of the Middle Ages, and one of the founders of modern rationalism, but who is also, in turn, a mouthpiece for C.S. Peirce, the American who founded semiotics) concludes that general laws are of weak help when it comes to analysing the complexity of particular events.

It is a very good novel, and a very instructive one. By conceptualizing, generalizing and turning our thoughts into dogma, we invented our own Beasts of the Apocalypse ... and then tried to deduce future developments in concrete history from their characteristics. In the sixties, we argued that the immutable laws of imperialism would inevitably widen the gulf between nations and that they would always lead to a polarity between wealth and poverty. And then we deduced an inevitable sequence of stages of development and underdevelopment. We forecast the impossibility of industrial development in the dominated countries. Yet what did we have to say when, in the seventies, Britain's decline accelerated, the USA slowed down, and the 'Newly Industrializing Countries' started to take off in imperialism's 'backyard'?

Some of us immediately began to retheorize everything and went back to other verses from the Apocalypse that prophesized a different but equally necessary future. Bill Warren dug out Marx's old text on how the Indian railways would bring capitalist relations in their wake just as surely as the productive forces were going to revolutionize the relations of production.[1] That, however, was one of the great prophet's more memorable howlers!

Others, meanwhile, began to reconceptualize history; forecasting that the Centre of the World Economy was going to shift to a vague but watery point somewhere between Tokyo and Los Angeles, and that a new international division of labour was going to emerge fully armed from some obscure upheaval in World Capital. And when in the 1980s the NICs began to be hit by the crisis, yet others who had believed all along in the old division of labour smiled knowingly and said, 'We told you so.' Needless to say, I did not avoid these traps either, and sometimes fell into all three at once.

The truth of the matter is that, as Lenin used to say, history has infinitely more imagination than we have. I mean by this the history of the human race, of an 'objective subject'[2] which makes its own history. It is not a subject with a project, but a vast body made of up millions of subjects struggling against one another. Its history is the history of their victories and defeats.

Marx, not to mention Mao Zedong, also warns us in very nominalist terms against the temptation to believe in the 'realism of concepts', against the idea that all we have to do in order to understand the Particular is to grasp the Universal. The Universal is no more than an intellectual systematization of our practical experience of the real, and it takes no account of the concrete nature of the real. According to Marx, concepts thus risk becoming fetishes: 'In the *language of speculative philosophy* ... I am declaring that "Fruit" is the "Substance" of the pear, the apple, the almond, etc. ... I therefore declare apples, pears, almonds, etc. to be mere forms of existence, "*modi*" of "*Fruit*". ... It is as hard to produce real fruits from the abstract idea "the fruit" as it is easy to produce this abstract idea from real fruits.'[3]

He makes the same point in the first version of the First chapter of *Capital*: 'If I say that Roman law and German law are both laws, I make myself understood. But if I say that law, that abstract thing, is realized in both Roman and German law, that is in concrete laws, the connection between the two becomes mystical.'[4] This methodological warning is not without its political implications; it is our capacity to analyse history that is at stake. In his critique of Mikhailovsky, Marx compares the proletarianization of the peasantry in Russia and in the Roman Empire: 'Strikingly analogous events which occur in different historical contexts can lead to very disparate results. If we study each of these developments in its own right and then compare them, we can easily find a key to understanding the phenomena, but we will never understand them by using the pass key of a historico-philosophical theory whose main virtue is that it is supra-historical.'[5] And as Engels argues in a letter to Schmidt, if we always define 'mammals' as animals which give birth to living young, we eventually have to 'beg the duck-bill's pardon.'[6] How much longer do we have to go on begging the poor thing's pardon?

The 'Habits of History'

Does this mean that no rational knowledge is possible in the face of the freedom of history? Are there no universal laws, no necessity, and therefore no science, no generalities and no concepts? Or as Adso, who plays Dr Watson to William's Holmes, says, 'If all laws limit God's freedom, can one conceive of necessary being which is totally polluted with the possible?' William (I mean the real William of Ockham) would say 'Yes'. Because, on the one hand, God in his freedom is subject to the principle of non-contradiction; therefore, not everything may happen. And because, on the other hand, the power of God is materialized in His creation, which is reified, objectified and therefore governed by identifiable regularities. It is a conditioned potentiality, conditioned by the habits of nature as it has been created.

Don't worry; I am not going to give a lecture on theology. But Spinoza did say 'God, or nature, if you prefer', thereby making a distinction between *natura naturans* and *natura naturata*. And Marx, who knew of only one science – that of history – made it quite clear that men make their own history, but on the basis of conditions inherited from the past.

If we cling firmly to dialectical materialism, there is then a scientific project for understanding history. It implies: 1) the study of the *regularities* which past struggles have imposed upon human relations; 2) the study of the *crises* which arise within those regularities because contradictions are only provisionally resolved; and 3) the study of the *changes* within those regularities that result from humanity's on-going struggles for or against freedom.[7]

In other words, the concepts we use do not drop from the

skies. Rather, they come from the partial systematization of a reality which is itself only partially a system. They then help us to recognize in other situations the general features they elucidate. Either they prove to be pertinent, and can help to liberate people who are oppressed by the habits of history. Or they prove to be ineffective and have to be modified or, if necessary, discarded. It also follows that a number of different partial systematizations or concepts can help to shed light on the same object. Neither sectarianism, concept-fetishism nor book-fetishism – which is even worse – are admissible in concrete analysis.

It is, of course, in studying the system of the world economy that we have to be most careful; Charles-Albert Michalet is quite right to stress that the system itself is no more than a process of partial totalization.[8] Economists study only certain aspects of it, even though we do flatter ourselves into believing (with some reason) that those aspects are 'determinant in the last instance'.

I would stress that our Masters were not unaware of the need for caution. I have quoted Marx and Lenin; now let me quote Cardoso and Faletto, the Fathers of dependency theory: 'The concept of dependence tries to give a meaning to a series of events and situations that occur together, and to make empirical situations understandable in terms of the way internal and external structural components are linked.'[9]

Unfortunately, it has to be admitted that the concept of Dependency, like the concepts of Modes of Production and Imperialism, soon takes on a life of its own. Too often these concepts plunge us into systems which are not intellectual servants which help us to understand the real, but masters which obscure the real, its specificities, its differences and its transformations. This is why fundamentalism must never prevent us from enriching our concepts, especially by using other concepts which are capable of grasping just what it is about the real that makes it stable enough to be amenable to conceptualization. This is the only way to come to terms with its evolution and its specificities.

Take the case of *the capitalist mode of production*. This is already a rich concept in that it identifies the stabilization of a certain system of human relations in certain countries at a certain time. We know its tendencies and countertendencies, the former from observation and the latter by deduction.

One of the great contradictions of this mode of production relates to its 'commodity' side. Although capitalists can organize production in their factories down to the last detail and can, given their habits and their calculations, establish there an 'iron law of proportionality',[10] in their dealings with the rest of society they behave like any other gambler: their products may or may not find a buyer at a price which makes production profitable (this is the famous 'realization problem'). Yet it works ... except, of course, when there is a crisis. In order to understand how it works we have to produce new concepts. A number of French research workers have proposed the concepts of *regime of accumulation* and *mode of regulation*.[11] I will describe these concepts in detail later, but we must first say a word as to their methodological status.

A *regime of accumulation* describes the fairly long-term stabilization of the allocation of social production between consumption and accumulation. This implies a certain correspondence between the transformation of the conditions of production and the transformation of the conditions of the reproduction of wage-labour, between certain of the modalities in which capitalism is articulated with other modes of production within *a national economic and social formation*, and between the social and economic formation under consideration and its 'outside world'.

In mathematical terms, a regime of accumulation can be described as a schema of reproduction. Regimes of accumulation exist because their schemas of reproduction are stable; therefore, not all regimes of accumulation are possible. There is of course no reason why all individual capitals should come peacefully together within a coherent schema of reproduction. The regime of accumulation must therefore be materialized in the shape of norms, habits, laws and regulating networks which ensure the unity of the process and which guarantee that its agents conform more or less to the schema of reproduction in their day-to-day behaviour and struggles (both the economic struggle between capitalists and wage-earners, and that between capitals).

The set of internalized rules and social procedures which incorporate social elements into individual behaviour (and one might be able to mobilize Bourdieu's concept of habitus here[12]) is referred to as a *mode of regulation*. Thus, the dominant regime of accumulation in the OECD countries during the postwar period – an intensive regime centred upon mass consumption – has a very different mode of regulation to that operating in nineteenth-century capitalism. In a gesture of homage to Gramsci, we now refer to it as *Fordism*.[13]

It should be noted that not every mode of regulation can regulate every regime of accumulation and that a single mode can take the shape of different combinations of *partial forms of regulation*. Indirect wages do not, for instance, have the same importance in the USA and in northern Europe.

The important point, however, is that the emergence of a new regime of accumulation is not a pre-ordained part of capitalism's destiny, even though it may correspond to certain identifiable 'tendencies'. Nor is the stabilization of a mode of regulation an expression of the needs of a regime of accumulation which emerges from Plato's cave and dictates its laws to us as though we were mere shades. Regimes of accumulation and modes of regulation are *chance discoveries* made in the course of human struggles and if they are for a while successful, it is only because they are able to ensure a certain regularity and a certain permanence in social reproduction. But, just as nature is full of oddities like duck-bills and toucans which survive in scattered colonies between the 'discontinuous equilibria' that punctuate the evolution of species, so the history of capitalism is full of experiments which led nowhere: aborted revolutions, abandoned prototypes and all sorts of monstrosities. It is pointless to attempt to fit all social formations into the framework of a regime of accumulation adapted to a model situation (such as Fordism). It is not simply that they do not necessarily all conform to *that* regime of accumulation; it may be that they conform to *no* stabilized regime of accumulation. In other words, they may simply be in a state of crisis.[14]

16

Pessimistic Functionalism

The above comments on the scarcity of examples of successful capitalism; on the scale of the contradictions it has to resolve if it is to get under way and go on reproducing itself; on the need to 'find' a suitable regime of accumulation and to 'set up' a suitable mode of regulation; and on the fact that the existence of concrete capitalisms is more improbable than necessary – should not be taken as meaning, *a contrario*, that 'if it works, it's because it has been designed to work', that the 'function' of a mode of regulation is to make a regime of accumulation work, that the Welfare State was invented 'in order to' make mass production go on smoothly, etc. ...

It is simply that a given regime of accumulation and certain forms of regulation stabilized at the same time because they allowed social relations to be reproduced for a certain length of time without a crisis arising. At best, we can adopt an *a posteriori* or almost metaphoric functionalism: 'It is as though ...'. It is as though the underdevelopment of the periphery helped capitalism to work in the centre. Which brings me to my second warning.

It is probably in theories of international relations that the tendency to lapse into functionalism or even finalism, which are both the outcome of a belief in systems, is most obvious, and that it inflicts most damage.[15] Ricardo and the supporters of the Heckscher–Ohlin–Samuelson theorem seem, for instance, to believe that the international division of labour is the result of some world conference at which brilliant economists explained to an admiring gallery of politicians that – given relative levels of productivity, collective preferences and the initial endowment of factors – the free play of market forces would ensure the optimal division of production, and that each participant then went home convinced not only of the virtues of free trade but that the law of comparative costs ensured that the lot that had fallen to his or her country was quite justified, and that they could therefore force it to adopt the requisite specialization.

The great achievement of the theoreticians of Imperialism and Dependency is to have swept aside these apologetic fables and to have shown that the undeniable empirical differences that exist between economic spaces are differences in wealth and power, and that those who found that this state of affairs worked to their advantage were more likely to rely upon the invisible handshakes of corruption or the eminently audible boots of the military to establish or maintain it, than upon the invisible hand of the market.

Going back to the tradition of Adam Smith rather than that of Ricardo, the Marxists and then the Dependency theorists demonstrated quite correctly that the existence of the 'uneven international development' of capitalism and the stabilization of a certain structure of trade did lead to a more rapid accumulation of capital in the centre because the contradictions of the capitalist mode of production were resolved in capitalism's favour in those countries. It is as though a regime of accumulation existed on a world scale, with the centre-periphery polarization acting as a regulator. They then baptized this state of affairs, or the tendency to impose and reproduce international relations which in one way or another favoured the accumulation of capital in the more developed countries, '*Imperialism*'. And they baptized the corresponding state of affairs or tendencies in countries with a less developed capitalism, '*Dependency*'.

Insofar as they are states of affairs, Imperialism and Dependency are realities: we can of course call a reality whatever we want to call it. But this is only one step away from saying that the regime was imposed (and I stress the impersonality of the grammatical form) on the dominated countries because certain zones *had* to perform the *function* of resolving capitalism's contradictions or, worse still, that 'someone' imposed those relations of domination *in order to* resolve its contradictions. As to whether one believes in finalism or in functionalism, that too is a question of style. One can either take the view that some conscious subject forced the periphery to serve the needs of the centre, or that some immanent world reality separated the centre and the periphery to serve its purposes in the same way that God divided the firmament from the waters of the earth.

Needless to say, the step in the direction of finalism and functionalism was taken very early. To restrict the discussion to the Dependency school, Cardoso took that step in very subtle fashion: 'There is no metaphysical distinction between internal and external conditions. In other words, the dynamic of dependent countries is one particular aspect of the more general dynamic of the capitalist world. That general dynamic is not, however, an abstract factor producing concrete effects: it exists both at the level of the particular modes of its expression in "the periphery of the system" and at the level of international capitalism's mode of articulation.'[16]

If matters had remained there, no real harm would have been done. Yet the belief in the 'realism of concepts' (the idea that there is some 'general dynamic' that exists *independently* of our intellectual reconstruction of the partial coherence which articulates countless particular dynamics) is already becoming a belief in systems (the whole is 'expressed' in the 'Particular modes' of its expression and in the articulation of their elements). This leads to both an implicit functionalism (which is not far removed from the belief that general dynamics create dominated modes in the same way that functions create organs) and a belief in the primacy of external causes.

Anyway, finalism and pessimistic functionalism are obvious from the outset of Baran's argument that 'the decisive point is that the economic development of the underdeveloped countries is profoundly antagonistic to the dominant interests of the advanced capitalist countries.'[17] This is certainly an admirable position, coming from an intellectual speaking from within the heart of the American Empire at the height of its power. And there are certainly enough arguments to back it up. But in theoretical terms, it is a very weak position. It provides the basis for a simplistic Third Worldism and, thirty years later, the revanchist New Philosophers had only to evoke the good conscience of the White Man choking back his tears to refute it.

I have no intention of exonerating Great Satans like America and Britain, Little Satans like France, or more abstract Great Satans such as Capitalism or the World Economy. I am simply saying that *results* should not be confused with *causes of existence*: that a body of partial regularities which 'forms a system' is not the same thing as a system which 'unfolds'. The formation of the international division of labour cannot be regarded as the deliberate or functional

organization of a system. Quite apart from the freedom of
history, the class struggle and competition between capitals,
we also have to take into account the way in which the
existences of nations and of State sovereignty compart-
mentalize the reproduction of social relations.

The State is in fact the archetypal form of all regulation. It
is at the level of the State that the class struggle is resolved;
the State is the institutional form which condenses the compromises which prevent the different groups making up the
national (or at least territorial) community from destroying
one another in an endless struggle (the point is not that
struggles come to an end, but that they rarely destroy
classes).

To argue that world capitalism has from the outset been a
single regime of accumulation with forms of global regulation is tantamount to saying that some sovereign power
established regular trade flows, codified and guaranteed universally applicable social norms and procedures, and then,
when the need arose, delegated its powers to local states
that were simultaneously established throughout the world.
It is tantamount to saying that every compromise and every
shift in the balance of power at any given point on the sur-
face of the earth corresponds to the need to adjust a totally
adaptable and perfectly homeostatic cybernetic system.

That image is as gloomy as it is unrealistic. The development of capitalism in any given country is first and foremost
the outcome of internal class struggles which result in
embryonic regimes of accumulation being consolidated by
forms of regulation that are backed up by the local state.
Within these national social formations, it may be the case
that relations with the outside world established long ago by
certain agents (trading companies, military expeditions,
etc.) proved not only acceptable but even useful to certain
dominant groups, and that they became decisively important
to the regime of accumulation insofar as the national social
formation can no longer function without them because
they resolve one or more of the contradictions inherent in
its mode of reproduction. When that happens, those
relations mould the local society's 'habits', become part of
its regular workings, and appear to have been 'designed
on purpose'. What has in fact happened is that certain

compatible relations have combined with one another. Other relations could have done so, but that would have been a different story.

We must, then, study *each national social formation in its own right*, using the weapons of history, statistics and even econometrics to identify its successive regimes of accumulation and modes of regulation. We must make a concrete analysis of their rise and fall, and see to what extent external factors did or did not have a role to play.

The stabilization of a regime of accumulation or a mode of regulation obviously cannot be analysed in terms of its economic logic alone. Such 'discoveries' are the outcome of social and political struggles which stabilize to form *a hegemonic system* in Gramsci's sense of the term: in other words class alliances based upon a consensus (and a varying degree of coercion) which shape the interests of the ruling classes, and sometimes some of the interests of the dominated classes, into the framework of a regime of accumulation.

The countries of the centre have often been analysed in this way, but the workings of the periphery (which is usually seen as a homogeneous reality, whereas it is in fact an infinite quantity of differentiated situations) are usually seen in terms of the needs of the centre.[18]

Does this mean that Satan (Imperialism as intentional practice) never intervenes in the underdevelopment of peripheral countries, or that national regimes of accumulation are simply juxtaposed and do not form a system? This brings us back to William de Baskerville's problems with the crimes of the mysterious Antichrist. He solved the mystery by looking for a chain of causes and for relations between signs, but he also realized that each situation was specific. It is true to say that in one sense all the murders were caught up in the contradictions of the same Benedictine institution and that, in a very specific sense, those contradictions did tend to generate an Antichrist. As to whether or not the hand of Satan was *directly* involved ... that depends which murders we are talking about.

I will say no more, as I do not want to give the plot away. It does, however, seem to me that this twofold answer applies equally well to imperialism. Capitalism does have general contradictions (though they are not always manifested in the same way, and their importance varies from one regime to another and from one dominant mode of regulation to another), and capitalism does 'work'. If imperialism did indeed find even a provisional solution for those contradictions, and if a particular chain of concrete causes did indeed generate and develop embryonic imperialist relations, then it is legitimate to say that imperialism developed because it resolved those general contradictions to the advantage of certain national capitalisms. But it was not created 'in order to resolve them'; it survived and developed *because* it resolved them. If other ways to resolve the contradictions are found, or if other contradictions appear, it may disappear, change, or persist out of habit. It is only in that sense that we can say that, the habits of History being what they are, the 'function' of imperialism is to resolve those contradictions (which is not to say that its 'function' is responsible for all the ills of the Third World).

Just as a manufacturer of machine-tools tries to do business rather than playing a role in 'Department One', but does at the same time fulfil that function, so class alliances in certain countries find it profitable to adopt international relations which give their country a peripheral function, or are forced to do so. And we can agree that, once centre–periphery relations have stabilized, there is indeed a world regime of accumulation (or an 'international division of labour') with specific forms of regulation (expeditions, wars, international treaties, subcontracting agreements, the international financial system ...).

How are we to reconcile 'national regimes of accumulation' and the 'world regime of accumulation'? As with the wave–particle duality, they are in fact two aspects of the same thing, depending on how we look at it. Thus, 'triangular trade' characterized both certain aspects of the Spanish regime of accumulation and certain aspects of the world economy's regime of accumulation during the Mercantile period, and what I will term 'peripheral Fordism' characterizes both certain NICs and certain aspects of the world economy in the seventies.[19] But in reality, struggles and institutionalized compromises tend to arise within the framework of individual nations; hence the methodological priority given to the study of each social formation in its own right (and in terms of its relations with the outside world) or, to take up the terms of an old debate, to *the primacy of internal causes.*

Just a moment. Someone is sure to object that 'external' and 'internal' are not mutually exclusive terms, that we cannot seriously overestimate the power of a young state's laws, and that uncertain frontiers are no real defence against the power of capital. I quite agree. We can see from the examples of Chile, Poland and Afghanistan that foreign intervention, and sometimes even the threat of foreign intervention, can interfere decisively with local struggles. It happens every day in Africa, and it has been known to happen in France, both under the Vichy regime and in the days of the Burgundians and the Armagnacs.

That is the whole point. If we regard the dominant strata within dominated countries simply as puppets of foreign powers or if we make a broad distinction between the 'world bourgeoisie' and the 'peoples of the world', we will be unable to analyse the infinite number of divergent interests which, intellectually, we group into force fields, but which are in fact simply pursuing local or locally materialized interests.[20] In reality they are no more than partially integrated, and it is through the State that they find their overall expression. Even if economic interests and transnational ideological pressures do abolish frontiers, it has to be remembered that the form in which those pressures and interests are integrated is still the State form (even though not all territories have 'reached' that form, and even though certain territories claim that it has already been 'transcended').

Can we go so far as to say that determinate agents such as foreign states or companies deliberately create or maintain imperialist relations because they know that they will resolve certain problems? Yes, of course, but this is not necessarily the case. Wars and coups d'état have been fomented to keep markets open, to get hold of raw materials or to keep control over a badly-paid labour-force. That has always happened, it still happens, and it will go on happening. But if we always explain the destiny of dominated nations in terms of obvious Machiavellian interventions by dominant groups, we confuse specific cases with generalities. Worse still, we confuse a state of affairs characterized by certain economic relations with the result of specific actions on the part of a limited sector, with actions designed to produce that result. In many cases, that sector may in fact have been pursuing non-economic aims, and it may have achieved results that were not intended.

First and foremost, the outcome is the result of internal conflicts or of a consensus (influenced by varying degrees of coercion) to 'choose' a particular regime of accumulation. In each case, the 'choice' induces the national social formation to a specific position within the hierarchy of nations, but that position itself is not predetermined. No matter how stable the hierarchy may seem, and no matter how coherently it may function, it is no more than the product of an uncertain process.

The 'needs of central capitalism' approach tells us nothing about the successes of North America, Japan or Prussia, and nothing about the relative destinies of Australia, Canada or Argentina. In fact it probably leads us wildly astray when it comes to both Canada and Argentina.

Matters are obviously rather different when it comes to colonies. These are territories without a State and they are subordinated to the policies of the metropolis, though not without considerable resistance, and therefore not without compromises. In terms of the needs of dominant metropolitan groups they are obviously functional (even though Spain certainly did not know the price it would have to pay for having certain colonies as opposed to others). Similar arguments apply at the regional level.[21] The 'needs of central capitalism' approach should be questioned primarily when applied to formally independent states with a relatively autonomous field of class struggle.

This is the case, then, with former colonies in Latin America from the early nineteenth century onwards and with some former British Dominions – particularly Canada and Australia – at the end of that century. It is significant that when Frank raises this issue, he uses the language of the Apocalypse, arguing that from the 1820s onwards, 'both Canning and Bolivar were giving expression to the historical process that, if not Providence, world capitalist development held in destiny for Latin America.[22] He then quite rightly reverts to the language of concrete analysis, providing a detailed description of the key role played by the defeat of an 'internal' bourgeoisie which wanted to develop manufacturing industry at the hands of a liberal bourgeoisie based in the import–export sector. If the struggle had been won by the internal bourgeoisie, there might have been a Latin American Prussia or a Latin American Japan. But in that case, what does 'world capitalist development' have to do with it? It is simply a concept which helps us to grasp and intellectually synthesize the outcome of concrete processes. It certainly does not predetermine the destiny of any particular country.

To Conclude: Beware of the 'International Division of Labour' and Other Labels

Whilst no immanent destiny condemns a particular nation to a particular place within the international division of labour, a provisional solution for the immanent contradictions of capitalism can at times be found (and I insist that is a matter of chance discoveries) in deviations and differences between regimes of accumulation in different national social formations. In such periods, a *field* of possible positions, in other words a range of mutually compatible national regimes of accumulation, does exist, but positions within it are not allocated in advance. The ruling classes of various countries can refer to a number of 'models'. The ruling classes of the dominant countries dream of reducing other countries (which may be already dominated or still autonomous) to a peripheral status devised in other circumstances. Social alliances within the dominated countries develop strategies which may, depending on the state of the internal class struggle, lead to either dependency or autonomy. But not all national social formations can be 'dominant' at the same time.

Having chased the ghost of World Capitalism out of the door, I am not about to let it come back through the window. Something which 'forms a system' and which we intellectually identify as a system precisely because it is provisionally stable must not, I repeat, be seen as an intentional structure or inevitable destiny because of its 'coherence'. Of course it is relatively coherent; if it were not, we would have international conflict and there would be no more talk of systems. But its coherence is simply the effect of the interaction between several relatively autonomous processes, of the provisionally stabilized complementarity and antagonism that exists between various national regimes of accumulation.

Centre-periphery relations, to use a widespread conceptualization, are not direct relations between states or territories which are caught up in a single process. They are *relations between processes*, between processes of social struggle and between regimes of accumulation that are to a greater or lesser extent introverted or extraverted. Relations between processes obey constraints of compatibility similar to those which regulate the process of capital valorization within a schema of reproduction: world output of equipment goods must equal world demand for equipment goods, and so on. And as we well know, schemas in which everyone produces and exchanges the same things do not 'help' to resolve the contradictions of capitalism.

World labour and its products are, then, unequally allocated between various countries. We refer to this phenomenon as the 'International Division of Labour', but we can now see that the term is as deceptive and probably as deliberately confusing as the concept of 'Actual Existing Socialism'.

When we speak of the International Division of Labour, we all too often imply that labour is internationally allocated in accordance with the 'iron law of proportionality', with the same principles and the same optimal level of organization that prevail within capitalist units of production. The international division of labour is in fact more akin to the division which exists *between* capitalist units. It does lead to a certain order (the famous 'schemas of reproduction'), but that order is mediated by the effects of arbitrary and unregulated competition, by generalized warfare and dirty tricks, and by relations of domination. Similarly, the actual existing division of labour is simply the outcome of various nations' attempts to control one another or to escape one another's control, of one or another class alliance's unremitting efforts to achieve or surrender national autonomy. It is not an expression of the needs of 'World Capitalism', except insofar as the existence of world capitalism does logically pre-suppose some regularity in the allocation of labour. It is, I repeat, a chance discovery, or rather the result of attempts to resist or adopt chance discoveries.

As we shall see, certain economic and financial groups do in fact try to manoeuvre their way across the chessboard of 'unequally developed' nations and regions by fragmenting the labour-process in their branch across pools of labour characterized by different types of wage relations (i.e., con-ditions of the sale and use of labour-power). They quite consciously organize an internal geographical division of labour, and it is true that the generalization of such practices does consolidate a new international division of labour.

It would, however, be quite wrong to conclude that this new international division of labour is simply the outcome of organizational activity on the part of multinational com-panies. The field can only be structured because the multi-nationals' project coincides with a decision on the part of the ruling classes of certain countries to gamble upon what we will term an 'export-substitution strategy', and that can, as we shall see, involve a number of different internal regimes of accumulation ('bloody Taylorism', 'peripheral Fordism'). The studies produced by Michalet's team show that multinational companies do not normally relocate cer-tain segments of the production process in order to establish a new international division of labour.[23] The capitalists of the centre are usually more concerned with getting around trade barriers erected by peripheral coun-tries and with off-loading their manufactured goods in accordance with the 'old' division of labour.

A final word has to be said about the objective nature of positions within the 'field' of unevenly developed national social formations. It is fairly easy to give a stylized des-cription of these positions by using conceptualizations such as 'centre of the world economy/semi-periphery/periphery', 'developed countries/underdeveloped countries', 'raw-material exporters/industrialized countries', 'introverted countries/extraverted countries', 'sub-imperialism', 'NICS', etc. It is much more difficult, and indeed dangerous, to apply any one of these labels to a given country, and it is still more dangerous to describe a country on the basis of the label we give it or which it adopts.

The 'field' itself varies as regimes of accumulation in different countries (and therefore the dominant international regime) change. This does not simply mean that one country takes another's place or that the 'centre of the world', as Wallerstein or Braudel would put it, moves from one country to another.[24] It is the very texture of the field which changes. The centre was once a city (Amsterdam), and then it became a country (England, the USA), but there is no reason why there should not be several centres or why the system should take the form of a network organized around a centre. Why should we try at all cost to find a predecessor for England or a successor to the USA?[25]

More seriously, the field is in fact a *quasi-continuum* of situations, local regimes and modes of insertion into the world economy. Certain countries appear to *typify* certain internal regimes of accumulation or certain modes of insertion, and we spontaneously tend to classify countries by referring to these models. Once they have been classified, we tend to think that it is the abstract category which determines the specific features of each country (even though we can never quite agree as to which country belongs to which category). But if we put Argentina into the same category as some Caribbean banana republic[26] on the grounds that 'its exports are mainly raw materials', we are going to have problems with Canada.

National situations are no more separable by classificatory barriers which define the essence of their position in international relations than are Boltanski's social classes.[27] There are of course typical cases, classic 'centres' and classic 'peripheries'. Both theoretical work and empirical criteria reveal certain similarities (the NICS). In other cases – 'OPEC', 'The Group of 77', etc. – self-designation comes into play. When a classification becomes widely accepted, it becomes an objective reality, if only because the countries that have been 'grouped together' try to form alliances with their 'fellows' in order to defend their 'common interests', though they may well alter their stance in the light of other character-istics which seem to justify other alliances. This real political solidarity or material recognition of being in roughly the same position must of course be taken into account.

But when labels make us forget concrete analysis, and when we enter into metaphysical debates as to whether such and such a country belongs in such and such a category because it is 'already fairly extraverted', because 'it exports so many raw materials' or 'so few industrial goods'; we are heading for disaster. Matters become even worse when basic characteristics are deduced from these categorizations; when we are so blinkered that we see only those aspects of the concrete reality of a country that correspond to the appropriate category (foreign companies controlling the export sector, etc.).

Beware of labels. Beware of the International Division of Labour. Look at how each country 'works', at what it pro-duces, and for whom it produces it. Look at how and why specific forms of wage relations and regimes of accumu-lation developed. And be very careful about 'casting a net' over the world in an attempt to grasp relations between regimes of accumulation in different national social formations.

2
The Fortunes and Misfortunes of the Central Regime of Accumulation: Fordism

Armed with these caveats, we can now attempt to make sense of the latest episodes in a tale full of sound and fury and drenched in blood and mud: the invention and diffusion of capitalism, the expropriation of the peasantry, 'bloody legislation' and forced labour, the rediscovery of slavery and serfdom, the violent colonization of the greater part of the world, crises, strikes and wars ...

In order to do so, we must first describe our conceptual tools (our 'scaffolding'), which we derive from the work of Marx. We will then further specify the notions of 'regime of accumulation' and 'mode of regulation' via a brief examination of the twofold rupture brought about in both the production process and overall regulation by the emergence (again from crisis and war) of a central regime which came into its own in the post-1945 period: Fordism. Then we will examine the international economic configuration when that model was in its heyday and outline the first stages in its crisis.

This chapter will of necessity be schematic. Quite apart from the fact that its major theses have been developed elsewhere,[1] its main purpose is simply to set the stage for the rest of the book. If we wish to understand what is happening 'on the periphery' (pragmatically defined as that part of the world in which the regime of accumulation found in the most developed capitalist countries has not been able to take root), we must begin by looking at what is happening in the advanced capitalist world. As we shall see, different things happen there at different times, as it is not always the same contradictions that come to the fore. We can therefore expect considerable mutations to occur in the relationship between the central regime of accumulation and the rest of the world, and we can expect those mutations to open up the *possibility* (not the necessity) for different periphery-centre relations and, given local social struggles, for the discovery of different models of peripheral development.

(In Chapter 3 we will go back to what was happening on the periphery while Fordism matured in the centre. Later chapters will take up the thread of the story by examining the development of its crisis, with particular reference to events on the periphery.)

Conceptual Reminders

Marx made his essential contribution by stressing the importance of the social relations established within the process of production. Both his theory of exploitation and his theory of the stages of the development of the capitalist organization of labour derive from that insight. At the same time, Marx was even more aware than most economists of his day of the specific problems raised by the circulation of revenue and products within a market economy. In particular he emphasized that the reproduction of a market (capitalist) economy implies a close connection between the production and circulation of commodities and revenue. It is not sufficient to produce commodities, a buyer must also be found.

Ay, there's the rub. We know that the capitalist mode of production is a combination of two basic relations: commodity relations and wage relations.[2]

Commodity relations. The owners of units of production organize the investment of labour and put the product of that labour on the market. The product of different labour processes takes the form of a value which has to be socially *validated* by being exchanged for money, in other words by being *realized* or sold.

Wage relations. The owners of the units of production buy labour-power from wage-earners in exchange for a quantity of money whose value is inferior to the value added by their labour, the difference between the two being surplus-value. The wage-earners do at least have the advantage of being paid, but in return they have to submit to the work discipline and the organization which the capitalist imposes in the factory.

For the capitalist matters are in a sense more complicated. The *individual* capitalist owns a sum of money which he exchanges for means of production, notably fixed capital (investment) and labour-power. He organizes the process of production, sells the commodities (if he can), and *accumulates* more capital and surplus-value. The initial value he owns is therefore a *value-in-process* and it will in time increase, *provided that he invests and valorizes it correctly.* At the same time, the wage-earner spends his wages and thus reconstitutes his labour-power for the next cycle. Both wage relations and the market division of labour are thus reproduced. We also know that, broadly speaking,[3] *the rate of profit* (the ratio of surplus-value to capital) is positively determined by *the rate of surplus-value* (the ratio of surplus-value to value-added) and negatively determined by the 'organic composition of capital' (the ratio of value added to capital invested). Both these factors are themselves determined by norms of production (which determine productivity and the coefficient of per-capita fixed capital) and by norms of consumption by wage-earners.

But what *social* guarantee is there that all capitalists (or if not 'all', the vast majority of them) will sell their commodities, and that all wage-earners will sell their labour-power? In classical terms, this is the problem of 'social demand'. Now demand is prestructured by the distribution of revenue and by the availability of money to buy the conditions of production. When the product is 'realized' in the form of money, the agents who control the units of production can expand production by reinvesting their turnover and can thereby help to recreate demand, and so on.

Moreover, the times of production and circulation are articulated with another form of temporality: that of technical change, which is itself an effect of the accumulation of capital under conditions defined by the present state of the conflict between those involved in production and distribution, in other words between wage-earners and capitalists. Those conditions are, however, further defined by other social classes (rentiers, small independent producers, etc.). in both 'value' and 'volume' terms, then, the structure of supply and demand is determined by the transformation of both norms of production (per-capita capital, increases in productivity), norms of distribution (division of economic surplus into wages, profits, rent, etc.), and norms of consumption (life-styles of different classes, etc.).

As we have already seen, the term *regime of accumulation* refers to a systematic and long-term allocation of the product in such a way as to ensure a certain adequation between transformations of conditions of production and transformations of conditions of consumption. A regime of accumulation can be defined in terms of a *schema of reproduction* which describes how social labour is allocated over a period of time and how products are distributed between different departments of production over the same period. *Departments* can be defined as divisions within the productive system based on requirements of reproduction and accumulation (but without any necessary reference to the technical constraints of concrete labour). A schema of reproduction is in a sense the skeleton of a regime of accumulation or a mathematical diagram of its social coherence.

In its simplest form, the division involves two departments: Department 1 (production of means of production) and Department 2 (production of articles of consumption). It can of course be further refined into sub-departments. Thus, Department 1 can be subdivided into 'production for Department 1' and 'production for Department 2', whilst Department 2 can be subdivided into 'production for wage-earners' and 'production for the ruling classes' (sometimes referred to as 'Department 3'). If international trade is taken into account, an export department can also be identified. In fact any macroeconomic function of production allows us to identify a corresponding department.[4] The existence within a socio-economic formation of other forms or modes of pro-

NB.

in articulation with capi-
...es of accumulation.[5] In such
...efined in terms of modes of
...us ways to perform macro-
...te the income of different
... not to be confused with
...which relate to the concrete

⇐

...nomic studies have revealed
...f regimes of accumulation. A
...primarily *extensive* or pri-
...hether capital accumulation
...f production (with constant
...ther the capitalist reorgan-
...ubordination' of labour to
...ivity or the coefficient of
...that the *centre* of the pro-
...ls the pole which structures
...on, may also shift from one
...loix notes,[6] capitalist pro-
...ntred upon the exchange of
...s-value (Department 3), for
...l) and for variable capital
...al distinction must be made
...oductive apparatus and its
...new norms of production

⇐

ext.
vs.
int.
regimes

✳ NB

...me of accumulation which
...capitalist countries between
...d the First World War was
...l upon the extended repro-
...n. Since the Second World
...regime has been intensive
...mass consumption.

⇐

...not, however, some disem-
...e ethereal world of schemas
...to be realized and to repro-
...e, there must also be insti-
...habits which either coerce
...nform to its schemas. These
...a *mode of regulation*. Not

mode
of
regulation
df'd

every mode of regulation is suitable for every regime of accumulation. Economic crises, which appear to interrupt extended reproduction for varying periods of time, may in fact be manifestations of a variety of conjunctures.[7]

'Minor crises' simply sanction a latent failure to adjust individual behaviour and expectations to the potentialities and needs of the regime of accumulation. Ultimately, they reestablish the unity of the circuit, and they are a normal element in regulation ('*crisis in regulation*').

'Major crises' indicate that the mode of regulation is not adequate to the regime of regulation either because the emergence of a new regime is being held back by outdated forms of regulation (as in the crisis of 1930) or because the potential of the regime of accumulation has been exhausted, given the prevailing mode of regulation (this is probably true of both the crisis of the late nineteenth century and of the present crisis).

The major crisis of the 1930s can in fact be analysed either as the first crisis in intensive accumulation or as the last crisis in '*competitive regulation*'. That mode of regulation was characterized by the *a posteriori* adjustment of the output of the various branches to price movements, and by price movements which were highly responsive to changes in demand. Wages were adjusted to price movements so that direct real wages were either stable or rose slowly. Such a mode of regulation was relatively adequate to extensive accumulation with only minor changes in norms of production and consumption.

Within that mode of regulation, the tentative search for an outlet for various capitals which could not forecast their collective growth with any accuracy was an ever-present problem, and the possibility of overproduction on either a local or a general scale was a persistent danger: hence the importance of the question of markets, particularly those 'outside capitalism', to which we will return in the next chapter. But in the aftermath of the First World War, the generalization of new forms of work organization (the Taylorist and then the Fordist revolutions) led to unprecedented rises in productivity (of the order of 5 to 6 per cent in France, as opposed to an average of 2 per cent since the first industrial revolution). Under competitive regulation final demand did not keep pace with the rise in productivity. The boom caused by the enormous increase in *relative surplus-value*[8] in the 1920s gave way to a major crisis of over-production in the 1930s.

Fordism: A Well-Regulated Regime of Accumulation

After the Second World War, an intensive regime of accumulation centred upon mass consumption became generalized because a new '*monopolistic*' mode of regulation incorporated both productivity rises and the corresponding rise in popular consumption into the determination of wages and nominal profits *a priori*. Thanks to the original insights of Gramsci and Henri de Man, this regime is now known as 'Fordism'. The term refers to two phenomena which are theoretically linked but which are also relatively distinct and subject to historical – and, as we shall see, geographical – variations.

In the 1920s, a revolutionary mode of work organization became generalized in the USA and, to a certain extent, in Europe. This was Taylorism, the process whereby the skills of worker collectives were expropriated and systematized by engineers and technicians using methods of 'Scientific Management'. A further step was taken when that systematized knowledge was incorporated into an automatic system, with machines dictating working methods to workers whose initiative had been expropriated. This was the 'productive aspect of Fordism'.[9] It should, however, be noted that the presence of skilled workers was still necessary at every level of the branches that were Taylorized and then Fordized. This was particularly true in the metal-working industries, and even more so in the key areas where 'incorporation' took place, the branches manufacturing industrial equipment goods and machine-tools that constitute the 'heart' of the productive apparatus.[10] It should also be noted that Taylorization presupposed *from the outset* that the labour-force possessed certain skills or at least a certain 'industrial culture'.

Once the process got under way, it led to a rapid rise in

labour productivity and, thanks to mechanization, to an increase in the per-capita volume of fixed capital.[11] As we have noted, this rise in productivity led to the over-production crisis of the 1930s. To use a famous formula, mankind had set itself a problem which it took fifteen years and a gigantic conflict between nations, classes and political projects to solve.

It did so by discovering a new mode of regulation which allowed Fordism to develop fully. A new element was introduced: the continual adjustment of *mass consumption* to rises in productivity. This adaptation led to huge changes in the life-style of wage-earners – to its 'normalization' and to its incorporation into capitalist accumulation itself.[12]

After the period of reconstruction in Europe, which was by its very nature extensive, and the Korean War, the OECD countries experienced a new intensive wave which was to last for twenty years and which was to result in a considerable rise in both productivity and in per-capita fixed capital. But this time the rise in the purchasing power of both productive and non-productive wage-earners matched the rise in productivity almost exactly. The rise in productivity was much the same in both departments. Both the organic composition of capital and the sharing-out of value-added (the rate of surplus-value) remained almost unchanged.

More detail will be given later. For the moment, these developments allow us to paint a stylized picture of the 'Golden Age'.

The Golden Age

There are two main aspects to the Golden Age model:[13]

1) Overall technical composition (a rough equivalent to per-capita fixed capital) and productivity in Department 1 rise at the same rate. This 'counteracting influence' of the rising technical composition of capital inhibits the tendency of the organic composition to rise (as the value of machines depreciates, their 'volume' increases).

2) Consumption by wage-earners and productivity in Department 2 rise at the same rate. Whilst this certainly limits the increase in the rate of exploitation, which would

otherwise 'counteract' the falling rate of profit, it also inhibits the tendency towards a crisis of overproduction and under-consumption. Given that the organic composition of capital does not vary, the general rate of profit remains stable, and accumulation can therefore continue at a steady rate.

Until the mid-1960s, these conditions were more or less met in the developed countries. But there was no *a priori* reason why that should have been the case. It was almost a miracle that the first condition was met,[14] and statistical data shows that in the major industrialized countries it was decreasingly true from the 1960s onwards. On the other hand, a more or less explicit policy of regulating wage relations by normalizing increases in purchasing power did help the second condition to be met, particularly as the stabilization of wage relations was accompanied by the extension of wage-earning to most activities, including management, market and financial regulation, and social control.[15]

The regulation of wage relations took different institutional forms in the various OECD countries, but it usually involved:

1) binding collective agreements applying to all employers within a given branch or region (and thus preventing competition from low wages); 2) minimum wages established by the State, with periodic increases in purchasing power; and 3) a social insurance system financed by compulsory contributions guaranteeing all wage-earners a permanent income, even if they no longer received a direct wage because of illness, retirement or unemployment.

Regulation of wage relations was accompanied by major changes in relations between banks and industrial firms. As a result, firms could transfer production from one branch to another and at the same time maintain prices in declining branches. Similarly there were important changes in the role of the State, above all in the management of wage relations (the welfare state and direct wage relations) and the management of money.

Private banks acquired the ability to issue money by providing credit for both firms and households. This 'credit money' anticipates the validation of values-in-process and is

wiped out when the loans are repaid; it is wagered against
the high probability that the borrowers will be able to repay.
The 'monetary mass' issued by the banks thus represents a
'*pre-validation*' of productively invested values-in-process.[16]
But the banks also require (at least to clear-off their balances)
a form of currency which is unconditionally accepted and
which has to be accepted when debts are repaid. In other
words, they require a currency issued by a State-controlled
central bank. Some of the currency issued by the central
bank (the 'monetary base') may represent an international
currency (such as gold or the currency issued by the central
bank of a hegemonic country, like the dollar), but most of it
represents the official pre-validation or '*pseudo-validation*' of
certain debts (debts contracted by the state treasury, or
privileged credits rediscounted by secondary banks). By
establishing the level of pseudo-validation and by using a
battery of rules to oblige secondary banks to hold back some
of their credit in the form of central currency reserves, the
central bank can influence their willingness to lend, or at
least the rate of interest at which they do lend, thereby influ-
encing other agents' willingness to borrow.

By using the weapon of monetary policy, the State can,
then, attempt to stimulate or slow down the economy. It can
do the same thing by juggling its spending and revenue.
When the economy requires a boost it can cut taxes and
increase spending, relying upon the revenue generated by
the subsequent recovery to cut its deficit. It can also mani-
pulate minimum wages and/or the budget of welfare
expenditure. Together these various devices constitute the
famous tool box of 'Keynesian policy'.

The working of this mode of regulation, together with
the generalization of Fordism within the labour-process,
meant that the two rules of the intensive accumulation of
the Golden Age schema could be respected *a priori*. For a
period of twenty years, the OECD countries enjoyed
exceptionally high and regular long-term growth. There
were of course conjunctural slow-downs ('recessions') and
there were also major differences between the growth rates
of different countries, but it can be said that each country
experimented with Fordism and developed it to its advantage by expanding internal demand. Being the most

advanced country from the outset, the USA obviously had a
lower rate of growth than countries with a younger Fordism,
but even so its economy still grew by almost 4 per cent per
year. The one exception was Great Britain which, because of
the strength of its craft unions and the industrial apathy of
its financial bourgeoisie, departed considerably from the
model of Fordist production and therefore had a lower rate
of growth.

The 'Implicit Hegemony' of the USA

As we have just seen, international trade was of secondary
importance to the Fordist model of growth. The driving
forces instead were the internal transformation of industrial
production processes and the expansion of the *internal*
market by increasing purchasing power. Foreign markets in
dominated countries which, as we shall see in Chapter 3,
were the traditional form of regulation under competitive
capitalism lost much of their importance. The ratio of manufactured products exported to those sold on the home
market reached a historical low in the sixties. Moreover, the
main growth in international trade occurred within continental blocs and within the OECD, in other words inside
and between Europe and North America.

The South was tendentially forced into the role of supply-
ing labour and raw materials. The primary task of US political
and military *domination* was to assure control over its raw
material resources. Certain countries in Latin America and
Asia did aspire to the Fordist model by sheltering behind
high tariff barriers: this was the famous 'import-substitution
policy', and we will look later at the problems it involved.

In the period 1945-65, then, international relations were
primarily 'North-North' relations.[17] Can we describe them as
constituting a world regime of accumulation or a world
mode of regulation? What in fact was happening was that
Europe and Japan were 'catching up' with the USA. Since they
started out from unequal, differentiated positions, the combination of 'differentiation/catching up' was in itself a regime
of accumulation and a mode of regulation providing the
basis for what Arrighi terms 'the implicit hegemony of the

USA'.[18] The USA emerged victorious from the Second World War enjoying great productivity advantages and producing 63 per cent of the GDP of the five major countries (USA, UK, West Germany, France and Japan) and 57 per cent of all value-added in 1950. It forced its model of development on the rest of the world, first culturally, then financially with the Marshall and MacArthur Plans, and finally institutionally with the Bretton Woods agreements and the establishment of GATT, the IMF and the OECD.

Under these conditions, there was no need for an international form of regulation of wage relations; the same principles (contractualization, a welfare state, increased purchasing power) were universally adopted, even though they took different concrete forms in different countries. The dollar became the international currency. It was pledged against the unchallenged validity of American values-in-process; the productivity gap was such that American equipment goods, which incorporated the most efficient production norms, would always find buyers in Europe and Japan. America therefore had a systematic trade surplus. The only problem was the ability of Europe and Japan to buy American producer-goods. At first, the problem was resolved by loans from the US government but increasingly it was solved by overseas investment on the part of US firms. As a result, the USA had a structural capital deficit. This deficit provided the 'base' for an international currency: 'xeno-dollars' (dollars held by non-residents). In theory, the xeno-dollar (née Eurodollar) was backed by US gold reserves; in reality it was backed by the undeniable validity of American capitalist production. And as we shall see, when its validity became problematic, the USA refused to exchange the dollar balances held by foreign residents for gold.

We do not, then, have an international regime of accumulation in the true sense of the term, but rather a *world configuration* that temporarily guaranteed the compatibility of a juxtaposition of similar regimes of accumulation with different growth rates, and which were inserted into the international framework in different ways. Very schematically, the USA re-equipped Europe (and Japan) in exchange for rights over European labour-power. Multinational companies purchased labour-power in exchange for the right to buy American producer-goods. The purchase of those producer-goods, together with the accelerated generalization of Fordism, allowed Europe[19] and Japan gradually to catch up with US levels of productivity.

As we shall see later, the world economy has not (yet?) developed beyond this implicit level of organization. No institutional form regulating world demand has been possible. No supra-national authority to control money supply has been created. The complementarities and antagonisms that exist between national economies remain unstable, constituting little more than partial and random *configurations*. We therefore cannot literally speak of a world regime of accumulation.[20]

From Latent Erosion to Open Crisis (1967-1974)

If the crisis can be characterized in terms of a general downturn in accumulation, slower growth in manufacturing output,[21] a general and continuous rise in unemployment and, above all, an absence of regular growth, we have to conclude that the premonitory signs were already visible from the 1967 recession.[22]

From that point onwards, a slight downward slope began to appear in the curve linking the 'peaks' in minor fluctuations in world industrial growth (6.6 per cent per year between 1963 and 1967; 5.6 per cent per year between 1967 and 1973). More significantly, the curve linking the 'lows', which had until then been running almost parallel to the 'peaks', began to diverge, falling from 4.8 per cent between 1967 and 1971 to 2.5 per cent between 1971 and 1974.

The Roots of the General Crisis in Fordism

Three different species of phenomena and events should be distinguished within the development of the present crisis: 1) those which relate to the general crisis in Fordism and which appear to some extent in all those countries which have adopted that mode of development; 2) the magnifying effects of the interconnections between the various socio-economic national formations; and 3) phenomena specific to each of the social formations in question.

We will not discuss national specificities here, even though they provide a fertile field for research inspired by the same problematic as this book.[23] The distinction between the first two series of phenomena must, on the other hand, be made very clear as it has obvious political implications. If we restrict the argument to the second type, the crisis appears to be simply a crisis within *national* monopolistic regulation, which has come into contradiction with the internationalization of production. If that is in fact the case, a concerted recovery would provide an answer to the crisis. If we also take into account the first type, it becomes apparent that the crisis also affects the very basis of an intensive regime of accumulation based upon Taylorist work organization methods and Fordist mass consumption. We will try here to synthesize both aspects.

The most obvious factor in the crisis in the regime of accumulation is the general downturn in rate of productivity growth. This began in the late 1960s and affected all branches, including the car industry, which is the most typically Fordist branch.[24] But how does that downturn lead to a crisis?

We could answer that question by stressing the contradiction between the downturn and the continued tendency to increase purchasing power. Thus, it could be argued that increased purchasing power has led to increased unit wage-costs, to a profit squeeze and then to crisis. The statistics for the early 1970s do not, however, support this argument for all industrial countries (Germany and Japan are temporary exceptions). To be more specific, the rise in purchasing power does not seem to have accelerated autonomously. The few cases in which purchasing power did rise faster than productivity can be better explained in terms of a slowing down of productivity growth. Besides, if wage/profit distribution were the origin of the crisis, it could have been warded off by simply slowing down direct or indirect wage growth.

A more convincing explanation takes into account the other component in the profitability of capital. By the mid-

1960s, the downturn in productivity growth had led to an increase in per capita capital in *value* terms or, in Marxist terms, to a rise in the organic composition of capital. Since then, productivity rises have failed to compensate for the rise in the technical composition of capital, in, that is, the per capita volume of fixed capital.[25]

Initially, the mark-up procedures characteristic of mono-polistic regulation (whereby firms add a marginal rate to prices) compensated for the fall in immediate profitability by producing a nominal rise in profits, but that had reper-cussions in that it led to a general increase in both prices and wages, and meant that a greater share of profits had to be ploughed into amortization. Increasingly, firms ran into debt and the cost of debt-servicing, together with the rise in the relative cost of investment, led to a latent investment crisis.[26] All this took place in an inflationary climate. The downturn in investment, together with the fact that each individual investment created fewer jobs, led to a rise in unemployment and therefore to increasing pressure on the welfare state.

No matter whether we emphasize the profit squeeze or the rise in the organic composition of capital, the present crisis in intensive accumulation is a crisis in *profitability*, whereas the crisis of the 1930s was a crisis of *over-production*. The institutional forms of monopolistic regu-lation do in fact inhibit the 'depressive spiral'. The increase in indirect wages offsets a fall in purchasing power (despite the numerical rise in unemployment). The soundness of credit-money allows values-in-process to survive. Firms which would have been reduced to bankruptcy in a gold-based banking system therefore survive too. The crisis there-fore takes the form of simultaneous stagnation and inflation, but neither prices nor production collapse.

But why does productivity slow down? It is here that the difference between the analysis we have been discussing and the theory of 'long waves of innovation' can be seen most clearly. It is very difficult to see any downturn in tech-nological innovation during the 1960s, indeed the emer-gence of microelectronics would seem to imply the opposite. On the other hand, the limitations of Taylorist and Fordist work-organization principles, which had been so successful in the 1950s and the 1960s, were gradually becoming obvious in purely organizational terms (not to mention their social costs).[27] At a deeper level, this form of work organization means that the majority of producers have no control over their own work and that the activities of engineers and technicians become the only sources of productivity. The only way in which they can increase overall productivity is to invent ever more complex machines. We can thus see why the downturn in productivity goes hand in hand with a rising coefficient of per capita fixed capital.[28] Which leaves us with the problem of why the latent crisis in Fordism, which was being undermined by minor but cumulative changes, degenerated into an obvious recession. In order to understand that, we have to take into account both the international dimension and the reactions of governments and employers.

From the Erosion of US Hegemony to the First Oil Shock

From 1967 onwards, a qualitative change radically altered the international configuration. Productivity in Japan and Europe (notably in West Germany and France) was now so close to US levels that, given the prevailing exchange rate, unit wage costs were beginning to have an unfavourable impact on US competitiveness.[29] The growth of multinational companies in Europe and the extension of Fordist methods in both Europe and Japan had allowed them to catch up. Investment levels were still much higher there than in the USA.

America now had a trade deficit. Fort Knox's gold reserves could no longer cover xenodollars. As American production became less and less competitive, xenodollars could no longer be regarded as representing a money currency (gold) or as representing values-in-process that would be unquestioningly validated at the international level. The dollar was therefore thought to be over-valued.

As a result the dollar gradually lost its role as an absolute standard and began to fall against all other currencies.[30] A trade war then broke out between the three poles of the capitalist world economy, which were roughly equally com-

petitive. The differentiated configuration of the 1950s and
the 1960s gave way to a configuration in which three poles
were synchronized in accumulation. Phases of expansion
and recession in any one pole were directly echoed in the
others, and their effects were cumulative.

The worldwide boom of 1973 strongly suggested that
there would be a general recession in 1974, but its main
effect was extreme tension in the raw materials market. At
the same time there was a nationalist upsurge in the Third
World as explicit American hegemony came under direct
threat in Indochina. It was in this objective and subjective
conjuncture that the Arab-Israeli War of October 1973 gave
the ruling classes of the oil-exporting countries an opportunity to take control of oil rents.

In theory, the increase in oil rents simply reflected a
change in the ownership of a tiny fraction of world surplus-
value.[31] But in the developed countries, which were already
threatened with recession and where the latent crisis in
Fordism was exacerbating tensions over the allocation of
value-added, the sudden rise in oil prices added an inflationary dimension to the struggle over its distribution.
Employers and governments used inflation as an excuse to
try to reduce wage-earners' purchasing power by cutting
wages and restricting credit. Their initial successes in that
direction led to depressed demand in the developed countries and that, combined with a panic off-loading of stock,
provoked the first great recession of the crisis.

In 1975, however, this austerity offensive was halted by
worldwide resistance from workers and trade unions. The
automatic stabilizers of the welfare state, which had been
strengthened by the precipitate extension of unemployment
benefits (the ruling classes had been all the more 'generous'
in that they did not believe that the crisis was serious),
helped halt the spiral of depression, ensuring that consumption remained more or less stable despite the rise in
unemployment. The 'safety net' thus prevented a depression
and by 1975 a general recovery was under way, particularly
as the oil levy, which had been financed by credit, was
recycled into a major increase in effective world demand.
Such is the strange configuration which we will examine
later.

Conclusion

The least that can be said after this rapid survey is that, whilst the contradictions of capitalism may well be permanent, they can be expressed and resolved in a variety of ways. Regimes of accumulation which are predominantly extensive and regimes which are predominantly intensive obviously relate to the 'outside world' in different ways. We may suspect that relations with the outside world were originally very important, that they became less important as capital created its own internal market; that, at its height, Fordism marks the extent to which developed capitalism can be autocentred; and that the crisis in Fordism will open up new possibilities. We will examine these issues below, beginning with the period that takes us from the origins to the triumph of central Fordism. But once again it has to be stressed that the 'needs' of the centre do not determine what happens in every peripheral territory!

3
The Old Division of Labour, Or What Did Capitalism Want With The Periphery?

While it is, as I have attempted to show, true that in the countries in which it first developed, capitalism did go through a series of different regimes of accumulation and modes of regulation, it is rather pointless to attempt to elaborate a general theory of centre–periphery relations by deducing it from 'the basic tendencies of the mode of production' without analysing the specificities of those regimes and modes. And it has to be admitted that, in face of historical developments which are blindingly obvious, theories of 'dependency' and 'imperialism' are out of date. If those theories continue to survive, it is only because they do contain a grain of truth pertaining to *past* stages in historical development. But even at the time of their elaboration, they had difficulty in explaining how previous stages had led to the existing configuration. And when, by some stroke of luck (or bad luck), new facts seem to confirm their theses, they had difficulty in identifying or understanding these emergent developments. This is true of both the 'classical' theories of imperialism elaborated at the beginning of the twentieth century and of the dependency theories which flourished between 1950 and 1960 (a period which appeared to prove them right). Their conclusions have to be revised considerably in the light of events in the 1970s.

The present chapter will be devoted to a schematic analysis of both the history of real events and the history of ideas.

The Periphery as Thermostat

The classical theories of imperialism were developed in a context of a specific historical reality: predominantly extensive accumulation and competitive regulation in the first countries undertaking capitalist industrial revolution. The philosophical core of these theories can in fact be found in Adam Smith, even though he and the theorists of imperialism differ as to the merits of the international division of labour.

The basic argument is that the capitalist wage system led to the emergence of relatively complex forms of cooperation in manufacturing which gave capitalism an absolute advantage over other modes of production in terms of productivity. But the extensive accumulation of capital in countries experimenting with this mode of growth was not accompanied by a parallel expansion of social demand (because, to use a modern argument, there was no monopolistic regulation of wages). In the absence of sufficient internal demand, demand *had* to be created 'in the outside world', which capitalism, in fact, *could* successfully do because of its absolute economic (and military) advantages. The search for new demand and the ability to create it (if necessary by coercion) are the mainsprings behind imperialism, which is seen as the need on the part of the most highly developed capitalist countries to control foreign economies.

At the time, the imperialism meant primarily outlets for commodities which could not find buyers in the home market, and the theorists of the day, including Rosa Luxemburg, understood it specifically in that sense. However once commodity production and the wage-system had developed sufficiently, the outside world became also an outlet for direct capital investment (as Lenin was to emphasize). The only truly fundamental point over which Marxists disagreed was the urgency or necessity of finding such outlets; it was taken for granted that 'outside capitalism' did not necessarily mean 'outside *the country*'.[1]

In his polemics against 'economic romanticism',[2] Lenin began by *denying* that there was an outlet problem, but at the same time he demonstrated that the development of capitalism in Russia meant the absorption of the 'outside

world' of agriculture and handicraft production.[3] According
to Lenin, the growing demand for constant capital within a
regime of extensive accumulation was sufficient to provide
capitalism with its own markets. Three years later,[4] he
admitted that there was an overall 'realization' problem and
stressed the importance of foreign markets. At the other
extreme, Luxemburg overestimated the difficulties of resolving the contradiction between production and realization
within a closed regime of capitalist accumulation.[5] For both
Luxemburg and Lenin, the function of the outside world was
to mop up a surplus which cannot be absorbed by the existing internal regime of accumulation (the product of
branches which develop more rapidly than others, excess
production which cannot be absorbed by popular demand).
In their conception the world market acts as an external
pole which validates production that is for the moment in
excess of social demand.

The outside world also acts as a *reservoir* providing
capitalism with items it can transform but cannot create
(raw materials) or can only reproduce (labour-power). The
theoreticians of the early twentieth century paid little
attention to this, as neither problem was urgent: industrial
capitalism could still find most of the reserves it needed
within its home countries, even though the 'industrial
reserve army' of the peasantry was already spilling across
national frontiers. It was only later that the 'plunder of the
Third World' (which can also take the form of emigration)
became an overarching theme. It was, however, at this time
that the term 'international division of labour' began to be
used (meaning that the South produced cheap raw materials
and that the North produced manufactures).

Under this regime of 'centre–periphery' relations, the role
of the periphery is effectively that of a *thermostat*, and it is
seen as such. The capitalist circuits of extended reproduction cannot be completed within the centre. The outside
world therefore supplies it with both hot and cold sources
(labour-power and raw materials, and markets). We can,
then, quite understand why the theoreticians of imperialism
took little theoretical interest in the concrete analysis of
peripheral social relations. These were usually described as
'primitive' or 'precapitalist' (forced labour, pseudo-slavery,

quasi-feudal agriculture, etc.) and, although they were destined to 'disappear', it was simply assumed that they would comply with the needs of the centre. Once again, theory was until the mid-twentieth century simply a reflection of the realities of the international mode of regulation: the periphery felt the repercussions of 'minor crises' in the centre and amplified them (at least in the commodity sector): from the onset, a characteristic movement of the colonial export-trade in raw materials.

It must be stressed, however, that centre–periphery relations were originally a *process* (whereby the capitalist manufacturing centre located markets, tapped a labour-force, and spread firms dependent on itself) and that it is only later that they were consolidated into a *structure* of unequal relations. It might in fact be more accurate to say that if structural relations are indeed involved, they are relations between processes. To use Lenin's sibylline but telling phrase, in the centre, capitalism develops '*in depth*'; in the periphery it develops '*in breadth*'.[6] In other words, the centre is characterized by increasingly interconnected processes of production within an increasingly clearly defined schema of reproduction (and is becoming auto-centred), whereas peripheral capitalist units of production develop in accordance with a coherence that is established elsewhere. In other words, they are 'extraverted'.

The fact that they were extraverted, together with the fact that the Marxist intellectuals were Europeans, meant that there was even less interest in the internal regimes of accumulation of dominated countries. It was not until the great anti-colonial revolution of the mid-twentieth century that theorists emerged from the Third World itself. Their emergence and the fact that links of economic dependency continued to exist once political independence had been gained led to an increasing theoretical interest in the concrete workings of dominated social formations. The result was a critique of earlier 'centro-centrism' and the beginnings of methodological work on the relative autonomy of peripheral regimes of accumulation. The debate over theories of imperialism, however, simply shifted from the needs of the centre to centre–periphery relations. Little attention was paid to the periphery itself, which remained a 'dark continent'.

To restrict the discussion to the debate in France, Rey emphasized the solidity of non-capitalist modes of production and the specific problem of their articulation with capitalism, showing that even though capitalism had an 'absolute advantage', its products could not penetrate economies which did not really take a commodity form.[7] Palloix revealed how the capitalism–outside world articulation took different forms at different times.[8] Amin anticipated later work on Fordist regimes of accumulation and modes of regulation by showing that the problem of markets gradually became less important as the centre became auto-centred, and as the relative growth of departments and income became increasingly subject to 'ex-ante' regulation.[9] He argued that on the contrary, the impetus for the capitalist sector of extraverted formations[10] came from the outside (in other words from the centre) and that forms or modes of production in other areas of the social formation (and the care with which Amin examines these was at the time unusual) played only a supporting role (by reproducing labour-power cheaply) or were parasites living off the export sector, when, that is, they were not simply marginalized.

Thus, rereading the canonical texts through the early seventies, one receives the overwhelming impression that, leaving aside countries embarked upon a 'socialist experience', everything is determined by the movement of world capital, that all the initiative for change comes from the centre, and that developments in the periphery are simply functions of the needs of the centre. Although Palloix and Amin clearly anticipated that peripheral industrialization was possible (and it was indeed beginning to happen at the time they were writing), they overemphasized its necessarily limited and dependent nature.

It must be stressed that these texts are highly pertinent for the period up to the 1950s. More emphasis might have been placed upon the class conflicts that arose on the periphery during and after the struggle for political independence, as these explain the 'irreversibility' of peripheralization, and some authors, especially those from the Third World, did stress their importance. The Third International had provided a schematic framework for a class analysis of such struggles. The framework was that of the classic opposition between a *national bourgeoisie* which wanted autonomous capitalist development and a *comprador bourgeoisie* based upon the primary import-export sector.

In any event, the Beast had already appeared in the heavens of the Apocalypse: *the 'first' international division of labour*, a division between a centre producing manufactures and a periphery exporting raw materials. As we have seen, this 'division' of labour is not really a division at all. If it could do so, the centre would produce everything and import nothing. Besides, in historical terms, capitalism developed where it could find its basic raw materials, namely iron and coal. In the early period of mercantilism, European capitalism even used raw materials (its own gold and then that of Latin America) to pay for handicrafts from the East. It was because it was *excluded* from the capitalist manufacturing centre that the periphery began to 'specialize' in raw materials in the nineteenth century. And by a historical contingency, those central capitals which were allied to fractions of the local ruling classes and which wanted to acquire monopoly rents or to over-exploit an indigeneous labour force realized that the increased exploitation of peripheral raw materials worked to their advantage. In some cases, the exploitation of the labour force took a capitalist form, but in others wage relations were scarcely developed at all. In yet others, strange 'pseudo-pre-capitalist' forms of exploitation were improvised. Whether the export capital was national or external (central) had little effect on its peripheral nature.

What, then, is the status of peripheral *production* in the classical theory of imperialism? It comes as no surprise to learn that Luxemburg, who always stressed the centre's problems with markets, tended to see it as producing currency to be exchanged for imported manufactures (though the historical interest she takes in peripheral production does mark a break with Kautsky's Eurocentrism). In the final analysis, the centre buys products from the periphery because it cannot, after all, give away its own products. The important point is to extend the commodity sphere and to realize 'excess' surplus-value which cannot be absorbed within the central schema of reproduction by exchanging it against products originating from outside capitalism.[11]

The debate gradually shifted to the monetary profits which central capitalism derived from productive enclaves inserted into these particular social relations. With the post-war rise of central Fordism, the question of external markets became less important, and the problems of growth in the decolonized periphery came to the fore. Interest therefore focussed upon the transfer of value from periphery to centre that resulted from North–South trade. Transfers of value could result either from price mechanisms or, at a more basic level, from differences in the value of labour-power, with the central (and not the local) ruling classes appropriating the differential surplus-value. The great debate of the 1960s thus centred upon 'unequal exchange'.[12]

It was generally calculated that trade flows corresponded to a transfer of value from the periphery to the centre and that they therefore helped to increase the rate of profit in the centre. But that simply exacerbated the realization problem. The search for super-profits may well have been the *motive* behind the export of individual capitals from the centre to the periphery (though the flow was in fact limited), but it would be incorrect to say that the 'plunder of the Third World' was in quantitative terms a major factor in growth in the centre, and it would be even more incorrect to say that the *function* of the periphery was to promote growth in the centre, either before or after the Second World War. In qualitative terms, it was of course vital to appropriate raw materials which, unfortunately, could not be found or produced cheaply in the centre, but the fact that those raw materials could be exploited in the periphery was in itself a coincidence. Besides, profitable raw materials were not found throughout the periphery. It was certainly profitable to plunder the Third World and to over-exploit its workers, but the discovery of Taylorism was even more profitable.[13]

In that sense, Latouche is perfectly right to criticize the tendency to attribute growth in the centre to a 'transfer of value' from the periphery. Leaving aside certain strategic raw materials, under the old division of labour the Third World was primarily (but decreasingly) functional to the regulation of central accumulation in that it facilitated realization. As

Latouche notes, the chemical metaphor of 'catalysts' would be much more appropriate than that of 'blood transfusions'. The 'plunder of the Third World' did of course have serious effects *on the periphery*, 'but the destruction wreaked on the periphery was out of all proportion to the benefits reaped by the North'.[14] It is perfectly clear that Bengal was looted for the sake of a few cargoes of gold and that French West Africa was sacked for a few bales of cotton.

Other discoveries proved to be more promising. Capitalism, its factories, its wage system and its modern farms could, for instance, be transplanted to settlement colonies such as Canada or Australia, where capitalist accumulation could amass its initial funds by exporting raw materials. One can do anything with agricultural or mineral raw materials, but it is dangerous simply to export them. The dilemma is whether to lavish the profits on commodities from the centre, or to buy machinery to extend the basis of wage relations and to embark upon a process of auto-centred accumulation, even if it means adopting protectionism to defend what List (the official economist of Bismarkian development) called the emergent 'productive power' against the encroachments of free trade. The decision rests with the configuration of internal class struggles, and the scars left on social structures by the colonial past (the famous 'habits of history') obviously have a major influence on that configuration.

Once this process reaches a certain stage, the extraversion of a peripheral nation-state naturally becomes a basic fact which it is difficult to reverse and which has profound effects on the whole structure of social relations. But if we conclude from this that its socio-economic structure is simply a *function* of the needs of the centre (an argument which does of course apply to colonization to a certain extent) and that all its problems are due to its dependence on the outside world, we come dangerously close to the shortcomings of 'dependency' theories which tried to modernize classical paradigms of imperialism.

The basic idea behind 'dependency' theory (or the 'South's view of imperialism') is that the nation-states of the periphery cannot develop within a capitalist framework because the developed countries increasingly require their under-development. At best, they may be allowed to pursue 'dependent accumulation'. This idea had its hour of glory when a number of explicit attempts to escape dependency during the era of triumphant Fordism ended in failure, most of them in Latin America. 'New industrialization', which we will examine later, has now obviously challenged the hypo-statized premisses of this theory. The long-term history of capitalism is not simply a destructive process whereby a pre-existing central capitalism invades the periphery and prevents it from gaining access to capitalist development. Even in concrete cases where attempts to achieve autonomy through import-substitution have ended in failure, a more relative view of the importance of dependence on the outside world has to be taken.

Imperialism Gives Birth to Capitalism

If we regard the periphery's difficulties as an effect of central capitalism, as a desire on the part of the advanced capitalist economies to export their own difficulties, we inevitably suggest that there are two stages to the history of capitalism, that it first creates its central 'territory' and then, being unable to resolve its contradictions within a closed circuit, projects itself outwards. In short, we suggest that capitalism gives birth to imperialism. In reality, things are rather different: indeed, almost the reverse is true. Braudel's historical survey of the birth of capitalism and Frank's study of the period between 1492 and 1789 both provide striking illus-trations of the relativity of the *territorial* notion of the 'centre'.[15]

At the end of what we call the 'Middle Ages', material pro-duction all over the world was essentially carried out in non-commodity form. At a local level, commodity and even wage relations had of course existed for centuries in and around the feudal estates of Europe, but they represented only a tiny fraction of the estates' material output, and it is by no means certain that the logic governing the mobil-ization of money rent was in fact either a capitalist or even a market logic. Capitalist activity as such (the investment of funds with a view to selling at a profit at some later but uncertain date) was essentially confined to international or even intercontinental long-distance trade and involved only a tiny proportion of world output, most of it directed towards the feudal or 'tributary' ruling classes,[16] rather than other capitalists or wage-earners. Some of the centres of these market networks began to transform the metals, spices and textiles in which they traded, and therefore developed a waged labour force, though it represented only a small proportion of their clientele. These cities or 'centres of world-economies' floated at the edge of tributary empires or feudal kingdoms.

The entire economic miracle of the seventeenth and eighteenth centuries revolved around the transition from city-centres to national economies, the key to the transition itself being the shift from Amsterdam to London. The market economy and the waged labour force centred upon these markets and metropoles grew sufficiently to create a *territorialized economic space* geared primarily towards internal consumption and accumulation.

There is obviously a difference between a territorialized economic space and a network established around a city by a world-economy. Territorialized spaces are usually consolidated via identification with a pre-existing nation-state (France, England), although in some cases obstacles to economic unification have to be removed by political unification (Germany between 1871 and 1945). It is, however, still difficult to identify certain central states with an individualized economic space (Belgium or even Canada).

Capitalism was, then, born of world trade, and it created first a waged labour force and then a home market for its manufactures. Initially, it was an eddy within the great ocean of the non-capitalist economy which sustained it, but it then grew into territorialized capitalist structures which gradually became individualized and auto-centred, to use the schema popularized by Prigogine.[17] The ratio of trade flows 'between the structure and its thermostat' to flows 'internal to the structure' was *initially* very high (in terms of manufactured commodities, but not of course in terms of overall material output), and it *fell* as the home market was consolidated (see Table 1).

The widespread view to the contrary notwithstanding, the

Table 1
Foreign Trade and Production

	1899	1913	1929	1937	1950	1959
A) Exports as share of manufactures: %						
France	33	26	25	12	23	18
Germany (Reich territory to 1937)	31	31	27	15	–	–
West Germany	–	–	–	–	13	23
UK	42	45	37	21	23	19
USA	5	5	6	5	5	4
Japan	25	40	29	40	29	23
B) Import content of supply* of manufactures: %						
France	12	13	9	7	7	6
Germany (Reich territory to 1937)	16	10	7	3	–	–
West Germany	–	–	–	–	4	7
UK	16	17	16	10	4	6
USA	3	3	2	2	2	3
Japan	30	34	21	11	3	4

*Imports plus domestic output.

Source: J. Mistral, 'Compétivité et formation du capital en longue période', *Economie et statistiques* 97, February 1977.

history of capitalism was until very recently the history of the *declining* importance of foreign trade. There is in fact nothing paradoxical about this. When territorialized capitalist spaces were established, and especially when the national economies of the centre began to make the transition towards an intensive regime of accumulation and monopolistic regulation, the 'thermostat' gradually lost its importance as an outlet, even though it did become more significant as a source (of oil or labour). The existence of a regime of accumulation centred upon well-regulated mass consumption provisionally allowed capitalism to solve its realization problems on an internal basis. Up to a point, manufactures were exported to the periphery solely in order to pay for raw material needs!

Whilst imperialism, in the sense of the imperative to find outside markets, may once have been a powerful factor within the dynamics of capitalism, it had lost much of its importance only thirty years after Lenin characterized it as capitalism's 'highest stage'. It is true that in *Imperialism*, Lenin defines imperialism in terms of five characteristics, two of which are relevant to regulation in the centre; the others relate to the partition of the world, to the preponderant role of capital exports and to the advent of an era in which finance capital, which is primarily interested in appropriating raw materials, will repartition the world. Many readers believe, however, that Lenin is saying that, once it has reached a certain stage in its internal development, capitalism needs to export commodities and capital.

It is this misinterpretation of Lenin that is criticized by Latouche.[18] Lenin himself was well aware of the fact that capitalism develops by creating a home market which did not previously exist and that originally there was only the 'foreign' market. He began his *Development of Capitalism in Russia*, his first major work on economics and the first concrete analysis of a regime of accumulation, by 'examining the question of how a home market is being formed for Russian capitalism.'[19] In this text at least, Lenin argued that extensive accumulation, which works to the detriment of the non-capitalist sector, is enough to create a market and that foreign trade is ultimately merely a residual historical effect of the fact that it was long-distance trade which gave birth to capitalism: 'The need for a capitalist country to have a foreign market is not determined at all by the laws of the realization of the social product (and of surplus-value in particular), but, firstly, by the fact that capitalism makes its appearance only as a result of widely developed commodity *circulation*, which transcends the limits of the state. It is therefore impossible to conceive a capitalist nation without foreign trade, nor is there any such nation. As the reader sees, this reason is of a historical order.'[20]

It is on the other hand clear that Lenin, like Rosa Luxemburg and like many of today's 'realizationists' (such as François Partant[21]), thought it impossible that demand from wage-earners could provide capitalism with its primary market: 'It goes without saying that if capitalism could develop agriculture, which today is everywhere lagging terribly behind industry, if it could raise the living standard of the masses, who in spite of the amazing technical progress are everywhere still half-starved and poverty-stricken, there could be no question of a surplus of capital. This "argument" is very often advanced by the petty-bourgeois critics of capitalism. But if capitalism did these things it would not be capitalism: for both uneven development and a semi-starvation level of existence of the masses are fundamental and inevitable conditions and constitute premisses of this mode of production. As long as capitalism remains what it is, surplus capital will be utilized not for the purpose of raising the standard of living of the masses in a given country, for this would mean a decline in profits for the capitalists, but for the purpose of increasing profits by exporting capital abroad to the backward countries.'[22]

We have already seen in Chapter 2 that monopolistic regulation of intensive regulation, which provides the basis for Fordism, implies the very 'rise in living standards' which Lenin thought impossible (at least in terms of consumption of capitalist products). It is, however, true that at the time Lenin and Luxemburg were to a large extent right and that their arguments were still valid during the crisis of the 1930s.

We now have to ask why it is that so few auto-centred spatial structures emerged during the era of predominantly extensive accumulation, when capitalism was developing 'in breadth'.

It should first be noted that some spaces of this type did in fact emerge when European capitalism spread to settlement colonies (the United States and, much later, Australia) or when protectionism allowed the model to become acclimatized (as in the case of Japan). It should also be noted that, even at the beginning of the twentieth century, it was not easy to classify the countries of the Southern Cone of Latin America or certain dominions. Moreover, certain countries which were never colonized remained marginal to the capitalist 'International Division of Labour'.

In most cases, however, the model could not become 'acclimatized' because the forms of *colonialism* (which is not to be confused with colonization) which had moulded social and political relations inhibited the development of an industrial bourgeoisie and a waged labour force. The main problem is the 'failure' of capitalist development in former colonies which, like those in Latin America, gained their political independence very early and made a real attempt to become auto-centred. Such countries provide fertile ground for theories of dependency, but those theories usually avoid identifying the concrete root cause of their 'failure'. A detailed explanation of their failure would involve a historical study of the social relations, the regimes of accumulation and the modes of regulation prevailing in the countries in question.[23] We will however try briefly to show how their failure is articulated with international conditions.

On the 'Failure' of Early Import–Substitution Policies

Certain populist regimes in Latin America took advantage of the great crisis of the 1930s to develop an 'import-substitution' strategy, and in the 1950s countries like South Korea followed their example. The object of this strategy was to shift surpluses derived from primary exports into the consumer-goods sector by restricting imports from the centre to capital goods and using very high tariff barriers to protect the emergent industries. It was hoped that it would then be possible to apply the same tactics to the production of consumer durables and capital goods.

An Incomplete Fordism?

Although initially successful, the strategy ran into serious difficulties in the 1960s. This model of peripheral industrialization, which implied the partial and often illusory adoption of the central model of production and consumption but not the corresponding social relations, failed to enter the 'virtuous circle' of central Fordism. There are three main reasons for its failure.

In terms of the labour process, technology is not a transferable resource which grows in the forests of the North. It is not enough to import machinery. The corresponding social relations also have to be constructed. These countries had neither the experienced working class nor the managerial staff required for the implementation of Fordist modes of operation. They, as we have seen, derive from a process of expropriation and systematization of *pre-existing* skills, and they can never dispense completely with those skills. As a result, the imported forms of production never achieved their 'theoretical' productivity. Once development has gone beyond the stage of 'easy substitution', which requires little fixed capital, and begins to involve mechanization, the cost of investment and of imported capital goods rises at a breathtaking rate. As a result, the profitability of capital falls, although the fall can be masked if national companies with a monopoly position succeed in imposing inflationary marginal rates.[24]

In terms of markets, the characteristic features of monopolistic regulation were restricted to the management of mark-up rates and credit-money. There were very few cases of any significant expansion of worker and peasant purchasing-power (Peronism and Christian Democracy, then Popular Unity, in Chile were the exceptions). Markets therefore remained restricted to: 1) The ruling and middle classes created by the export economy. This market was in any case limited, but it was also sociologically stratified and resistant to the consumption of standardized articles.[25] 2) The foreign market, in other words the centre itself. But, wage differentials notwithstanding (and they were at this time lower than they would be in the late 1960s), peripheral manufacturing activity was not yet competitive because of its low productivity.

In terms of foreign trade, while the famous question of the 'terms of trade' applying to the raw material exports used to finance industrialization and to capital goods imported from the centre is still controversial (particularly where unit price effects are concerned[26]), climbing the productive ladder and going beyond the final assembly stage implied a rapid increase in the *volume* of investment, and therefore an increase in imports. Increased raw material exports could not make up for that.

Import-substitution policies therefore inevitably came up against the obstacles of trade deficits and debts, with domestic inflation (as in Chile), or ended in stagnation and destruction of the model (as in the Philippines). These experiments did, however, result in a real social transformation and in the emergence of a modern working class, modern middle strata and modern industrial capitalism. They might, then, be described as a '*sub-Fordism*', as a *caricature* of Fordism, or as an attempt to industrialize by using Fordist technology and its model of consumption, but without either its social labour processes or its mass consumption norms.

'Dependency' did have something to do with this failure, but its effects were much more mediated than vengeful slogans would have us believe. The missing link has to be sought in the *internal* social structure, which was consolidated by the survival of a very unequal distribution of income in the primary export sector, by the failure of agrarian reform to redistribute wealth, and by the failure to expand the manufacturing sector or to incorporate mass consumption into the regime of accumulation. Leaving aside the question of the scars left on internal social structures by colonization, however, it was the very fact that the centre had become so 'auto-centred' that had the greatest impact. The diffusion of the intensive regime of accumulation led to an increasing gap between centre and periphery in terms of competitiveness, and expelled the periphery from the international trade in manufactures. Yet it was precisely because the centre had been so good at developing its model of production and its norms of consumption that import-substitution fell into the trap of trying to imitate it.

It has to be remembered that, even in the OECD countries, the Fordist revolution did not take place overnight. The extent to which new norms of production, consumption and management of wage relations were invented or adopted varied from one country to another, with the USA being the most developed country, leading the way. The 'uneven diffusion of intensive accumulation'[27] worked wonders in continental Northern Europe, Japan, Australia, Canada and New Zealand. But Great Britain almost missed the Fordist boat because its finance capital was too internationalized to be devoted to a revolution at home. Argentina, which in the 1930s had a per capita GDP comparable to Canada's, did miss it because in the face of working-class resistance its ruling class chose to fall back on agricultural exports.

If we have to talk about American imperialism in countries which developed intensive accumulation and mass consumption, the term has to be restricted to meaning cultural imperialism, which was designed to impose the American model of development and not to perpetuate a situation of under-development. In the period between 1945 and 1960, the Marshall and MacArthur plans financed the import of American machinery into Western Europe and Japan. Fordist norms of consumption, work organization and contractualization were imported at the same time. As Boltanski[28] points out, the importation of those norms was quite explicitly made a precondition for Marshall aid, and at the time the Americans generally regarded France as being half-way between the US itself and an underdeveloped country.

Once Fordism had taken off in these countries, no one would have dreamed of describing France – and still less Japan or even Italy – as being part of the periphery. The case of Italy is even more remarkable than that of France (which, between the wars, was regarded as one of the most powerful countries in the world) or that of Japan, which had in the thirties sided with Germany and against the USA in the 'War of the English Succession' and which had almost conquered the entire Asia–Pacific zone single-handed. It is true that Italy had benefited from a twenty-year period of nationalist industrialization under Mussolini, but there is no *a priori* reason why Getulio Vargas or Peron should not have produced similar results in Brazil and Argentina respectively. *Desarrollismo* failed in Latin America but similar policies almost succeeded in Italy (except in the South, where they precisely failed because of the internal social structures). And what are we to make of Spain?

Excessive Theorizations

In 1951, twenty years after some countries had first taken
advantage of the crisis and the war to adopt an import–
substitution strategy, the Economic Commission for Latin
America (ECLA) published its *Economic Survey of Latin
America – 1949* and brought a team of Latin American
economists, including Raul Prebish, into the limelight. For
the first time, an articulate critique of the old division of
labour, of the 'organically uneven development of the world
economy', and of the 'centre-periphery opposition' had
appeared in the official literature on economics. The document denounced the way the periphery specialized in the
export of primary goods, the subordination of its economy
to fluctuations in external demand, and the way in which
productivity gains in the primary sector were translated into
worsening terms of trade and unemployment. It also criticized the restriction of import–substitution to the production of consumer goods required by the ruling classes of
the export sector; there again, productivity gains could only
lead to job losses, and the tendency to create alternative jobs
in the capital-goods sector was blocked because there were
no such industries in the periphery. The solution was to
create a domestic capital-goods sector or, to use a term that
was soon to become popular among development theorists,
to 'put the national matrix of inter-industry trade into the
black'.

The foundations for all the doctrines of economic
national independence that were to emerge over the next
twenty years had been laid. As Joao Manuel Cardoso de
Mello remarks, 'The ECLA problematic is a problematic based
upon achieving national independence in a peripheral situation.'[29] In other words, it means the Nation versus the IDL,
St George against the dragon of the Apocalypse. I would add
that this basic document is also characterized by a purely
technological vision of intensive accumulation (which is
seen in terms of industrial techniques becoming generalized
as they spread out from a centre) and that it implicitly
restricts intensive accumulation to a regime centred upon
the production of investment goods, in other words to the
regime which characterized the centre in the 1920s. It aims

at replacing external demand with internal demand for investment goods; the possibility of a prior expansion of the consumer goods sector is not considered. From the outset, two aspects of developed Fordism were ignored (changes in social labour relations and expansion of mass consumption), though that may well have been excusable in 1951.

The ECLA theorists responded to the difficulties they encountered by refining their doctrine, denouncing structural stalemates, appealing for rational planning in the construction of the industrial sector, and calling for 'every stage in the pyramid'[30] to be built at the same time to prevent development in any one sector leading to increased imports at a higher level. As a result of their advice, some countries looked to the Soviet model for inspiration and began to industrialize from the top, beginning with heavy industry. This strategy was extremely expensive in capital (which had to be raised by enforced savings or by borrowing from abroad), and it meant that production was diverted into areas which had no effect on the masses' standard of living for an intolerably long time.

By the 1960s, import–substitution was increasingly regarded as a failure; it had either led to inflation and a foreign deficit, or had failed to deliver what had been expected of it (national independence and an escape from poverty). The subjective failure was in fact more obvious than the objective failure, and it was that which upset ECLA's problematic. The refrain was no longer, 'This is where we are, on the periphery of the IDL, and this is how we will get out of that position', but 'This is what we are, a periphery of the IDL, and any attempt to get out of that position will bring us up against the realities of our dependency; all we can do is adjust the form of our dependency to what the centre wants to retain or reform.' Using what Cardoso de Mello calls 'a radicalized reproduction of the ECLA problematic', the theoreticians of 'the development of underdevelopment' defined the infinite paradigm of dependency and listed the curses of the Apocalypse: colonial dependency, dependency on primary exports, technological dependency, financial dependency ....

Others like Cardoso, whose more open position was noted in Chapter 1, stressed the local roots of dependent capitalism. The Campinas school (Maria de Conceiçao Tavares and especially Cardoso de Mello) turned even more decisively towards the study of internal regimes of accumulation. Cardoso de Mello himself explains the reason for the break with the ECLA problematic and its silences: the periphery should not be studied in relation to the centre, and its capitalism should not be seen as peripheral. It had to be seen as a *specific capitalism* which had reached a specific phase *in its own history*; it had to be seen as a 'belated' capitalism.[31]

This is not the place to enter into a debate over the pertinence of either this concept or that of the Brazilian regimes of accumulation identified by the Campinas school. The adequacy or otherwise of concrete analyses of concrete regimes of accumulation is a matter for specialists of the countries concerned. The main point is that a promising methodological shift was under way. The more caricatural forms of dependency theory continued to flourish simply because they allowed everything to be lumped together: American intervention in the Dominican Republic (on behalf of the dominant classes in the agro-export sector), pro-American coups against failed import–substitution strategies (as in Korea in 1961), coups against regimes which were tempted to radicalize the strategy (as in Allende's Chile in 1973), or which were simply suspected of wanting to do so (as in Goulart's Brazil in 1964), and even military operations with no consistent economic objective, like the 'unimportant tragedy' of Cambodia.

In the case of the Dominican Republic, America did indeed use its big stick to defend particular agro-export interests (those of United Fruit, to name names), but the other cases involved an *internal* reaction to the internal socio-political effects of the radicalization of policies of national independence, though support was of course forthcoming from at least some sections of the US administration. But can we therefore say that the USA is *opposed to* the industrialization of the Third World, even if wage relations are managed in social-democratic fashion? After all, it was the USA that encouraged the development of that model in the ruins of Europe.

In postwar France and Italy, Fordist models and norms

'took' *with* US aid; in Latin America, they failed to 'take', *despite* US aid. Covert or military intervention on the part of the USA was not directed against the threat of successful industrialization on the periphery (and nor was it designed to perpetuate dependency). It was directed against *political* attempts to depart from that model or to subvert it.

It was in fact in the interests of the USA to promote peripheral industrialization. American policy, especially after the launch of Kennedy's Alliance for Progress, was to attempt to force a Fordist model of accumulation on to the countries of the South, provided that it could be done without taking socio-political measures that would harm the interests of American firms connected with archaic elements in the export sector. This involved a contradiction in terms. Import-substitution implied certain reforms and certain difficulties and local governments were therefore forced to take measures that were 'too radical', and strayed dangerously far away from the US model. It was at this point that the policeman intervened, especially if the radicalization of a desire for independence seemed to suggest the possibility of an alliance with the Soviet Union. In certain cases, however, the USA did originally intervene to ensure that the plunder of raw materials could go on (the Dominican Republic, the fall of Mossadegh in Iran, etc.). But its subsequent attitude towards Shah Reza showed that it was not in principle opposed to an inflow of capital to the underdeveloped countries, to industrialization or to the transformation of local ruling classes ... provided that such developments conformed to and were bound up with the American model.

Conclusion

On reflection, the classical theory that imperialism reproduces dependency and an International Division of Labour with a centre–periphery division between the manufacturing and primary sectors is both realistic and contingent. It is realistic in that this was true of the extensive accumulation epoch in the centre, provided that it is interpreted correctly. This is still true, as a description of *reality*, where relations between the Fordist regimes of the centre and primary-export states of the periphery are concerned (and most peripheral states come into this category).

Insofar as it describes the *logic* of an international regime, it is contingent in that it is true only of one period. It is true of the period that stretches from the consolidation of territorialized capital spaces into nation-states in the mid-nineteenth century to the constitution of intensive regimes centred upon the growth of the home market in the mid-twentieth century. Insofar as it describes the old IDL as resulting from attempts on the part of an extensive central regime to resolve its contradictions, it is quite simply wrong. The central regime emerged as territorial economic spaces crystalized within an existing world capitalist economy. Its crystalization was one of 'History's chance discoveries'; it could have taken a different form, and it could have taken place elsewhere.

The 'Dependency' dogma's ability to explain why import-substitution did not really lead to industrialization in the 1950s is largely an illusion. An alternative explanation which concentrates upon 'internal causes' and upon the time lag between the success of Fordism in the centre and the appearance of 'incomplete Fordism' on the periphery is more likely to provide an explanation of the real dynamics involved. If that is true, the fact that the prognoses of the 'development of underdevelopment' dogma appeared not to be completely falsified by the real problems of capitalist industrialization on the periphery is not merely contingent. It is misleading. It led a whole generation of militants to deny the possibility – and even the reality – of relatively independent capitalist development on the periphery and to claim without further ado that the military men who had put an end to the early 'nationalist–populist' strategies for industrialization in dominated countries were simply '*gorillas*' and 'puppets of the comprador bourgeoisie'.[32] What was worse, it meant that any strategy for national industrialization could be seen as a progressive attack on imperialism and as a step towards socialism. In the event, subsequent developments were to put the clocks right.

4
Towards Global Fordism?

When central Fordism was at its height in the mid-1960s, it seemed that the periphery's role of providing a market for manufactured goods was no longer decisive to the dynamics of accumulation in the centre. During this period, the share of exports in the manufacturing output of capitalist countries reached an all-time low. Most foreign trade took place within the centre, or within the continental blocs of the centre (USA–Canada, the EEC). Exports of manufactures to the periphery fell to 2 per cent of GDP in the EEC, and to 0.8 per cent in the USA. If the 'search for markets' for capitalist products had *caused* both imperialism and the enforced stagnation of the periphery, we can only conclude that the centre no longer needed the periphery.

At this time, the share of manufactures in imports from the underdeveloped countries to all industrialized countries was negligible (less than 0.2 per cent). It was, however, in this area that the periphery was to regain its importance.

We will look first at those tendencies that stimulated the resurgence of industrialization in the former periphery, which seemed to have been condemned to export nothing more than primary commodities. We will distinguish two main logics which express the tendency to extend Fordism's geographical base, and will situate them within the context of the crisis in the centre. We will then demonstrate the scale of the phenomenon, which is far from being restricted to the famous 'NICS' or to the relocation of labour-intensive industries. We will thus see that a 'new division of labour' has emerged and has been superimposed upon the old; it has to be theorized with all the nuances and all the caution we applied to the old. Finally, we will attempt to identify certain forms of partial regulation within this quasi-international regime of accumulation. In this chapter, we will not, however, concentrate upon the overall conditions which allowed it to develop.

A Limited Extension of Central Fordism

The rising share of exports and imports in domestic production in the 1960s shows that the historical process of the international diffusion and integration of capitalist relations was once more under way. This was due to a combination of *two* series of factors: one having to do directly with the logic of central Fordism; the other, with the character of peripheral political regimes.

In the first case the internal dynamics of central Fordism in its emergent crisis phase led to new socio-spatial strategies whose clear forms can begin to be recognized in the early 1970s: the attempt to raise productivity by expanding the scale of production, and the search for cheaper wage-zones. The former tendency represents an authentic attempt to consolidate Fordism on the basis of its own resources. Insofar as rising productivity is, for Fordism, combined with an expansion of the market via an extension of mass production and economies of scale, the development of international trade *within the centre* leads to new productivity gains as capitalism becomes more centralized and as the developed economies become increasingly interdependent.

The process whereby productive systems 'overstep' national boundaries leads to the emergence of major continental blocs and even begins to affect the 'first periphery': the under-industrialized countries of the Mediterranean area and the eastern fringe of Europe. The same phenomenon can be observed in the American South and in the area around Japan. We will return to this point in a moment. But it should also be noted that internationalization within the centre also has the serious effect of weakening the regulation of growth; as each country strives to improve its competitiveness at the expense of domestic purchasing power, the world market as a whole grows more slowly.

For the purposes of the present discussion, extension to the 'first periphery' is more important, as it corresponds to the second objective of finding cheaper wage-zones. This in fact coincides with the objective of expanding the market by gaining a foothold in countries protected by high tariff barriers. In a sense, this is simply an extension of one of Fordism's intrinsic mechanisms: spreading 'branch-circuits' over several pools of unevenly skilled, unevenly unionized and unevenly paid workers.

From the point of view of the labour process, Fordism is, as we have seen, characterized by a disjunction, or by the division of activities into three levels: 1) conception, organization of methods, and engineering, all of which become autonomous; 2) skilled manufacturing, which requires a fairly skilled labour force; and 3) unskilled assembly and execution, which in theory requires no skills.

The possibility of articulating these three levels with a geographical distribution of the productive circuit within Fordist branches across three different labour pools is of course very attractive. The major differences between the labour pools relate to levels of skills and of exploitation, but there are also differences in terms of density of industrial network, proximity to major markets, and so on. The first experiments in relocating unskilled tasks took place in 'peripheral regions' within the centre,[1] and in the 1960s the process was extended to the countries of the immediate 'outer' periphery, that is, to Portugal, Spain, Eastern Europe (in some senses: Poland, Rumania), Mexico and the free-trade zones of East Asia, where hourly wage-rates were considerably lower and where the working class was less organized.

A *new, vertical division of labour* between levels of skill inside branches of industry was thus superimposed upon the old horizontal division between sectors (primary, mining, agriculture/secondary, manufacturing), and it was a way of expanding and reorganizing the regime of accumulation, rather than a change in its relations with the 'outside world'.

Once again, there were two reasons for this expansion. On the one hand, the object was to extend central Fordism's scale of production and therefore the market in which it was present, and tariff barriers designed to enforce import-substitution often meant that it was inevitable that the final assembly plants would be located in specific countries. The second factor was more important. Fordism was affected less by the absence of markets than by the strain on its rate of profit, and countries or regions with a high rate of exploitation allowed it to produce for the central markets at a low cost.

The countries (and regions) in question had to meet some further conditions, and this brings us to the *second series of factors*. If it was to expand, Fordism required the existence of political regimes whose ruling classes controlled a 'free' labour force and were prepared to play that card. Not all countries on the periphery met these conditions. A proletariat which is poorly organized but available for Taylorized (and *a fortiori* Fordized) labour is not merely a labour force which has recently been driven off the land. What E.P. Thompson calls the 'making of a working class' is a difficult process involving the mobilization and stabilization of industrial discipline.[3] A local political regime's freedom to 'choose' this strategy is more limited than one might think. This regime must be autonomous in three senses.

First, the regime must be politically autonomous from traditional forms of foreign domination. We have already stressed that a nation-state is always potentially autonomous in the sense that the ruling classes of dominated countries are never simply 'puppets' of imperialism. The extent to which they choose to be puppets (because it reinforces their class or fractional interests) expresses the form taken by national and international class alliances.[4]

Secondly, the political regime must be autonomous from ruling classes connected with earlier regimes of accumulation in sectors connected with either the primary export economy or the growth of the home market. The development of an export-orientated manufacturing industry can conflict with the interests of *latifundistas* or with those of industrialists who have opted for import-substitution. Such contradictions are not insoluble, but a balance has to be struck between the growth of an industrial waged labour force, an increase in wage levels, the requisite degree of competitiveness, priorities in allocation of capital resources, and so on. The Ivory Coast is a case in point.[5]

Finally, the regime must also be autonomous from the popular masses. This form of autonomy may be limited. There may have been, for instance, an earlier experiment with populism, and there may be trade unions to defend certain limited working-class interests, even if they are linked to the state apparatus (as in Goulart's Brazil or Peron's Argentina). Memories of the popular mobilizations that took place during the struggle for national liberation may still be alive.

In short, it usually requires a *dictatorship* to break the old balance and to use the state to create managerial personnel who can play the part of the ruling classes within a new regime of accumulation. A vast market and a labour force freed from its old peasant loyalties are not in themselves enough. Conversely, a strong and resolute regime can embark upon a strategy of 'pirating central Fordism' even if it does not have a strong home market, provided that it does have a labour force that can be mobilized cheaply.

The term 'pirating' (or 'grafting on to') can refer to a number of possible *strategies* for industrialization. These can be combined in specific ways with other strategies to produce a different regime of accumulation for *each* NIC. One combination might involve a new version of import-substitution; a different combination might lead to the promotion and integration of the old primary-export sector. It seems to me, however, that regimes of accumulation in the NICs are now characterized by the presence of what has been termed '*export-substitution*':[6] this strategy implies a decision to break with the primary-export model and to develop exports of manufactures produced at level three of the tripartite Fordist division of labour (labour-intensive activities). This strategy may be articulated with other elements within the local regime of accumulation, with central Fordism, or with regimes of accumulation elsewhere in the periphery. This may involve a number of different logics,[7] but two appear to be particularly significant: 'primitive Taylorization' and 'peripheral Fordism'.

From Primitive Taylorization to Peripheral Fordism

What are NICS? The OECD classification uses two pragmatic criteria: NICS are countries in which manufactured products represent 25 per cent of GDP and at least 50 per cent of exports. This gives us the following: Portugal, Spain, Yugoslavia, Israel, South Korea, Singapore, Taiwan and Hong Kong. Brazil, Mexico and Greece are usually also included in the list, presumably so as to give them a 'second chance'. Israel, on the other hand, should probably be deleted, since it is a settlement colony like Australia, whereas certain state-capitalist countries in the Eastern bloc (Poland) might be included. It is noteworthy that, according to these criteria, an immense agricultural country like India is not an NIC, even though in absolute terms its industrial and export capacities are as great as those of the official NICS.

Whilst all the classic NICS may well be industrializing in a new way, they do not all obey the same logic.

'Primitive Taylorization'

'Primitive Taylorization' refers to the transfer of specific and limited segments of 'branch circuits' to states with high rates of exploitation (in terms of wages, length of the working day and labour intensity). Most products are re-exported to the centre. In the 1960s and the early 1970s, the free trade zones of South Korea and Taiwan, and the workshop states of Asia (Singapore and Hong Kong) were the best illustrations of the strategy, but it is now becoming more widespread.[8] Relocation occurs mainly in textiles and electronics. There are two reasons for describing this logic as 'Primitive Taylorization'.

1) It involves 'Taylorism' rather than Fordism. The jobs that are transferred are fragmented and repetitive, but they are not linked by any automatic machine system. The equipment is light and requires only one operator (sewing machines in the textile industry, microscopes and tweezers in electronics). In short, they are labour-intensive in the strictest sense of the word.

As Salama points out,[9] even within these countries, there is a great contrast between the composition of capital in industries working for the home market and export industries. In South Korea (1974), per capita fixed capital was four times lower in export industries than in manufacturing as a whole; it was 23 times lower in 'electrical and electronic machines', and 192 times lower in the 'textiles and clothing' branch. Unlike import-substitution, 'export-substitution' costs local capital almost nothing in terms of capital goods. The 'mega-tools' required by the heavier segments of the branch circuit tend usually to remain in the countries of the centre, and in the hands of technicians and skilled workers. But there is no need for Ivan Illich to worry; micro-tools can, given the appropriate social relations, be perfectly suitable for the alienation and exploitation of human labour.

There is no difficulty in finding a labour force that can be Taylorized. The working class's relationship to material production does not make it the sole repository of skills. Since the dawn of patriarchy ('the most widely distributed phenomenon in the world', as Descartes would say), women's exploited role in domestic production has prepared them for the twin requirements of Taylorized industries: acquiescence in the goals of the labour-process, and complete involvement in the job. Even the body movements involved in basket-making and weaving are similar to those needed in the two key relocated branches: textiles and electronic assembly.

According to a Malaysian investment brochure, 'Oriental women are world famous for their manual dexterity. They have small hands, and they work quickly and very carefully. Who could be better qualified by both nature and tradition to contribute to the efficiency of an assembly line? ... Wage rates in Malaysia are amongst the lowest in the region, and women workers can be employed for about US $1.50 a day.'

In the free trade zones of Asia, which are the most typical examples of this type of 'development' (if it can be called that), women make up 80 per cent of the work force, and they are paid accordingly. They are also young; 90 per cent are under thirty and 50 per cent are under twenty. They do not work for long in the Gulag Archipelago of the free trade zones. If these young women who have fled from poverty and forced marriages become pregnant, they are dismissed (or deported from Singapore in the case of Malaysian women). The reserve supply of labour is inexhaustible if we also take into account the NICs' 'hinterland' of Thailand, the Philippines, Indonesia and, now, the People's Republic of China.

2) This logic, like that of 'primitive accumulation' in Europe, is designed to extort as much surplus-value as possible, and no attempt is made to reproduce the labour force on any regular basis. Markets are sought wherever there is a pre-existing demand; primitive accumulation relied upon the revenue of the gentry, and primitive Taylorization relies upon that of central Fordism. At least some surplus-value is accumulated within the country, and it often provides the first major source for autonomous accumulation. But this, as we have already noted, implies '"bloody" exploitation' – 'bloody' in the sense that Marx speaks of the 'bloody legislation' which launched primitive accumulation in England at the beginning of the modern period. All too often, we can speak just as well of *bloody Taylorization*.

In their respective studies of Asia and Brazil, Salama, Tissier and Mathias,[10] all come independently to the same conclusion: the implementation of an export-substitution strategy always implies the use of centralized measures (wage freezes plus inflation) to hold down or even to cut drastically the living standards of urban workers (as in Brazil after 1964). In general, the authors stress the role of the State in labour management: regulation (legislation, or rather the absence of social legislation, establishment of free trade zones), repression (the dismantling of autonomous trade-union organizations, police controls, company unions, use of torture, etc.), and regimentation (thanks to the war in Vietnam, South Korea acquired a veritable army of workers whom could be exported for public-works projects).

The results are as spectacular as the means used to achieve them. The rate of surplus-value rises sharply, whereas it remains stable in the central 'Fordist' regime. The rise is due to the opening of the 'scissors' between stagnant purchasing power and rising apparent productivity. Per capita production rises, not only in hourly, but in annual terms, thanks to the lengthening of the working day and to the production of absolute surplus-value. In South Korea, 30 per cent of all women workers were working more than fifteen hours a day in the mid-1970s. Under these conditions, accidents become more common (disability resulting from work accidents has been rising at an annual rate of 17 per cent since 1970). It is not difficult to understand why firms discard their women workers when they reach the age of thirty; their hands and eyes can no longer meet the required norms. They then fall back into the 'traditional sector' or into prostitution.

This model of accumulation (or, to be more accurate, the dominant logic within the regime of accumulation) is extremely profitable, but it cannot escape its narrow limitations.

In world terms, these nineteenth-century enclaves in certain segments of twentieth-century branches can only temporarily increase the amount of surplus-value extracted from what are, after all, only tiny segments of world production. The foreign capital invested in these enclaves does increase its profitability, but it is usually a matter of multinational companies sub-contracting a link in their branch circuits to local capitalists.[11] According to Salama,[12] in 1974 Japanese conglomerates still controlled 40 per cent of South Korea's foreign trade, and 56 per cent of Taiwan's. In 1971, 80 per cent of Brazilian and 90 per cent of Mexican electronics exports represented 'captive trade' between contractors and sub-contractors.

But although this model helps to restore the profitability of the contractors in the centre (and to increase working-class purchasing power without increasing wages), it raises other problems for central Fordism. The relocation of certain branches of production does not increase world demand, and it may lead to (not very) well paid workers in the centre being replaced by women workers who receive minimal wages.[13] In a branch like textiles, this is a zero-sum game in which the loser is employment in the centre. Hence the protectionist reactions which suddenly put an end to increased textile exports from the NICs.[14]

The local ruling classes, for their part, know only too well that they cannot remain warders of capitalist prisons for ever. The model is redolent of the nineteenth century, and it will not be long before the working classes begin to react in nineteenth-century fashion. As the model exhausts the locally available labour force and has to bring in more and more immigrant labour from the countryside or from neighbouring countries, the social question is further complicated by an urban question and a racial question. Having attempted to solve the problem by using truly 'bloody' methods (the forced sterilization of Malay women, for instance), the workshop states of Asia are now attempting to improve the technological level of their exports by increasing wages and at the same time sub-sub-contracting unskilled, labour-intensive work to their hinterlands. In more densely populated countries like Taiwan and South Korea, where the task is to establish a reasonably cohesive regime of accumulation and a hegemonic bloc (in Gramsci's sense of the term), the ruling classes are being forced to follow the example of Brazil and to adopt a rather different logic which we can describe as 'peripheral Fordism'.

Peripheral Fordism

In the 1970s a new pattern emerged in certain countries. It was characterized by the existence of autonomous local capital and by the presence of a sizeable middle class, and significant elements of a skilled working class. In some cases, its origins lay in an earlier import-substitution policy or in a peripheral form of merchant capitalism (Chinese in Eastern Asia). In other cases, it emerged from the 'miraculous' promotion of exports of raw materials such as oil or from an earlier stage of primitive Taylorization. This conjuncture allowed certain states to develop a new logic which we will refer to as 'peripheral Fordism'. The *political* nature of the choices involved must again be stressed; as they are bound up with an internal class struggle which makes the State truly autonomous from the classic ruling classes. Korea in the 1970s, Mexico and Brazil are all cases in point ... but so were Opus Dei's Spain and Gierek's Poland.

Why peripheral Fordism? First, this is a true Fordism in that it involves both mechanization and a combination of intensive accumulation and a growing market for consumer durables. Secondly, it remains peripheral in that, in terms of the world circuits of productive branches, jobs and production processes corresponding to the 'skilled manufacturing' and engineering levels are still mainly located outside these countries. Its markets represent a specific combination of consumption by the local middle classes, with workers in the Fordist sectors having limited access to consumer durables, and exports of cheap manufactures to the centre. Growth in social demand (which means *world* demand) for consumer durables is thus anticipated, but at the national level it is not institutionally regulated or adjusted to productivity gains in local *Fordist* branches.

We have, then, a combination of import-substitution *and* export-substitution in varying proportions.[15] Finance, when required, comes from the proceeds of the old division of labour, from the promotion of raw materials exports, from tourism, from the money repatriated by emigrant workers, and so on. At the same time, industrialization is accompanied by an increase in imports from the centre; most of them are capital goods produced at levels 1 (conception, engineering) and 2 (skilled assembly) of the new division of labour, and they have to be paid for by exporting level-3 (unskilled assembly) products to the centre.

Insofar as it is a logic of accumulation, or a component element in concrete regimes of accumulation, peripheral Fordism can, then, be analysed as: 1) an element within each NIC's internal regime of accumulation; and 2) an element within the regime of accumulation which links the centre to the NICs in terms of the overall production process and in terms of all markets.

It must be stressed that the regimes of accumulation which we are proposing to group together under the heading 'peripheral Fordism' can in fact vary enormously. Thus, the ratio of exports (manufactures) to internal demand varies from 4.1 per cent in Mexico to 25.4 per cent in South Korea (1978 figures). The ratios between 'growth in domestic final demand', 'import-substitution' and 'industrial re-exporting' are obviously not the same in every concrete regime of accumulation as they reflect major differences between their modes of regulation, particularly in wage relations and forms of ruling-class hegemony. Significantly, Mexico (or at least the urban sector) is relatively 'democratic',[16] whereas South Korea is a dictatorship.

Yet, the term 'peripheral Fordism' should only be used when growth in the home market for manufactured goods plays a real part in the national regime of accumulation. In this context, it should be noted that South Korea, which some writers insist upon calling a workshop country because of the primitive Taylorization that exists in some segments of the transferred labour-intensive industries, departed from the Taylorist schema long ago. That schema characterized its growth in the period between 1962 and 1972. Since 1973, growth has centred on the home market; the share of exports fell from 28 to 23 per cent and then stabilized. An active policy of import-substitution then helped the country to 'climb the ladder' and further reduced the share of imports from 27 to 20 per cent of the home market. Real wages, which had been rising more slowly than productivity, took off in 1976, so much so that they began to threaten South Korea's competitiveness vis à vis Taiwan.

In a very subtle analysis of these developments, Benabou identifies five groups of industries in South Korea by tracing the relative movement of export/domestic (X/D) and import/domestic (I/D) ratios:[17]

1. Domestic industries (X/D and I/D low).
2. Export industries (X/D high and rising; I/D low).
3. Import-substitution industries (X/D low; M/D low and falling).
4. Extroverted industries (X/D and I/D high and both rising).
5. Internationalized industries (X/D and I/D average; X/D rising, but I/D falling).

Groups 2 and 4 (clothing and electronic components) are characterized by bloody Taylorization. The difference is purely statistical; it is only because the 'thread and fabrics' branch (import) has been separated from the 'hosiery and clothing' branch (export) that the textiles sector can be broken down into an export industry and an import-substitution industry. In the electronics sector, however, the 'transferred' segments cannot be identified by using Benabou's classification. Thus, electronic components are classed as an extraverted industry, whereas home electronics and vehicles are classed as 'internationalized industries'.

Two developments are, however, typical of peripheral Fordism. Whereas 'extraverted industries' are moving backwards along the bi-sector, 'internationalized industries' are moving perpendicular to it (see Graph 1 overleaf). Whilst South Korea continues to export Fordist goods at either the final or intermediary stages (groups 4 and 5), it is increasingly producing them for the home market. At the same time, pure exports (group 2) are falling, whilst import-substitution (group 3) is increasing.

Scale and Limits of the Movement towards Global Fordism

Danger! Danger! The spectre of the Beast of the Apocalypse is prowling around. As soon as it is unleashed, the concept of 'peripheral Fordism' tends to take on a life of its own and comes back to haunt us, leaving its mark on everything that comes within its reach. It must therefore be made perfectly clear that:

* Insofar as it is a regime of accumulation, Fordism is not taking over the whole periphery.
* Insofar as it is a form of industrialization, it is not the only form operating in the periphery or even in the NICs.
* Equally important developments are taking place in agriculture.
* On the other hand, primitive Taylorisms and even peripheral Fordism exist outside the NICs.

We need, first of all, to get at least a rough idea of the scale of the phenomenon of peripheral industrialization. We will then look at a number of objections which ought to temper the enthusiasm that such suggestively named concepts are likely to inspire. Finally, we will take the thesis seriously and look at its real implications: the establishment of a new international division of labour.

Graph 1
South Korea: Position of Five Groups of Industries 1970-79

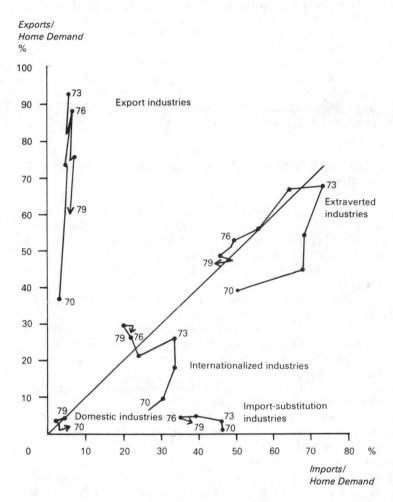

Source: R. Benabou, 'La Corée du Sud ou l'industrialisation planifiée',
Economie Prospective Internationale, 10, August 1979.

A Widespread, Uneven and Precocious Phenomenon

The easiest way to gauge the extent of the phenomenon is to refer to World Bank statistics (which deal with virtually the whole world, notably excepting Taiwan). With a disarming methodological placidity, the World Bank ranks countries in terms of GNP per head of population, and then uses arbitrary distinctions to classify them into groups of twenty to thirty countries. The only countries which are not classified in this way are high-income oil-exporters (Libya, Saudi Arabia, Kuwait and the Emirates) and 'Eastern European countries with planned economies'. For 1981,[18] this classification gives us:

1) Low-income countries ranging from Kampuchea (less than $80 per head of population per year) to Ghana ($400). Total population: 2 billion, 200 million.

2) Lower middle-income countries ranging from Kenya ($880) to Paraguay ($1,630). Total population: 1 billion, 130 million.

3) Upper middle-income countries ranging from South Korea ($1,700) to Trinidad and Tobago ($5,670). Total population: 464 million.

4) Industrial countries with a market economy, ranging from Ireland ($5,230 – less than Trinidad or Singapore!) to Switzerland ($17,430). Total population: 719 million.

Preliminary comments. Both the countries and categories are so heterogeneous that the average indicators relating to 'categories' do not mean a great deal and that those relating to certain countries do not mean a great deal more. Thus, China and India together account for more than half the total output of the first category. But in terms of per capita income, India comes into the same category as Upper Volta, Ruanda, Somalia and Tanzania.[19] It is an old industrial country and it does have a Fordist sector, but it is swamped by an impoverished peasantry. The World Bank gives statistics for the category 'low-income countries, excluding China and India' – and we will be using them – but the same category includes Bangladesh and Pakistan, which are classic examples of 'primitive Taylorization', and which are also swamped by an impoverished peasantry.

The 'lower middle-income' group (which takes in Senegal, Morocco, Bolivia, the Philippines and Indonesia) includes some countries which are characterized by the promotion of traditional exports, others characterized by import-substitution and still others characterized by bloody Taylorization. The 'upper middle-income' group contains all our NICs, with the exception of Spain, which has been promoted to being an industrial country. But it also takes in most of the most densely populated OPEC countries and 'Newly Deindustrializing Countries' like Argentina and Chile, which began to deindustrialize in the seventies. Ireland, for its part, is a perfect example of the logic of peripheral Fordism, but it can scarcely be described as an industrial country.

This classification does, however, provide us with a starting point. In terms of Table 2, the 'industrial countries' can be regarded as representing the centre, the 'upper middle-income countries' as classic NICs and 'lower middle-income countries' as 'the second wave of emerging NICs'. The category of 'low-income countries excluding China and India' can be regarded as being outside the Fordist world regime of accumulation. On the other hand, we shall also identify three typical NICs: Mexico, Brazil and South Korea.

Bearing in mind all these provisos, let us look at what happened in the periods 1960-70 and 1970-81. These periods are generally held to be typical of 'before the crisis' and of the first phase of the crisis itself.[20]

We note first that Gross Domestic Product increased in all categories, including the poorest. This is not true of all countries, especially after 1981. That in itself does not mean a great deal; in purely statistical terms, rural depopulation and the break-up of 'natural' economies lead to an increase in GDP.[21] Nor does it necessarily imply a rising average standard of living; population growth can more than wipe out an increase in GDP, and, I repeat, GDP does not give a measure of all the forms whereby the means of existence are reproduced.

The important point is that, whereas the crisis put an end to growth in the countries of the centre, growth scarcely

Table 2 (continued overleaf)
Changes in World Production, 1960-81

	Industrial Countries	Upper Middle Income	Lower Middle Income	Low Income[1]	South Korea[2]	Brazil	Mexico
GNP per head of population $ 1981	11,120	2,490	850	240	1,190	2,220	2,250
Annual growth of GNP per head of population 1960-81	3.4	4.2	3.4	0.8[3]	6.9	5.1	3.5
Annual growth of GNP							
1960-70	5.1	6.4	5	4.7	8.6	5.4	7.6
1970-81	3.0	5.6	5.6	3.6	9.1	7.6	6.4
Growth in manufacturing sector							
1960-70	5.9	7.8	7.1	5.9	17.6	n.a.	10.1
1970-81	3.1	6.3	5.8	2.8	14.5	7.8	7.1
Growth in gross investment							
1960-70	5.8	7.5	7.9	4.3	23.6	6.1	9.9
1970-81	0.9	7.2	8.2	3.7	11	6.5	9.0
Share of agriculture in GNP							
1960	6	18	36	48	37	16	16
1981	3	10	22	45	16	13	8
Share of manufacturing in GNP							
1960	30	23	15	9	14	26	19
1981	25	24	17	10	28	27	22

Table 2 (continued)

	Industrial Countries	Upper Middle Income	Lower Middle Income	Low Income[1]	South Korea[2]	Brazil	Mexico
Exports/GDP							
1960	12	18	15	15	3	5	10
1981	20	23	23	12	39[2]	9	13–17[2]
Structure of exports % 1960-81							
Primary	34 → 28	84 → 55	96 → 82	91 → 71	86 → 10	97 → 61	88 → 61
Textiles	7 → 5	4 → 10	1 → 5	4 → 21	8 → 30	0 → 4	4 → 3
Machinery and transport	29 → 35	2 → 13	0 → 2	0 → 2	0 → 22	0 → 17	1 → 19
Other manufactures	30 → 32	10 → 22	3 → 11	5 → 6	6 → 38	3 → 18	7 → 17

1) Excluding China and India
2) 1982 figures
3) China: 5%; India 1.4%
All growth rates are given as annual percentages.

Source: World Bank, *Report on World Development*, 1983, 1984.

slowed down at all in the 'upper middle-income' group, which had been growing faster than the centre in the 1960s. The 'lower middle-income group', in which growth had been slower than in the centre, began to catch up with the upper middle-income countries. Growth in the manufacturing sector is even more significant;[22] growth in this sector was still stronger in the middle-income countries than in the centre, and it scarcely slowed in the seventies. The upper middle-income countries did, however, begin to grow faster. Growth rates in low-income countries, which were weaker than those in the centre, fell at the same time.

Changes in investment rates were even more spectacular: the crisis interrupted the dynamics of accumulation in the centre, but in the middle-income countries accumulation sped up. In low-income countries, accumulation fell, but it did so more slowly than in the centre. From the early 1960s onwards, there was, then, real accumulation and growth – including industrial growth – in the whole middle-income category, in countries ranging from Kenya[23] to Trinidad. Growth in that category was not affected by the crisis in central Fordism until at least 1981. On the other hand, the vast majority of low-income countries were stagnating when compared to the centre, and they appeared to have been affected by the crisis in the centre.

The only middle-income countries in which manufacturing output did not increase in the 1970s were Senegal, Zambia, El Salvador, Nicaragua, Congo, Peru, Jamaica, Panama, Argentina, Chile and Trinidad, which all performed less well than the average in the centre. On the other hand, the following performed at least three times better than the centre in terms of growth in manufacturing between 1970 and 1981: Bangladesh (the fifth poorest country in the world!), Kenya, North Yemen, Indonesia, Lesotho, Thailand, Nigeria, Equador, Tunisia, South Korea, Malaysia, Algeria, Hong Kong and Singapore. Brazil and Mexico performed almost as well.

In the 1960s, no middle-income country had done so well, but if we use 11% growth as a criterion (twice the average of the centre), Iran, Nicaragua and the Ivory Coast have to be added to the list (reclassification can sometimes be significant!). Conversely, Indonesia, Nigeria and Tunisia have to be removed, as, presumably, do all those countries (with the exception of Thailand) which were not then 'official' NICS.

We can already begin to see that new-style industrialization was a widespread phenomenon and that in some countries it began very early. In some, it also failed at an early date.

We also note that, whereas the respective shares of agriculture and industry in GDP determine the position of any given category in the wealth scale from the outset (1960), and whereas the share of agriculture declines in all categories, there is no great change in the share of manufacturing (in the centre it declines as the modern tertiary sector grows). The real difference between, on the one hand, the lower middle-income and low-income countries and on the other, the upper middle-income and industrial countries relates to the relative shares of primary goods and manufactures *in exports*.

Whereas the share of primary goods scarcely falls at all in the two poorest categories, in the upper-middle income countries it falls from 84 to 55 per cent. In the poorest countries, the only category of manufactured goods in which there is any significant growth is 'textiles and clothing' (mostly due to Pakistan and Bangladesh, where this sector represents 37 and 49 per cent of all exports respectively). In the typically Fordist domain of machinery and transport equipment, the upper middle-income countries are increasing the gap. In terms of exports as a share of GDP, on the other hand, the lower middle-income countries are catching up. In low income countries, the ratio of exports to GDP is falling.

The main change relates, then, to the international division of labour. Many countries increased their exports of manufactures, but in the poorest the increase was restricted to textiles (presumably because of the logic of primitive Taylorization), whereas the richest reached the heights of exporting cars, even if, like Brazil, their total exports remain relatively modest.

This brings us to our final observation. Even without studying their internal regimes of accumulation, it is obvious that there are enormous differences between the various

NICS. Mexico and Brazil are still closer to the primary-export model (oil, soya, coffee ...) than most countries in the upper middle-income category, whereas South Korea seems still more remote from it than an industrial country. South Korea probably compensates for that by relying more on primitive Taylorization than Pakistan (if we take the share of 'textiles and clothing' in exports as an indicator). On the other hand, Mexico and Brazil appear to be auto-centred to a remarkable degree (although from 1982 onwards Mexico did launch a major export drive in order to repay its debts).

Size is obviously a major factor in itself. In a 'continental federation' like Brazil, the export/GDP ratio for the South-east region alone must be similar to South Korea's. On the other hand, the ratio of exports to GDP is 65 per cent in Belgium and 200 per cent in a 'trading-post' economy like Singapore.

The size factor is not, however, simply a statistical trap. Brazil has such a vast unitary market that it has sufficient room to manoeuvre to develop a truly auto-centred regime. The dictatorship in fact made poor use of this advantage: with a population of 120 million, a bigger market for consumer durables and even luxuries than that available to Belgium, can develop if only 10 per cent of the population appropriates two thirds of the country's wealth. In South Korea, on the other hand, there is a more 'egalitarian' distribution of wealth. As South Korea is, on average, a poorer country, it consumes less of the consumer durables it produces. These differences had a certain effect on the two countries' uneven ability to 'adjust' to the upheavals of the 1980s.

Diffusion of Accumulation Outside Fordist Industries

The unthinking application of the labels 'Taylorist' or 'Fordist' to industries in countries which are developing through capitalism will no doubt annoy the economists and sociologists of work. And they are right to be annoyed. Of course industries which export clothing are Taylorist, and of course industries which export machinery and vehicles are Fordist.[24] It would, however, be an exaggeration to say that all emergent national industries involve an export-substitution strategy, that all exports come from manufacturing industry, or that, in terms of work organization, all Third World industries are either Fordist or Taylorist.

First of all, the export-substitution strategy is not the only factor contributing to capitalist development in these countries. Traditional exports themselves have undergone significant changes, and have in many cases been actively promoted. The most obvious example is oil. OPEC's rise to power did not simply allow the exporting countries to control the fixing of oil rents. Some of them adopted a policy of downstream integration by establishing a refining and petrochemicals industry. Now that it has reached maturity, the Saudi industry is a threat to the world market, which was previously dominated by the advanced capitalist countries. The same could be said of the Brazilian steel industry (which recently purchased the remains of Kaiser Steel in California – Brazilian 'imperialism'?).

A less familiar example involves the extension (albeit on a limited scale) of the agribusiness model developed in North America to certain Third World countries, with Brazil producing soya and Thailand producing manioc. In these cases, we can speak of a fully capitalist industrialization of agriculture and of a labour force which has been 'freed' from working on small-holdings, and which is even more exploited than it would be under bloody Taylorization.[25]

Import-substitution is equally important. This is an integral element in the logic of peripheral Fordism, but it also applies to basic industries producing for local markets, be they Fordist or not. It applies particularly to energy and to the production of cement and the other materials needed for the construction industry and the public works programmes that go hand in hand with urbanization.[26]

Neither agribusiness nor basic industries (which are often processing industries; they use, that is, automated physico-chemical processes) derive their work-organization principles from Fordism or Taylorism. On the other hand, forms of a division of labour *similar* to the tripartite division of Fordism and even logics of accumulation *similar* to those of peripheral Fordism do tend to develop.

Take the case of steel and heavy engineering. We have

already seen that in the sixties, a variant of the first import substitution policy led certain countries to prioritize the development of basic industries. The idea, which derived from Soviet forms of industrialization and which at the time found support in the theory of 'industrializing industries' and 'poles of development', was to short-circuit the perverse effects from 'downstream' substitution: any industrialization based upon import-substitution in consumer goods leads to increased imports of intermediate and equipment goods. The answer was to begin 'upstream'. It was also hoped that the creation of a local supply of basic commodities would stimulate the growth of 'downstream' users.

This strategy was doubly mistaken. First of all, there is nothing really 'upstream'. Basic industries are usually very capitalistic. They require an enormous accumulation of fixed capital and relatively skilled collective workers to set them in motion. Either one reenacts the entire history of steel-making (from village furnaces to modern blast furnaces) at great speed, as during China's highly controversial 'Great Leap Forward' experiment, or one buys fully equipped factories. In the absence of a skilled work force, of equipment and of maintenance teams, one has to hire them from abroad. Technological dependency will no doubt become a thing of the past as a collective worker eventually emerges, but the macroeconomic aim (import-substitution) has not been achieved. Besides, in economic terms, it is cheaper to import steel as and when it is needed than to develop a steel plant which is expensive, difficult to maintain and which creates very few jobs.

This does not mean that such strategies are to be condemned out of hand. When a country has a major but *non-renewable* source of income (such as oil), it is obviously unreasonable to use it to develop consumption, and it makes sense to develop a relatively complete industry for the day when the rent runs out. The mistake, which is common to most import-substitution strategies, is the belief that the problem can be solved simply by *importing* factories. In terms of its social effects, this policy is open to criticism in that it has no immediate spin off in terms of employment or living standards, but that is not so much an 'error' as a political choice which reflects the ideology of a ruling class such as a nationalist military bureaucracy.[27]

It is equally erroneous to believe that other activities will 'spontaneously' develop alongside the basic industries. On paper, a complete industrial system can be built, either 'in accordance with a plan' or 'in accordance with the demands of the market'. The theory of 'industrializing industries' tries to have the best of both worlds. Either the planner will 'already' have the steel at his disposal when he decides to do something with it, or the captains of private industry will seize the opportunity of that supply. But no matter how brilliant he may be, the planner can never forecast future 'downstream' demand for semi-finished products, and the non-existent user industries cannot provide detailed orders, complete with technical specifications. All too often, the basic industries are therefore cathedrals in the desert, unless of course they respond to world demand, like mere component industries, and adopt the macroeconomic logic of peripheral Fordism.

Third World basic industries begin by ordering fully-equipped factories, but they have problems with maintaining or even running their plant. The lack of spares, the absence of a fully skilled workforce, and marketing all lead to further problems. They then begin to order 'full products', with the purchase contract covering maintenance teams and in-service training. Finally, they order 'factories with markets' (with sell-back clauses). But this involves a logic which is very similar to that of peripheral Fordism: buying equipment goods and engineering plant from the centre, manufacturing on the spot with a labour force which is less efficient (and which will be less efficient for at least ten years) but much lower-paid than that in the centre, re-exporting and then, if the rest of the national economy develops, using the products at home. The difference is that the 'know-how' remains elsewhere, and that far fewer jobs are created than in Fordist or Taylorist industries.[28]

We find similar parallels where modern agribusiness is transplanted. Selected soya seeds, fertilizers and technicians are imported from the centre and the product of the labour of a super-exploited peasantry is turned into oil cake, which is used to feed the livestock owned by the peasants of Europe, and to accelerate both concentration in livestock industries and rural unemployment.

Fordism, which began as a type of labour process (characterized by a division between conception and fragmented and deskilled execution, with mechanization incorporating a systematized social know-how), has become a social technology and has given its name to a regime of intensive accumulation centred upon mass consumption because it represents both the dominant model and the leading sector, even though not all activity in the centre is Fordist. Similarly, the logic of peripheral Fordism, in a specific way, is being forced upon other peripheral industries (and even agricultural activities) not only as an economic logic but also as a new form of the international division of labour.

The New International Division of Labour

It is now time to gauge the extent to which the partial industrialization of what was once a periphery exporting primary commodities has revolutionized the international division of labour. We will look first at the *results*, without raising the question of whether or not the division is functional or intentional. We will then turn to a discussion of the strategies of the agents involved and of the institutional forms which gave rise to this configuration.

Two Superimposed Divisions of Labour

It is important to remember that, whilst Fordism is becoming a global phenomenon, the old international division of labour continues to function. In lower-income countries (excluding China and India) which have a total population of one billion 700 hundred million, including almost the whole of Africa, the share of primary goods in exports remains almost constant, and primary goods account for more than half of all exports. The same is true of the lower middle-income countries, and it is overwhelmingly true of the high-income oil-exporters.

But this ratio measures only specialization within that

fraction of the product of world labour which is internationally exchanged. According to this indicator, the positions of China and India within the old division of labour are changing; manufactures now represent 47 and 59 per cent of their respective exports. The greater part of the labour performed in those countries is, however, agricultural, and much of it is not even destined for a market. Asia – and even the Asian NICs – continues to export one highly specific 'primary commodity', namely labour.[29]

Even so, things are changing considerably in two senses. As we have already seen, the rapid industrialization of the entire middle-income category has led to a spectacular increase in exports of manufactures from the upper middle-income categories. But it has also led to a reversal of trends within the trade in primary goods: the North now feeds the Third World. The agribusiness model which was developed in the USA and then introduced into Western Europe after World War Two seems to have led to a repetition of the 'victory' which gave the manufacturing industries of the northwest its absolute advantage over the rest of the world in the last century. Between 1970 and 1981, the share of 'North–South' exports in all agro-food trade rose by 6.7 per cent, whereas the flow in the other direction fell by 4.2 per cent.[30] Yet the North's new food hegemony (which is in fact primarily that of the USA) has, as we have seen, come up against increased competition from capitalist agriculture in some countries in the South.[31] Paradoxically, this relates directly to the 'new international division of labour'.[32]

What we have termed the 'new international division of labour' is an intra-industrial (or even intra-agricultural[33]) division resulting from what we have previously characterized as the Fordist tripartite division between: 1) engineering and advanced technology; 2) labour-intensive activities requiring a certain level of skills; 3) activities involving easily acquired skills.

This new international division is the great novelty of the postwar period, and it reflects the uneven international distribution of both intensive accumulation and crisis. It is the result of two developments. We deal in this book with the first: the logic of industrialization in what was (and to a large extent still is) the periphery of the first division of labour. But it should not be forgotten – and we will return to this point – that a symmetrical process of stratification is also occurring in the old manufacturing centres. One of the major issues of the period is whether the old industrial countries of Europe, in competition with the USA and Japan, will be closer to level 1 or level 2 when they emerge from the present crisis.[34]

The importance of the new international division of labour should be neither overestimated nor underestimated.[35] Whilst Third World industrialization is more widespread and occurred earlier than one might think (Singapore was already a NIC in the early sixties; Argentina is no longer a NIC, but new NICs will emerge from the middle-income category), very few countries have become export-based industrial powers. East Asia's 'Gang of Four' accounts for 60 per cent of the South's exports of manufactures; if we also take into account Brazil and India, the total rises to 70 per cent. Conversely, the South produces only some 3 to 4 per cent of all manufactured commodities consumed in the North. But it does export over 16 per cent of such typically Taylorist goods as clothing, shoes and electronic components, and 8 per cent of all optical goods and home electronics.

We are, it will be remembered, talking about a *division* of labour. Thus, it is not only the South which is increasing its exports (level-3 exports to the North). The North finds buyers for its level-1 and 2 products in the South (or should we say that it has rediscovered old customers?[36]). In terms of world trade in capital goods, the share of North–South exports rose from 20 to 30% in the seventies, whereas that of North–North exports fell from 60 to 50 per cent. Yet the South's increasing share in the international trade in industrial goods has to be distinguished from the old 'battle for markets', even though OPEC does absorb them (this is in accordance with the 'old division of labour'; OPEC in fact absorbs almost as many capital goods from the North as the NICs), and even though the logic of peripheral Fordism does, I repeat, have something to do with markets.

The increase in the flow of manufactures works in *both* directions, and it reflects a geographical shift in *both* tendencies within the internationalization of Fordism. At the beginning of this chapter we noted that until the 1960s both tendencies were at work primarily in the North, and that they are now being extended to the North-South dimension. Thus, the market share of the South in the US imports rose from 12 to 25 per cent between 1970 and 1981; in clothing, and electric and electronic components and equipment, the South's market share rose to 80 per cent and 46 per cent respectively. Canada and Europe were the losers.

It must again be stressed that it is not because its industries are stagnating that the South is once again becoming a major market for the North's industrial products; on the contrary, industry is growing faster in the South than in the North. But the pattern of world growth is such that the South also supplies the North with a market (within the new international division of labour). Table 2 (p. 85) shows that, whilst the South now competes with the North on the world market, it also provides more of a market than the crisis-ridden North. Whilst the share of exports in GDP has risen from 12 to 20 per cent in the industrial countries, it has risen by only a few percentage points in the upper-middle income countries and it remains very low in Mexico and Brazil, which absorb their own surplus products. It is, however, true that exports now have a major share in the GDP of South Korea and its East Asian associates, and that the markets of the North cannot absorb them unless there is a corresponding rise in demand. Needless to say, it is the 'old' periphery which will provide the missing outlets.

'South-South' Relations

The emergence of peripheral Fordist countries and the accumulation of liquid assets in certain OPEC countries has led to a veritable explosion of the former periphery. The hierarchy is being reshaped before our very eyes. The periphery was never homogeneous, but the new factor is the increased flow of commodities between the NICs and those countries which are still primarily exporters of primary goods. This flow is *similar* to that which occurred under the old division of labour. In terms of basic Fordist and Taylorist commodities and in intermediate branches like steel, the NICs are becoming very competitive, and in the former periphery they are even competing with the industries of the centre.[37] A potentially triangular trade in raw materials, emigrants and manufactures is developing between the countries of the South. Significantly, NIC exports to the South are at once more 'regional', more 'sophisticated' and more 'capitalistic' than exports to the centre.[38]

In 1980, South–South trade accounted for 37.4 per cent of all the South's exports of manufactures. Sixty-eight per cent of all South–South trade took place within continental blocs, 37 per cent of it within Asia alone. But 'Asia – other continents' trade already accounted for one quarter of all South–South trade. This trade is organized by the NICs and is directed mainly towards OPEC countries. The dominant role of Asia is explained by its export-based NICs.

Year by year, the 'old division of labour' becomes more pronounced, but it now exists 'within' the old periphery. The rate of cover in Brazil's industrial trade with the South, for example, rose from 153 per cent to 555 per cent between 1973 and 1980, generating a surplus of 3.2 billion dollars (the corresponding figure for South Korea was 4.5 billion). The regional nature of this trade is a good illustration of how peripheral Fordism promotes 'common markets' of middle-class demand. In structural terms, it is very different to the export trade between the NICs and the North; capital goods represent 41 per cent of the total, as against 31 per cent in NIC–North trade, and clothing represents 5% (as against 21 per cent). The capital coefficient is twice as high in regional trade. The NICs (including India and Pakistan) are now beginning to achieve technological dominance in regional markets. They may not have reached the top of the technological ladder, but they are now exporting cheap professional equipment and engineering products.

Competition between the 'North inside the South' and the traditional centre also should be neither overestimated nor underestimated. It is, of course, because they earn such low salaries ($358 per month in Taiwan, as against $2,900 in West Germany[39]) that the engineers and skilled workers of the NICs are so competitive. But they have in some cases developed new technologies which are appropriate to their countries and which can easily be transferred to their clients in the South.[40] Both India and South Korea, for instance, are now winning major civil engineering contracts, whilst Mexico has developed original metal-working and oil-exploration techniques. In world terms, however, their share at levels 1 and even 2 of the new international division of labour remains minimal. Benabou rightly notes that whilst South Korea exports 4 per cent of its machine tools, 65 per cent of home demand is met by imports.[41]

We are witnessing *a reduplication of the new international division of labour*. In terms of bloody Taylorization's strategy of relocation and re-exporting, the 'first-wave' NICS are becoming less competitive as wages begin to rise, and increasingly the centre is using import quotas against them. With the help of multinational companies, a second stage of 'bloody Taylorization' is emerging, and it is directed towards what the *OECD Observer* (November 1982) calls 'the new wave of industrial exporters': Malaysia, the Philippines, and, in a sense, China.

Finance and Partial Regulation: The Role of Banks and Transnational Companies

The reduplication of the international division of labour, the distribution of world circuits of productive branches across the NICS and their superimposition upon old relations between the 'manufacturing centre' and the 'primary-exporting periphery' by no means lead to the emergence of a 'world economy' with a single hegemonic centre. Quite apart from the fact that Japan and Europe are still fighting the 'War of the American Succession' (to use Wallerstein's expression) and that the state capitalisms of Eastern Europe have a peculiar status within the 'system', the Third World now looks like a constellation of special cases. It is characterized by vague regularities, elements of a logic of accumulation which more or less complement one another, and by flows which emerge and then disappear within the space of a few years without a stable mode of overall regulation ever being established.

As one might have expected, the new division of labour is no more of a division than the old, if by 'division of labour' we mean a rational project drawn up by some Beast of the Apocalypse. It is a random configuration resulting from the myriad strategies adopted by different companies and states, from a miraculous harmonization of the very different regimes of accumulation adopted as a result of the impersonal process of class struggle between the multiple social formations of the North and the South. Some very poor countries export very little; in accordance with the logic of bloody Taylorization, others like Bangladesh export a great deal. Some countries have an advanced capitalism and have mastered level-3 and level-2 activities, or even level-1 activities. Some of these export one third of their total output, as does South Korea, whilst others, like Brazil, export relatively little. Once again, we see the need for concrete analysis, for the study of the economic and social history of each specific country, for the study of their modes of regulation, their forms of class alliance and their successive hegemonic systems. I do not have the heart to attempt to outline a typology of regimes in the South here.[42]

On the other hand the new division of labour does seem to deserve its name more than the old, in that the Beast of the Apocalypse is now embodied in the material form of agents and institutions which not only 'own' many centres of production, but which actually 'possess' those centres and which are therefore able to divide the labour of manufacturing *between them*.[43] We have already mentioned their names: the banks and multinational companies. They bring with them the Curses of the Apocalypse, in other words technological and financial dependency.

By the end of the seventies, a rich and well-documented body of literature on the *reality* of these dependencies was available.[44] But the argument had already moved from the realities that result from multiple processes back to functionalism and intentionality. The new division of labour tended to be reduced to the relocation of the unskilled levels of the tripartite Fordist division; it was described as working to the advantage of the centre alone and as resulting from decisions taken by companies in the centre. Unfamiliar duckbills like Korean ships and Brazilian rolling mills did nothing to shake dogma. It was assumed that the Third World is dependent in the same way that mammals are viviparous. The other tendencies at work within the move towards global Fordism were overlooked. As markets and production expand at the same time, final demand in the Third World also rises and has a greater effect on the behaviour of agents, banks and companies. And as usual, the autonomous actions of nation-states were ignored.[45]

So What Were Multinational Companies Doing in the Periphery?

The simple answer is 'relatively little'. They had certainly become more multinational:[46] direct foreign investments rose much faster than average fixed capital formation in the centre. They are certainly extremely powerful: the top 866 multinational companies control 76 per cent of world manu-facturing output. Thirty per cent of all international trade takes place *within* multinational companies. The problem is that all this relates mainly to the way in which the eco-nomies *of the centre* are interconnected and to the central-ization of capital *within the centre*. During the seventies, roughly 25 per cent of all direct investment by multinational companies took place in the South: 21 per cent at the beginning of the decade, 29 per cent in the middle, and 23 per cent in the late seventies. Between 1960 and 1980, the share of capital invested directly in the South *fell* (from 60 to 47 per cent in the case of Japanese companies and from 40 to 25 per cent in the case of American firms). Naturally enough, there were considerable variations and flows were very unevenly distributed. The USA 'exported' 50 per cent of all direct transnational investments, and Latin America 'imported' 50 per cent of all investments exported to the South.

In any case, in almost all developing countries, the flow of direct capital imports represents less than 3 per cent of all fixed capital formation (2.1 per cent in Brazil for example). In short, it is negligible.[47] Nor is it true that the subsidiaries of multinational companies have a major share in the export sector of their host countries. The exceptions are Singapore (92 per cent) and the free trade zones, which exist for that purpose but which employ only one million workers worldwide. Elsewhere, multinational companies are content with a modest role: 40 per cent in Brazil, 35 per cent in Mexico, 30 per cent in Korea, 10 per cent in Hong Kong and 5 per cent in India.

This is of course still a great deal, and the example set by the multinationals probably did encourage countries to export. They may even have led the way. 'New forms of investment' also have to be taken into account.[48] Multinationals based in a developed country may take a minority share-holding in local firms (state or private), and this may involve the transfer of technology or subcontracting agreements. But economic ownership, and therefore the initiative to invest capital and social labour, remains largely in the hands of the local ruling class. The examples of Brazil and Korea suggest that multinational subsidiaries are no more export-oriented than local firms. Indeed, the NICs are now becoming bases for new multinational companies.[49]

Multinational companies do not in fact look to the Third World simply in order to find cheap labour for central markets. They are primarily interested in finding markets there. Nor do they simply establish workshop subsidiaries (the 'world market factories' of the 'new international division of labour' orthodoxy). They tend, rather, to establish 'relay-subsidiaries', producing and selling on the spot.[50]

In both 1971 and 1981, CERM carried out surveys in which major French companies were asked why they had established foreign subsidiaries.[51] The majority (87 per cent of all respondents in 1971; 72 per cent in 1981) said that they wanted to establish their presence in an important market. The second reason they gave was equally significant; 31 per cent said in 1971 (38 per cent in 1981) that they invested in Third World countries because 'local producers are protected by local governments.' This, no doubt, is one of the Beast's ruses: it is import–substitution policies which 'cause' the new international division of labour. 'Reducing wage costs' was only the eighth most popular answer, but the number of companies giving this as their reason doubled between 1971 and 1981 (28 per cent, as against 15 per cent). But within the NICs in particular? The answers were broadly similar ... with some variations. In 1981, only 58 per cent of all companies said 'markets', whereas 40 per cent now mentioned protectionism (which proves that this is a good way to increase the number of industrial jobs!). 'Reducing wage costs' was now the fifth most common reason (23 per cent), and 're-exporting to countries other than France' was the seventh (19 per cent).

We therefore have to agree with Madeuf and Ominami when they conclude that, '*In a context dominated by Fordism, even if it is in crisis, it is difficult to break the link between valorization and realization. Most direct investment in the Third World is governed by the logic of the international diffusion of Fordism, which presupposes the simultaneous expansion of productivity and real wages.*'[52] We do, however, have to add one qualification: it is *consumption* that has to be linked to the rise in productivity. In the North, that condition was met by monopolistic regulation of wage relations. In the South it can be met (and has been met) by an increase in the income of the middle class alone, provided that the middle class is sufficiently large.

Whilst the international division of labour between countries does not result from the international division of labour within companies,[53] the latter does obey *the logic of peripheral Fordism*: plants (which are planned in the centre and tooled up by the centre) are set up *both* to provide access to a growing market (this consideration applies to most investment in Brazil: it is probably less so in Korea) *and* so as to reduce costs, including the cost of re-exporting.

The Example of the Auto Industry

The case of the auto industry (which is analysed in detail in CEPREMAP's 1980 report[54]) exemplifies the combined logic of peripheral Fordism: import-substitution plus export-substitution.

The problem with car-assembly in type 3 regions outside the countries of the centre is that it requires a qualified labour-force and, more generally, semi-skilled male workers with some industrial experience. Large markets must also be close at hand, as cars cannot be transported as easily as T-shirts or pocket calculators. For the motor industry, the ideal region-3 labour pool allows the labour-force to be reproduced cheaply, is close to markets, and provides skilled workers. In terms of the logic of Fordism, which links local consumption norms (and therefore wages) to productivity, finding such a region is rather like squaring the circle. Regions in economies which are 'too' dominated are out of the question, because there is no adequate local market. Given transport costs and the relatively minor share of the cost of labour-power in total costs, it is impossible to use Third World pools simply as 'bases for reexporting', even with the relative advantage of very low wages. Bearing these simple points in mind, two 'poor' forms of relocation therefore seemed possible.

First, replacing vehicle exports with the assembly of completely knocked down sets of parts. Vehicles for the local ruling class can then be assembled in Third World countries. This is an unsatisfactory alternative because of the loss of economies of scale and because of the cost of acclimatization. But since the importer-countries insist on local assembly, other forms of imports are often impossible. It is probably this consideration which determines this form of relocation.

Second, the marginal use of low-wage labour pools close to a central market as a base for assembling light vehicles which can be re-exported to the centre. *Deux chevaux* assembled in Galicia are, for instance, sold in France.

But two 'conceptual breakthroughs', both of them made by Ford, a company which truly merits its eponymous role, cast the problem in a totally new light in the seventies.

Considerable economies of scale had already been achieved by distributing branch circuit across Northwest Europe, with large plants producing standardized components for the entire European market. The key transfer-section was no longer final assembly, but component assembly (or even the manufacture of components) and engine assembly (engines, gear-boxes, axles). The proximity of markets, low regional costs, economies of scale and the concessions granted by the states which 'benefited' from the opening of the plants combined to dictate the choice of location.

The system would have remained internal to the industrialized countries if there had not emerged a new type of country: the 'dominated industrial country'. In the period 1960-70, the emergence of countries which were technically integrated into the world branch circuits of Fordism but which had not mastered its overall logic within an autonomous national framework and which had not assimilated its mode of social regulation helped to resolve the contradiction we described above. Here, Fordism could find both a working class and managerial elements; standards of living did not force up wages, but there was already a sizeable middle-class market. Most of the countries involved had authoritarian regimes: Spain at the end of the Franco period, Brazil, the countries of the 'immediate periphery', NICs emerging from the 'wider periphery' ….

The difficulty was that these countries had an eye to development and usually demanded a high rate of integration. They insisted, that is, that the final product must contain as many local inputs as possible. In extreme cases, they even expected companies to establish a national industry for them. In most of these countries the home market was too small for the advantages of local production to outweigh the loss of economies of scale, but relocation was the only way to avoid losing the market altogether. Besides, the export market for fully equipped factories was of considerable importance to two related branches in which motor companies are often involved: engineering and machine-tools.

Once again, Ford made the 'breakthrough' by reaching an agreement with Spain that laid the foundations for a new conception of relocation. It involved neither pure import-substitution for an inadequate local market nor the use of the country as a base for reexporting operations (which could not be justified because of the costs involved), but a combination of the two. Spain provided a market which was expanding even though norms of working-class consumption were low. Spain also agreed to accept a lower rate of integration (which removed the need to disperse production) in exchange for a clear commitment that the plants would be used to reexport certain components on a mass scale.

The 1972 'Preferential Interest Decree', otherwise known

as 'The Ford Law', reduced the minimum rate of integration from 95 to 66 per cent. In exchange, Ford agreed to re-export two thirds of its total output and to increase its sales in Spain by no more than 10 per cent. Major facilities for importing machine-tools were also granted. Thanks to this agreement, Spain became the great 'Region 3' of the European motor industry. US companies were the main beneficiaries, and General Motors also set up local plants.

In Portugal, Renault negotiated a variant on the Ford Law. Four vehicle and engine plants were expanded or built, providing 13,000 jobs. The Portuguese government extended a degree of protection to the Renault subsidiary, whose share of the local market rose from 12 to 30 or 40 per cent. On the other hand, three-quarters of the 300,000 engines built were reexported to northern Europe.

In more general terms, the manufacturers estimated at the end of the seventies that this new relocation strategy would involve 15 per cent of world output within ten years. This will lead to the loss of 15 per cent of all jobs in manufacturing in the industrial centre; the expansion of conceptual and administrative employment in the tertiary sector of type 1 regions cannot offset this completely. If output remains constant, the balance-sheet of employment will be very negative for the centre. Unless, of course, the market, and especially the peripheral market expands. But that is another story, and we will come back to it later.

The Question of Finance

The above criticisms of the 'new international division of labour' orthodoxy do not alter the fact that the tripartite division of Fordism has *resulted in* an uneven distribution of activities. The former 'centre' has gradually been polarized between levels 1 and 2, whilst most NICS remain at level 3 despite some remarkable (and promising) breakthroughs to levels 2 and 1. The flow of international trade does tend to follow this division, to say nothing of the flow of patents and royalties.[55] The North exports level-1 and -2 products to the NICS; the NICS export level-3 products to the North and level-2 products to other countries in the South.

But this outcome is not simply the effect of a division internal to multinational companies; indeed, one might say that they are in fact responding to a change which has largely been brought about by states and local companies. Local firms often find themselves in the position of sub-contractors or suppliers, and if they wish to export to the centre, they have to accept drastic conditions of subordination to import-capital in the centre. The subcontracting relationship means that they have to give up much of the 'extra surplus-value'[56] they derive from exceptional conditions of exploitation.

How, then, is this local accumulation, which far exceeds direct investment from outside source, financed? In the glorious period between 1965 and 1980, when peripheral Fordism was expanding, much of the investment was supplied by *borrowing* on the international bank capital market, though considerable amounts of local profit were also ploughed back. Most of the loans were in xenodollars or petrodollars, and they were pledged against: 1) future income from traditional exports (including oil, tourism and emigration); 2) the 'promise of work',[57] which in turn depended upon the profitable launch of new production processes in the NICs and upon the existence of markets for their future output; and 3) the recycling of borrowed capital to buy capital goods from the North. This was made almost obligatory.

Virtually the entire international community of lenders decided that they could gamble on this regime, particularly as after the first oil shock there was an explosion of available liquid assets. OPEC had deposited its surplus with private bankers, and borrowers were needed at any price. International bank finance began to replace direct investment, leading to the emergence of *an international credit economy.*[58]

Take the case of South Korea. In 1960, direct investment accounted for 82 per cent of all capital in-flow, and borrowing on the international money market only 18 per cent. By 1975, the proportions had been reversed. France's 'contribution' to the industrialization of the Third World in 1976 broke down in exactly the same proportions.

This change, which went hand in hand with a relative fall

in state development aid and grants, finally put an end to the classic picture of dependency. The centre (or capital and firms from the centre) no longer 'decided' to invest in the Third World; the ruling classes of the dominated countries chose[59] a strategy which required a rapid in-flow of capital. They found that capital in one of two ways.[60] First they used export credits to import capital goods. between 1971 and 1980 Third World debts corresponding to export credits rose from 26 to 110 billion dollars. Secondly they borrowed from the banks, and issued debentures. These debts rose from 10 to 145 billion dollars and from 4 to 15 billion respectively.

Over the same period, the total debt rose from 86 to 445 billion dollars, 64 per cent of the total being provided by private credits. The North's total direct investments abroad rose from 160 billion dollars in 1971 to 500 billion in 1980; the South accounted for some 53 billion in 1971 and 120 billion in 1980.

This change in the structure of outside finance must be clearly understood. In the case of direct investment, a 'captain of industry' from the centre takes the 'risk' of exploiting a peripheral force and tries to sell the product, either in the centre or elsewhere. He may have borrowed the money himself, but in any case he is acting on his own initiative and will repatriate any profits he might make. In the case of bank loans, the bank prevalidates the borrower's future income. More specifically, when the loan is advanced to finance the import of capital goods, the bank pre-validates[61] a given strategy for industrialization, but it is the firm or State which chooses that strategy.

In terms of transferring value from the periphery to the centre, the new system is as efficient as the old, provided that we regard the OPEC banks as belonging to the central financial system (an assumption which raises theoretical and political problems which cannot be dealt with here). The NICS' exports do not simply pay for their imports; increasingly, exports are also used to pay the interest on debts. The NICS have to bear a heavy burden of debt-servicing on top of the classic problem of 'the repatriation of profits by the multinationals'.

We will have time to come back to all this later. For the

moment, we will simply note that the world banking system faces an overwhelming task of regulation: it has to pre-validate the investment of world labour in the disparate and uncoordinated strategies of the Third World, and it has to reconcile them with the anticipated growth of world demand.

Multinational companies certainly help the banking system; as we have seen, their internal planning mechanisms control much of international trade flows. The banks also get help from the international trade system, which discovers both markets and suppliers. The fact that the NICs do not put everything they produce on the world market also helps; they absorb most of their growth (or at least more of it than industrial countries). The system of multinational banks and companies thus introduces elements of world regulation, and various NICs adopt different internal forms of regulation, which we cannot even begin to describe here. The world regime of accumulation of the seventies, or at least its 'peripheral Fordist component', is not short of forms of regulation.

'Private bank regulation' is, however, extremely vulnerable. Private institutions are given the task of evaluating both 'risk sectors' and 'risk countries', but they are at the same time subject to the pressures of competition. As a result, they all lend, or refuse credit, at the same time. When the monetarist shock, or the second phase of the crisis, came along in the eighties, this resulted in a wide variety of debt situations.

The *total* amount of capital available to finance Fordist industrialization is of course determined by the state of the international money and financial markets, and their profitability is determined by fluctuations in world demand. Neither multinational banks nor sovereign states in the Third World can control these factors. This brings us to the problem of the *overall regulation* of the world regime of accumulation or, to put it more modestly, to the study of the successive configurations in the world economy that are partly responsible for the fortunes and misfortunes of peripheral Fordism. That will be the subject of our last chapter.

Conclusions

'Towards Global Fordism', 'Primitive Taylorization', 'Peripheral Fordism', 'New International Division of Labour' ... all these concepts have to be handled with care, though I do hope that I have shown that they are useful, that they provide both a net and a ladder to help us grasp how phenomena relate to one another. We have gauged the extent of the phenomenon of Third World industrialization, and we have tried to grasp its underlying logic. But concepts are like coordinates on a map: they give only a superficial picture of the concrete realities of the national social and economic formations of the Third World. As Newton would say, we are trying to drain the ocean with a shell.

We have made no attempt even to outline a concrete typology of how these logics combine within real regimes of accumulation. Whilst there is obviously all the difference in the world between Mali and Argentina, Brazil and South Korea *do* have something in common. Within each country, we find a combination of highly diverse strategies and logics. Mexico exports oil and labour power, and has turned its northern borderlands into a vast free trade zone of sweatshops working for American firms. Mexico exports car components to the USA and Europe, and is developing revolutionary steel-making processes. The sexual division of labour means that primitive Taylorization (women working in the electronics and textiles industries) can often coexist alongside peripheral Fordism (men in the motor industry).[62]

As for the international division of labour as a whole, even if we restrict the argument to the new division, it is by no means as simple as both old and new orthodoxies would have us believe. It simply cannot be reduced to a division of manufacturing labour which is introduced by multinational companies because of different levels of skills and differing labour costs. It is the outcome of a process which unevenly distributes between countries capitalist relations and the Fordist model (now, as we have seen, extended to non-Fordist activities). That model affects work organization, but also the growth of markets and changes in life-styles.

This does not mean that we have to revert to the staggered diachronies of Rostow's schema, or to the view that all countries are involved in the same venture, that they will all move from take-off to the post-industrial era, and that the only problem is that they did not all set off at the same time. In synchronic terms, there is a certain complementarity, between the huge markets that have already been developed, and the countries that are gambling on the conditions under which they can exploit their own labour force, importing capital goods and exporting labour-intensive commodities, in an attempt to gain a foothold at the less skilled levels of the division of labour and to hitch themselves to the Fordist regime.

The regime of accumulation which emerged in the 1970s is in some ways reminiscent of postwar industrialization in France. Initially, there was a phase of reconstruction, with imports of equipment goods and 'transfers of technology' from the USA being financed by Marshall loans. The loans were repaid with 'bottom of the range' exports. During the second phase, a home market was developed. Wage relations were extended to take in the peasantry and internal control over Department 1 was reestablished (at least until 1968).

But the differences are blindingly obvious. France already had a skilled industrial base. The institutional forms which could integrate wage relations and provide a home market for the products of growth had already been established. The postwar transitional regime and Marshall aid simply anticipated the establishment of a relatively auto-centred regime of accumulation and of regulation procedures which depended upon national sovereignty.

Peripheral industrialization is very different. In terms of its regime of accumulation' and its mode of regulation, it is heavily internationalized from the outset. To modify Cardoso de Mello's criticisms of F.H. Cardoso, we could say that Brazilian Fordism is not only 'late'; it is also 'peripheral'. It is not following the 'bicycle – moped – small car – big car' trajectory which *all* fractions of the wage-earning population – from unskilled workers to young engineers – followed in France and Italy as mass-production increased. In Brazil, where workers still go on foot, the motor industry began by making large and medium-sized cars designed in Germany for a middle class that already existed in both Germany and Brazil.

In terms of international trade, a 'late-comer country' has to be 'complementary' with others, even if the fact of being 'peripheral' is a result and not an explanation. But complementarity is no more than a transitory, changing configuration, a truly miraculous 'chance discovery'.

It remains for us to look at the chain of events which allowed this 'chance discovery' to stabilize. We have already said something about the elements of partial regulation which ensured it a certain stability in the seventies, about the minor, but no doubt innovatory or even structuring role played by multinational companies and sub-contracting agreements, about captive trade, and about the role of private banks. But none of these institutional forms can resolve the problem of overall regulation; nor did they ensure the possibility of the international logic of peripheral Fordism being 'completed' at the world macroeconomic level during the first phase of the crisis in central Fordism. And if we do not understand this 'successful configuration', we will have difficulty in understanding why it was that the crisis became so general in the eighties. That will be the object of our last chapter.

But before we go on to that, let us make a digression for the benefit of sociologists, political scientists and – why not? – political militants. At a time when the dictatorial regimes which presided over the development of peripheral Fordism appear to be collapsing under the irresistible weight of pressure for democracy everywhere from Brazil to South Korea, it might be useful to see what light the economic theory we are outlining can shed upon the similar events that occurred in Southern Europe's three 'early NICS'.

5
Peripheral Fordism in Southern Europe

In the mid-seventies, three dictatorships collapsed in Mediterranean Europe. Both the speed of the process and the degree of pressure brought to bear by the working class varied in Portugal, Greece and Spain. Outside contingencies did not play the same role in all three cases, but by the end of the decade all three countries had made the transition to a moderate and modernizing form of social democracy (which brought together many of the radicals and even the Marxist-Leninists who had been involved in the anti-fascist resistance), with a traditionally-based Communist Party (which then was reduced to ten to twenty per cent of the vote) to its left, and a conglomeration of traditional notables and modernist technocrats to its right. Specificities aside, it is obvious that the same tendencies were at work in all three countries. Social forces (and not only popular forces) developed under and by the dictatorships had undermined their base.

From 1980 onwards, the dictatorships in Brazil and South Korea began to be shaken by repeated blows from the popular masses or from elements within the ruling classes. In Brazil, the struggle for *Direitas* (direct elections) led to the appointment of a civilian president with a background in the popular opposition on 15 January 1985. A few days later, on 12 February, Chun Doo Hwan's dictatorship failed to prevent the democratic opposition making considerable advances in the elections it had rigged so carefully. The Korean New Democratic Party (the equivalent to Brazil's PMDB) immediately launched the struggle for direct suffrage in the 1988 presidential elections.

Hypothesis: the same economic causes (the maturation of peripheral Fordism) had the same effects in the early NICs (Southern Europe) and, ten years later, in the 'NICs of the seventies'.

There is no need to worry: I am not suggesting that we lapse into vulgar economic determinism. But it might be useful to use the concepts we developed in relation to what we now call the NICs to shed some retrospective light on the events of the seventies. And in terms of the socio-political outlook for the present NICs, it might be helpful to look at the example of Southern Europe.

Such is the object of this chapter. It is in no sense intended to replace a concrete analysis of the socio-economic formation and of the political conjuncture of either Southern Europe in the seventies or the NICs in the eighties. The task of making such an analysis can be left to better qualified specialists. In this chapter, we will simply be comparing figures and concepts, and outlining hypotheses.

The Internal Bourgeoisie and Peripheral Fordism

The Greek sociologist Nicos Poulantzas described the phenomenon of the 'crisis of the dictatorships' in Portugal, Greece and Spain as resulting from the emergence of an *internal bourgeoisie*.[1] By introducing this concept, he attempted to break with the traditional distinction between the 'national bourgeoisie' and the 'comprador bourgeoisie'. The classic distinction is only meaningful in terms of the old image of the international division of labour and of capitalist accumulation. According to that image, the imperialism of the dominant countries blocks 'normal' industrial development ('normal' in the sense of 'led by a national bourgeoisie') in the dominated countries, and uses a 'comprador' group of feudal elements, bureaucrats and import-export traders to ensure that the countries in question go on exporting primary commodities.

By breaking with an instrumental conception of the state and, more specifically, of dictatorship (traditionally seen as a mere instrument in the hands of the comprador group), Poulantzas was suggesting that in these specific cases the relative autonomy of the state (vis à vis both the local ruling classes and foreign imperialism) allowed a new industrial bourgeoisie (and therefore a new petty bourgeoisie and a new working class) to emerge. This *internal bourgeoisie* is inserted in a novel way into a new international division of labour which cannot be reduced to an opposition between 'primary' and 'manufacturing'. Although it has emerged from totalitarian conditions,[2] the new social bloc necessarily aspired towards the democratic and trade-union liberties enjoyed by the most highly industrialized countries.

Poulantzas's definition of the internal bourgeoisie was somewhat confused. Having abandoned the canonic division inherited from the Third International (and the old division of labour), he had no difficulty in making a distinction between the internal bourgeoisie and the 'oligarchy', that is, the bloc formed by 'agricultural' and 'comprador' interests. Internal bourgeoisie is primarily industrial, and it is developing true capitalist relations of production. The issue of the appropriation of surplus-value and its desire to conquer (or win back) the home market for industrial goods are enough to make it hostile to foreign capital. On the other hand, it is unclear how it differs from the national bourgeoisie, except insofar as '*its development coincided with the internationalization of capital*'. It is, then, dependent upon the process of internationalization itself, both in terms of technology and markets, and in terms of share-holding, patents and sub-contracting.

We recognize here the characteristics which we have ascribed to peripheral Fordism, and which make it so radically different from both the old division of labour and early import-substitution policies. Poulantzas did not really grasp the principles behind this regime because he was still influenced by economic representations which were current amongst the Marxists of the early seventies: intensive accumulation was reduced to heavy industry, and internationalization to imperialism and to the presence of American multinational companies. Little attention was paid to wage relations or to the various ways in which they are regulated. But the concept of an internal bourgeoisie did allow him to grasp the main political point: real capitalist development did take place under the dictatorships of the sixties, and they were not simply 'retrograde'. Nor, of course, were they anti-imperialist, but they did encourage the development of bourgeois democratic forces (the internal bourgeoisie) which were neither anti-imperialist nor truly nationalist (this precluded the emergence of either Stalinist or Maoist anti-imperialist united fronts led by the national bourgeoisie or the proletariat respectively).

Poulantzas was quite right as to what would become of the anti-fascist fronts led by the internal bourgeoisie. Although he did not know it, he was also right about the petty-bourgeois radical developmentalists, who were well represented in Spain by a proliferation of 'Marxist-Leninist' groups which even found a toehold in the state apparatus itself, and, in Portugal, by elements of the MES. In historical terms, they became modernizing movements which brought the political (and ethical) superstructure into line with the emerging economic base: an industrial economy which had Fordist tendencies, even if it was not yet Fordist as such. In short, they brought it into line with a European version of the American model, or, to be more specific, with European social-democracy.[3]

According to Poulantzas, the ruling classes of Europe could collectively be regarded as an internal bourgeoisie – but an internal bourgeoisie which has 'made it' and which is on good terms with American imperialism. This implies that we have to take a new look at the postwar transition to Fordism in Europe. We have already alluded to that process by drawing a comparison between France and Italy in the sixties and Latin American attempts to industrialize by adopting first an import-substitution policy and then the logic of peripheral Fordism. We now have to go further and ask why it was that these countries provided such a favourable terrain for the emergence of analyses of modern capitalism.

The studies I refer to produced the concepts of 'Fordism' and 'peripheral Fordism',[4] and they emerged in two European countries which lie midway between Southern

Europe and 'Mittel-Europa': France and Italy. This is not a coincidence. For various reasons, France, Italy, Greece, Spain and Portugal are all very old market civilizations and once enjoyed a worldwide influence. They were almost 'centres of a world economy', and some were in fact 'centres', albeit never as nation-states.[5] They emerged from World War Two with industrial and social structures that were archaic compared with the American model; even before the war that model had already been described as 'Fordist' by both Gramsci and Henri de Man.[6] For a variety of historical, social, political, economic, cultural and geographical reasons, France and Italy took advantage of the Liberation and Marshall Aid to embark upon an imitative process which, by the fifties and sixties, admitted them to the 'virtuous circle' of central Fordism. It was only in the sixties that Portugal, Greece and Spain embarked upon the same course. It is therefore not surprising that the theorization of the Fordist model of accumulation and of its spatial and inter-regional dimensions should have occurred primarily in France and Italy.

Conversely, the study of the processes of 'new industrialization' in Southern Europe, the East, Latin America and Asia sheds retrospective light on the specificities of the French and Italian miracles (and even the Japanese miracle). The virtuous circle of auto-centred Fordism was *never* fully completed, either in the postwar Fordist countries or in the NICs of the sixties and eighties (and it is becoming less and less likely that it will ever be completed). Foreign markets and foreign sources of technology always played an important role, as did the reserve army of labour provided by the break-up of archaic regional socio-economic blocs.

If we pursue the analysis at the regional level, the distinction outlined in the last chapter between 'Fordism' and 'peripheral Fordism' becomes less pertinent. In Italy, for instance, a whole range of situations can be found, from the dominated, archaic and comprador structures of Sicily, to Emilia Romagna, which produces numerically controlled machine tools for the whole of Europe. As for France, it has been shown elsewhere that its Fordism is still marked by the rapid absorption of the peasantry and the archaic middle classes, and that it still has a marked tendency to import professional equipment and to use what is in Northern European terms an under-paid labour force to produce labour-intensive commodities. I myself have described this as 'bottom of the range' Fordism, and it has often been pointed out that the state (and the 'developmentalist party') played an autonomous role in France's postwar growth.[7]

Are France and Italy examples of a successful peripheral Fordism? There is no point in jumping to conclusions. I have stressed in Chapter 4 that France started out with an advantage: between 1945 and 1968, it made a serious attempt to achieve 'introversion', and wage relations were *already* subject to monopolistic regulation.[8] These factors may, however, simply be preconditions for any transition from peripheral Fordist to Fordism as such. A comparative study of France in 1955, Italy in 1960, Spain in 1975, and Brazil and Korea in 1985 would no doubt produce fascinating results.

For the moment, however, we will restrict ourselves to comparing our three Southern European NICs, leaving aside Yugoslavia, which is still a fairly classic NIC, Albania, which really is a special case, and Turkey, which only became an OECD member by a stroke of luck.

Similarities and Differences

What follows should not be seen as an attempt to develop a new classification which ranks countries in terms of a scale ranging from 'imperialism' to 'underdevelopment', or to rate concrete realities in terms of 'peripheralization of Fordism'. I simply wish to demonstrate that the concepts we elaborated in previous chapters (the old and new divisions of labour, primitive Taylorization and peripheral Fordism) can shed light on concrete situations, revealing both similarities and differences. Without going into a concrete analysis of our three social formations (far beyond the scope of this study), we shall see that a rapid examination of the macroeconomic statistical data immediately brings out major differences between economic regulation and regimes of accumulation in Spain, Portugal and Greece. Those differences may help specialists in political science to understand the startling differences in the transition to democracy in these three countries.

It should first of all be noted that, although it played a central role until the beginning of the modern period, Southern Europe has been 'peripheral' for a very long time. As the international market economy developed, the Byzantine Empire, Italian city-states like Amalfi, Venice and Genoa, and then the Iberian kingdoms played pioneering roles, thanks to the ideal support provided by the Mediterranean.[9] But the fall of Constantinople, the discovery of America and the Cape route, and then the inability of Castille and Portugal to control their colonial empires led to the 'centre of the world' being transferred to the North Sea, initially to Bruges, Antwerp and Amsterdam.

At the same time, Greece (which had already been dismembered and pillaged by the Italian cities during the Fourth Crusade) was reduced to playing a peripheral role and was then cut off from the Atlantic world economy by the Turkish invasion.[10] The 'first international division of labour' was already taking shape within that world economy. Because it was based upon trade between independent states, the polarization seemed to imply mutually advantageous specialization and cooperation. David Ricardo theorized this deceptive appearance with his theses on 'comparative costs', illustrating it with the famous example of English textiles and Portuguese wine. Greece or Spain would have served his purposes equally well.

A detailed study of our three countries in the eighteenth and nineteenth centuries would obviously reveal major differences between them. On the other hand, it would also become apparent (and it is in this sense that Greek independence is significant) that they gradually converged and adopted a political regime appropriate to this regime of accumulation: a free-trade monarchy underwritten by 'the international community'.

Between the two world wars, their paths diverged again. Portugal and Spain festered under fascism, whilst Greece maintained its ties with Great Britain (though it did not enjoy democracy as a result). The history of the two fascist regimes is complex. Whilst they obviously had a reactionary political base, they did attempt to pursue an auto-centred policy (as did De Valera's Ireland, under more democratic conditions, from 1932). Spain even tried to achieve autarky by using corporatist regulation. They did not, however, emulate the successes of Peron or Vargas, precisely because the popular classes were politically and economically excluded. The survival of its colonial empire also means that Portugal is a very special case: it was both one of the poorest peripheral countries in Europe and the poorest imperialist power.

In the course of the sixties, they began to converge again with the 'normalization' of the dictatorships in Spain and Portugal, and with the America-inspired colonels' coup in Greece. As Jorge Semprun put it, 'the war was over'. And Fordist penetration had begun.

Although we cannot go into details as to the transformation of industrial production processes in all three countries,[11] or undertake a comparative concrete analysis of their socio-economic formations, we can discuss some indicative figures. It should, however, be remembered that the concept of 'peripheral Fordism' owes a lot to Spain and Portugal. It was in Spain that Ford negotiated the model agreement which removed the barriers (bequeathed by the Francoist phase of import-substitution) to importing machines and parts for its assembly lines in exchange for a commitment that part of its output would be re-exported to Northern Europe. Renault and General Motors subsequently reached similar agreements in Portugal and Zaragoza. Let us see, then, what we can learn by applying the criteria we used in the last chapter to the figures. In terms of the World Bank's classification, Spain and Ireland (another NIC!) are at the bottom of the list; Portugal and Greece come more than half-way up the table of 'upper middle-income countries'.

We can see from a glance at Table 3 that Spain, Greece and Portugal were indeed '1960s' NICs, with higher growth rates, particularly in industry, than the 'old' industrial countries and even (with the exception of Portugal) than the 'upper middle-income countries'. In the seventies, however, the rate of growth declined (especially in Spain) and was similar to that in the 'centre'. The downturn in manufacturing output and investment was even more pronounced. It is as though the crisis in Fordism had already

Table 3 (continued overleaf)

Changing Production: Portugal, Greece, Spain

	Industrial Countries	Upper Middle Income	Portugal	Greece	Spain
GNP/head of population 1981	11,120	2,490	2,520	4,420	5,640
GNP/head of population: growth 1960-81	3.4	4.2	4.8	5.4	4.2
Growth in GNP					
1960-70	5.1	6.4	6.2	6.6	7.1
1970-81	3.0	5.6	4.4	4.4	3.2
Growth in manufacturing					
1960-70	5.9	7.8	8.9	10.2	8.0
1970-81	3.1	6.3	4.5	5.5	3.7
Growth in gross investment					
1960-70	5.8	7.5	7.7	10.4	11.3
1970-81	0.9	7.2	2.3	1.3	1.2
Share of agriculture in GDP					
1960	6	18	25	23	7
1981	3	10	12	17	
Share of manufacturing in GDP					
1960	30	23	29	16	29
1981	25	24	35	20	

Table 3 (continued)

	Industrial Countries	Upper Middle Income	Portugal	Greece	Spain
Exports/GDP					
1960	12	18	17	9	10
1981	20	23	27	20	17
Structure of exports %					
1960 → 81					
Primary	34 → 28	84 → 55	45 → 28	90 → 53	78 → 28
Textiles	7 → 5	4 → 10	18 → 27	1 → 17	7 → 5
Machinery and transport equipment	29 → 35	2 → 13	3 → 13	1 → 3	2 → 26
Other manufacturing	30 → 32	10 → 22	34 → 32	8 → 27	13 → 41
Current balance of trade 1981 $ billions			−2.6	−2.4	−5
Funds repatriated by emigrant workers 1981 $ billions			2,896	1,177	521
Debt service as % of exports 1970 → 82		10.7 → 16.9	n.a. → 20	7.1 → 13.1	24.6[1]

1) OECD figures; total debts, whereas World Bank figures give only publicly guaranteed debts.

Sources: World Bank, *World Development Report*, 1983, 1984. All growth rates are given as yearly averages.

matured in these countries. The agricultural sector had declined considerably, and Spain appears to have reached the point where the modern tertiary sector grows faster than manufacturing.

If, however, we look more closely at the figures, we can see that we do not have to go back to Rostow's rather crude chronological scale (take off/industrialization), which would suggest that Spain was first in the race and that Greece was last.

There are major differences between the three in terms of wealth and population. Spain, for instance, is much wealthier than Portugal. Spain, like South Korea, has a population of 38 million; both Greece and Portugal have a population of 9.7 million. It is only in Spain that the home market has always played an important role; Spain in fact exports less than the average 'industrial' or 'middle-income' country. Portugal, on the other hand, has been a 'manufacturing' country for much longer than either Greece or Spain.[12] Spain manufactures more than the average industrial country, whereas Greece depends more upon agriculture and less upon manufacturing than the average 'middle-income country'.

One immediately assumes that (in relative terms), Greece is closest to the 'old international division of labour' (producing and exporting primary commodities), that Portugal is characterized by a form of 'primitive Taylorization' (exporting cheap industrial goods, and with a weak home market) and that only Spain represents a fully developed form of 'peripheral Fordism'.

If we examine the structure of exports, these differences become more pronounced, and they seem to confirm the initial diagnosis. By the early 1960s, Portugal was no longer primarily a 'primary exporter'; that sector was already less important than it would be for the 'upper middle-income' category in 1981. Besides, Portugal was at the time a colonial power in its own right. Greece on the other hand relied upon the primary export sector to the same extent as the upper middle-income countries, and was to continue doing so. Portugal was from the outset a major exporter of textiles, and that sector continued to expand. Greece had begun to export more textiles than the average upper middle-income country. That in itself is not, however, an index of higher development; on the contrary, Greece and Portugal were simply approaching the textile specialization rate for low-income countries and lagged far behind India and Bangladesh.[13] Unlike Greece, Portugal began to export machinery; its exports in this sector were average for a middle-income country but much lower than those from the major NICs we discussed in the last chapter. By 1981 Spain was specializing in machinery exports; it exported twice as much as the average middle-income countries, almost as much as the industrial countries had been exporting in 1960, and more than the Third World NICs, including South Korea. Portugal – and more so Spain – was exporting other manufactures (intermediate goods, etc.) to the same extent – if not more – than the industrial countries, and much more so than the average middle-income country.

The geographical structure of exports, and especially exports of manufactures, has also developed in different directions.[14] Portugal has ceased to be an English colony and an African metropolis, and has become primarily a manu-

Table 4
Changing Geographical Structure of Exports: 1960 → 1981
(% of all exports)

	Portugal	Spain	Greece
All commodities			
Industrial countries with market economy	56 → 77	80 → 56	65 → 56
Eastern bloc	2 → 2	2 → 4	21 → 8
High-income oil-exporters	0 → 1	0 → 5	1 → 13
Developing countries	42 → 20	18 → 35	13 → 23
Manufactures			
Industrial countries with market economy	56 → 81	57 → 57	52 → 56
Eastern bloc	0 → 1	1 → 2	6 → 5
High-income oil-exporters	0 → 11	0 → 5	3 → 13
Developing countries	44 → 17	42 → 36	39 → 26

Source: World Bank, *World Development Report*, 1983.

facturing platform for the EEC (mainly for France and West Germany). Spain, on the other hand, has increased its 'top quality' exports to the South, as one might expect of a developed peripheral Fordism (the change is not quite so marked in terms of manufactures), though it has also broken into the French market. Greek exports remain stable, the only change being a slight redeployment towards the oil-exporters of the Middle East rather than to the USA and Eastern Europe. It is rather as though Greece's insertion into the international division of labour remained unchanged, with only its clients changing.

The last indicator of differences in the regime of accumulation operating in these three countries (to restrict the discussion to their 'international insertion') is growth measured in terms of 'international value'. Domestic growth, expressed in volume terms, has to be corrected to take into account 'unequal purchasing power'; at any given rate of exchange, the same amount of money will buy different amounts of commodities in different countries.[15] To calculate the difference, we need a weighting index which it is not easy to establish. Very schematically, the 'higher' a country's position within the international division of labour, the more 'expensive' its products. Conversely, if a country sells its products cheaply, a fall in the real exchange rate may offset an adverse effect on its volume of output.

Table 5 (overleaf) shows that, as the crisis developed, home growth (measured in volume) slowed down in all three countries, Greece still growing faster than Portugal, then Spain. But whereas Spain's output was increasingly revalorized on the world market, Greece's output was devalorized until the crisis. Prior to the crisis, Portugal's output was valorized, but that soon ceased to be the case.[16] It was as though Spain had joined the ranks of 'countries benefitting from the terms of trade' (countries which get wealthier even though they are stagnating), whereas Portugal had joined the ranks of 'countries working at a loss'. Whilst the volume of output rose, it fell in international value.

The internal reasons for these divergent modes of insertion are too complex to be analysed here. We will restrict our discussion to two basic determinants of the regime of accumulation: changes in real wages and changes

Table 5
Conditions of Growth: 1963-80. Deviation from OECD Average.
(average annual rates)

	Real exchange rate		Domestic growth (volume)		Growth in international value	
	1963-73	1973-80	1963-73	1973-80	1963-73	1973-80
Spain	+1.19	+3.5	+1.33	−0.48	+2.53	+3.01
Portugal	+0.61	−3.13	+1.81	+0.45	+2.43	−2.67
Greece	−0.72	+0.16	+2.52	+1.19	+1.81	+1.35

Source: F. Freire de Souza, *Contrainte extérieure et régulation macroéconomique dans les économies semi-industrialisées*, Thesis, Université de Paris I, 1983.

in productivity (Table 6). All three countries experienced 'super-Fordist' productivity rises in the sixties, and then a definite downturn after the crisis. But whereas real wages rose faster than productivity in Spain (a sign that a 'consumer society' was developing at the expense of the archaic sectors), in Portugal, capital increased its share of surplus-value at a rate of 1.8 per cent a year, both before and after the restoration of democracy. This made it more competitive on the foreign market, but restrained the home market.[17] In Greece, the crisis and the restoration of democracy seem to have swung the balance in favour of wage-earners.[18]

All three countries are deficit countries (Table 3). Peripheral industrialization always presupposes that sources of finance can be found within the 'old' division of labour and from international credit. Between 1967 and 1980, the funds repatriated by emigrants, and tourism, accounted for 96 per cent of Portugal's trade deficit; the figures for Spain and Greece were 87 and 52 per cent respectively. There were, however, major differences between the three. Emigration was Portugal's main source of income, whilst Spain's was tourism and Greece's, commissioning ships. The balance had to be found, and like all NICs, Spain, Portugal and Greece found it by borrowing. Only Spain received any significant inflow of private foreign investment during this period (£5,700 million in Special Drawing Rights, as against £800 million for Portugal and £500 million for Greece). The

Table 6
Division of Relative Surplus-Value.
(average annual rates)

| | Productivity | | Real wages | |
	1963-73	1973-80	1963-73	1973-80
Spain	5.46	4.14	6.38	4.40
Portugal	6.81	3.05	4.99	1.20
Greece	7.51	3.42	6.98	5.06

Source: Freire de Souza, *Contrainte extérieure* ...

total inflow was, however, still below 5 per cent of the level of gross domestic investment.[19]

If, then, we adopt the sinister system of ranking countries in terms of debt-servicing, Spain ($5.7 billion in 1982) comes fourth after Brazil ($18.5 billion), Mexico and Venezuela. Spain (25 per cent) is also very badly placed in terms of the debt-service/exports ratio (Brazil: 32 per cent; Mexico: 28 per cent; Chile: 27 per cent). In terms of these indicators, Greece and Portugal were much closer to the average of middle-income countries. But, like them, they were threatened with economic strangulation and with the possibility that their young democracies would be made wards of the IMF.

Conclusion

The mid-seventies 'crisis of the dictatorships' in these three Mediterranean countries does seem to have been one of the early effects of the industrialization of the 'NICs of the sixties'. Unfortunately, the restoration of democracy coincided with the global crisis in Fordism, and it hastened the crisis in peripheral Fordism by denying these countries the advantages enjoyed by Asian countries in terms of the exploitation of the labour force.

There are, however, major differences between the three in terms of their insertion into the world economy. Greece is still the closest to the agricultural export model, whereas it is Portugal which relies most heavily on industrial exports based upon low wages (primitive Taylorization). Spain has developed a home market by raising wages. Even if we do take into account the wretched state of the peasantry in the South and that of the agricultural proletariat, Spain strongly resembles the Italy of the 1960s. The purchasing power of the working class in the teeming shanty towns of the industrial belts has increased out of proportion to average productivity. Cheap housing is available, and in 1984 25 per cent of the working class owned television sets – to use only one of the indicators chosen by *L'Etat du monde* to gauge the spread of mass consumption – as against 39 per cent in Italy, 16 per cent in Greece, 27 per cent in Korea and 12 per cent in Brazil. In terms of car-ownership, Spain is well launched upon the postwar 'Franco-Italian' trajectory.

I will not be so foolish as to attempt to deduce explanations for the different political processes that followed the crisis of the dictatorships from a handful of figures. That task can be left to sociologists, political scientists and militants. Nor should we forget the contingent factors that influence historical processes: the role played by colonial wars and the radicalization of a sector of the military in Portugal, the role played by Juan Carlos in Spain, and the Greek colonels' unfortunate experiences in Cyprus (the Greek equivalent to Argentina's Falklands affair). But the differences we have noted (but not analysed!) in their regimes of accumulation may provide a starting point for future work.

Greece changed little during its short-lived dictatorship. Being a small agro-exporting country, it was able to negotiate entry into the EEC on not unfavourable terms under a government of notables from an earlier period in its history. With the emergence of PASOK, the time had finally come for an interclass bloc dominated by the internal bourgeoisie, and it was stable enough to bring social legislation into line with European norms.

In Portugal, on the other hand, the fall of the dictatorship led to a real national crisis in the Leninist sense of the term. The ruling classes could no longer rule in the old way, and the working classes were no longer willing to obey in the old way. 25 April 1974 was Portugal's February Revolution: the entire country rose up against a discredited regime, demanding bread, freedom and peace in the colonies. Between 28 September and 11 March neither the ruling classes nor the internal bourgeoisie, which had rallied around Soares's PS, could control working-class unrest. The gap between working-class aspirations and the low wages imposed by the logic of primitive Taylorization was so great that European norms of consensus could not be applied.

The only alternative to a revolutionary breakthrough was a brutal normalization. The Portuguese October never came because there was no revolutionary leadership, even though the people did have some access to arms. There were also divisions within the people, and differences between the North, with its small farms and its reliance upon agricultural exports, and the South, with its modern industries and its large waged labour force on the latifundia.[20] On 25 November 1975, power was restored to various fractions of the internal bourgeoisie, but Portugal's unfavourable insertion into the international division of labour forced them to adopt a stop-go policy.

In Spain, the transition did not pose any serious problems for the internal bourgeoisie, thanks to the skill of the king, thanks to that of Prime Minister Suarez and thanks, above all, thanks to the leaders of the Communist Party and the trade unions, who agreed to exchange the interests of democracy against those of social peace rather than return to the horrors of the civil war of 1936. The PSOE came into its rightful inheritance. And like the French Socialist Party, it did so during the dark days of the general crisis in Fordism.

But neither Portugal nor Spain are out of the woods yet. Portuguese industry, like Spanish agriculture and Spanish fisheries, remains dependent upon wage relations which have more in common with primitive Taylorization than with social democracy. Spanish industry still enjoys the protectionist measures adopted under Franco. The entry of both countries into the EEC will create more economic and social problems for them than for their partners. It will also seriously compromise the position of other EEC partners such as the Maghreb countries. Spain and Portugal will find it very difficult to clamber aboard a train which set off in 1957, when the countries of what was once Lotharingia decided to pool their Fordist growth. They will find it all the more difficult in that the EEC's archaic institutions are making the crisis even worse.

Thousands of miles away, other dictatorships are being shaken as the demand for democracy grows, probably for the same reasons. It is to be hoped that the women and men of today will learn from the lessons of the past, that they realize that the crisis in Fordism has entered a new phase, and that it now affects peripheral Fordism too. This will make the transition all the more difficult for Brazil and, perhaps one day, for South Korea. It is to this changing conjuncture that we now turn.

6
From the Configuration of Success to Crises in Peripheral Fordism

The spectacular successes enjoyed by Brazil, South Korea and Mexico in the seventies, and, in rather less unexpected fashion, the crisis of the dictatorships in Southern Europe, have completely discredited the thesis of the 'development of underdevelopment'. The 'periphery' can indeed industrialize, grow and successfully compete with the centre, even in the most modern manufacturing branches. Betwen 1970 and 1978, average yearly growth in manufacturing output in the NICS ranged from 4.6 per cent in Portugal and 6.8 per cent in Mexico to 18.3 per cent in South Korea. In South Korea, per capita GDP rose from $70 to $2,281 between 1960 and 1980. Life expectancy in Hong Kong (75 years) is now higher than in West Germany. If we compare these figures with those for countries in the centre, the 'socialist' countries, or the old import-substitution countries, 'peripheral Fordism' appears to have been an overwhelming success, and the more of it as exports play a more important role in its growth.

It might be objected that inequalities are increasing, that primitive Taylorization involves atrocious working conditions, and that happiness cannot be measured in terms of GDP. These are valid arguments for citizens and militants, but they are irrelevant to an economist. The argument of the sixties was that autonomous capitalist growth in manufacturing was simply *impossible* in dominated countries. It has to be answered in the same terms, in other words in capitalist terms.

It must, however, be stressed that in world terms, we can count the number of successful NICs on our fingers. India is a giant and the seventh greatest economic power in the world (France is the sixth greatest), and its exports are mainly industrial, yet it provides its population with an average individual income lower than that of Burundi. Individual incomes in China are 20 per cent higher. Nigeria, Iran and Turkey, which were expected to play a 'sub-imperialist' role, have either become bogged down in spectacular fashion or have exploded. 1980 saw the rise of workers' struggles and an end to growth in South Korea, Brazil and Poland. In 1981, Mexico showed that the model was financially bankrupt, and a host of other countries suspended their debt payments. Factors relating to the local and the global crisis in Fordism were beginning to combine with peripheral factors.

In order to understand the chain of events leading from the configuration of success to the configuration of crisis,[1] we have to go back to the particular form taken by the general crisis in Fordism, and to how the states of the North managed the crisis in the seventies, after the first oil shock. This does not mean explaining what happened on the periphery in terms of the needs of the centre. In Chapter 4 we analysed industrial growth in the South, after we had simply noted at the end of Chapter 2 that the crisis, which affected the North first, was not yet catastrophic. We now have to see how this non-catastrophic stage of the crisis could, in macroeconomic terms, contribute to the expansion of peripheral Fordism insofar as it is an element within an international regime. We will then return to the South in order to show that, even before the turning point of the crisis in the North at the end of the 1970s, the storm clouds were gathering over peripheral Fordism – the dominant logic within local regimes – and that its subsequent crisis cannot simply be explained in terms of the evils of monetarism. Finally, we will demonstrate that central monetarism can nonetheless be held largely responsible for the strangling of peripheral Fordism.

Social-Democratic Management of the Crisis and Compulsory World Keynesianism

The second half of the seventies was marked by a strange contradiction. On the one hand, the crisis in Fordism was getting worse. On the other hand, Keynesianism was still a force, even though it had lost its base in both national and international terms. Its survival was the main element which gave the period its flavour, and we must therefore begin our analysis with Keynesianism.

Social-Democratic Management of the Crisis

In my *L'Audace ou l'enlisement*, I describe the first phase in the management of the crisis as 'social democratic'. Social democrats were in power in both Germany and Sweden. In Britain, Callaghan's Labour government was in power. The United States had Carter, a Democrat, as president. In France, Italy and Japan conservative governments adopted similar policies, either because trade-union pressure forced them to do so, or because their economic convictions led them to do so. In general terms, the dominant idea was that Keynesianism was still a valid policy. The mainstream was to borrow (like Sweden) or to issue an international credit money (like the USA) and wait for the oil shock to wear off, for supply to adjust to the deformed structure of world demand, and for the OPEC countries to begin ordering civil and military equipment goods.

At the national level, it was the Carter government which followed the policy of 'absorbing' the oil shock most consistently. Carter's USA was the 'locomotive' (to use the fashionable OECD terminology of the day), and it supplied the world with an internationally recognized credit money, even if its international purchasing power was increasingly coming under threat. In the domestic sphere, the USA succeeded in creating millions of jobs, most of them in the tertiary sector, despite, or because of, the conspicuous absence of increases in productivity. Western Europe and especially Japan supplied machinery and household equipment goods not only to the USA but also to the OPEC countries and to those countries in the South which had in their turn adopted peripheral variants on the Fordist model we examined earlier.

Naturally enough, America's 'lax monetary policy' led to a rapid fall in the value of the dollar, but the USA was not concerned; the devaluation helped to finance expansion at home. Because of the low import coefficient, it produced only a slight rise in inflation. The dollar's nominal fall against other currencies thus led to a *real* devaluation of American costs and restored American competitiveness, which had been compromised because the dollar had been over-valued for so long. And American expansion was so great that both Japan and Europe took good care not to protest too much.

Finally, international advisory bodies on economics, and especially the OECD, were recommending a policy of 'rotating Keynesianism'. Each of the three poles would take it in turn to play the role of 'locomotive', stimulating home demand so as to promote world growth. At their regular summit meetings, the 'Big Seven' and clubs of leaders like the Trilateral Commission argued that a coordinated policy of Keynesianism could act as a substitute for an explicit institutional form of monopolistic world regulation.

Relative Paralysis in Europe

Whilst the USA protected its rising employment by means of a rapid devaluation and paid the price of stagnation in productivity, Japan adopted the same devaluation policy (and again, it had no dramatic effect on internal inflation, and for the same reasons: the low share of imports), but used it to increase its market share and to flood the world with Fordist manufactures (cars, hi-fi equipment, optical equipment, etc.). Taking 1970 as a base of 100, US industrial output reached 141 at the beginning of 1979, whilst Japanese output reached 148. European countries certainly experienced remarkable growth for a period of crisis, but their rates of growth were lower than those of either the USA or Japan. In 1979, the index for France and Italy was 130; that for Germany and the UK, which had started out from a lower level in 1975, was 116.

The reasons for this slow growth are of course deep-rooted, and relate to the gravity of the industrial crisis as well as to the fact that European varieties of Fordism are both 'heavy' in terms of capitalist intensity and 'rigid' in terms of social relations. As the present study is deliberately confined to the 'non-specifically national' dimensions of the crisis, we will concentrate on only one major obstacle to implementing the 'Keynesianism + devaluation' tactic in Europe: the perverse mechanisms of 'austerity + internationalization'.

At the industrial level, Europe is increasingly integrated but it is still fragmented into distinct national spaces, *each* of which has to solve its balance of payments problem. In terms of production, these spaces are increasingly 'complementary'; they are, that is, obliged to buy from one another. Under these conditions, devaluation loses much of its efficacity because 'price effects' are not so marked. In order to improve its balance of payments, each country has to import less, consume less and invest less. Even as 'substitute products' are concerned (goods produced and exchanged by all countries), competition through pricing and volume adjustment within Europe, which has become a vast free-trade zone with no common social policy, leads to a remarkable form of protectionism which operates through wages restrictions and 'competitive stagnation'. In other words, it leads to austerity.

Unit wage costs (the ratio between the purchasing power of wages, direct or indirect, and productivity) had until now been the key variable in the monopolistic regulation of Fordism. Unit wage costs had to be regulated in such a way as to compromise neither the valorization of capital nor the realization of output. Compulsory measures therefore had to be used to prevent firms within the same national space from competing with one another by reducing their unit costs. Hence the institutional forms of monopolistic regulation of wage relations: guaranteed minimum wages, collective agreements, etc. No such mechanisms exist at the European level; there is simply an undertaking, which is, it is true, written into the preamble of the Treaty of Rome, to promote 'an *accelerated* rise in the standard of living' (my emphasis).

The various European countries therefore found themselves in a situation of competitive regulation against each other, which meant that the efficacy of internal Keynesianism was compromised earlier than in other countries. We will see later how this configuration of stagnation became more widespread as a result of the second oil shock. But for the moment, this local configuration existed with the favourable context of world Keynesianism. As we have already seen, its most spectacular effect was the rise of peripheral Fordism. We will return to that topic later, but first we will look at the changes that were taking place at the very heart of the regime of accumulation.

The Deepening Crisis and the Search for a New Way Out

Gambling on a stimulation of effective demand, without any corresponding rise in productivity at a time when per capita investment was still growing, was not without its effects. It meant that the nominal revenue distributed was in excess of the real growth of socially-produced value. Elsewhere I analyse the divergence between nominal values and underlying economic developments in terms of the distinction between 'exoteric' and 'esoteric'.[2] It is this divergence which leads to the take off of inflation. Values-in-process were prevalidated, but their overall growth could no longer be ensured as compatible. This did have a positive effect: the prevalidation of values-in-process 'come what may' warded off the imminent crisis, and in fact growth reached the maximum levels permitted by the rise in the 'capital co-efficient', in its organic composition. But inflation spiralled back on itself, increasing capital costs and gradually strangling investment. Very few jobs were created, and the increasing cost of the welfare state as expenditure per head of active population rose, reduced overall profitability still further. The question had more to do with profitability than with demand. There were three possible solutions: cutting wages (which was for the moment out of the question), restoring productivity, or reducing the cost of constant capital and especially fixed capital per worker.

Relocation to the Third World was, as we have seen, one

of the means used to achieve the first two objectives (by extending the scale of production). As relocation was accompanied by increased demand in the former periphery, its effects were not particularly recessive. But at a deeper level, wage relations in the industrialized countries were beginning to be affected by two different developments, one regressive and the other potentially progressive.

The first was an 'indirect' attempt to reduce wage costs. It was made not by a frontal assault on the central core of the working class or on wage-earners in the tertiary sector, but by segmenting the labour market, by increasing the number of jobs which were not covered by collective agreements, etc. This well-known tendency will not be analysed here.

The second development was a search for new sources of productivity within the labour process itself. The 'tech nological revolution' of electronics promised some new sources; other sources implied a challenge to Taylorist principles. Tasks were combined in new ways, and individual and collective interest in increased efficiency was promoted.

This obviously takes us away from the area of 'developments within the crisis' and into an almost unexplored world of blind alleys. The object of this tentative search was a new principle of work organization that could provide the basis for a new regime of accumulation. It was no longer a matter of catching up with or imitating a pre-existing model (the model of the USA in the fifties). Graph 2 (overleaf) shows that at this time Japanese productivity rose in spectacular fashion. Japan left standing those competitors who were still trying to catch up with the USA (France and Germany). This is even more obvious if we look at the different branches in more detail (Table 7 overleaf). Japanese capitalism did not simply catch up with the USA; it overtook it by discovering a new post-Fordist way of translating the skill of its producers, both manual and intellectual, into productivity.

But, as with Taylorism, these seeds of the future need a favourable social and macroeconomic environment if they are to grow. The monetarist shock was to prove the point in negative terms.

At the time, however, what was striking was the differ-

Graph 2
Per Capita Levels of Productivity in Manufacturing Industry: 1950-81.
Base 100 = USA

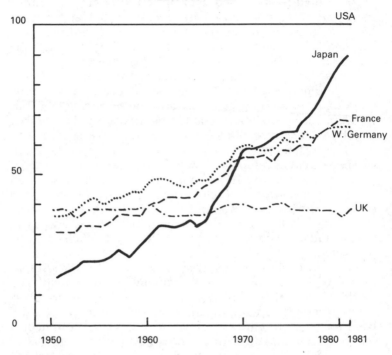

Source: CEPII.

entiation taking place within the former centre. Whereas France and Germany continued to catch up with the USA in Fordist terms,[3] and whereas Japan made a spectacular leap forward, the UK, which had gained no ground during the period of Fordism's maturity, fell seriously behind. The fact that central Fordism was being reshaped was obvious from the *difference* in productivity levels, but that in itself tells us nothing *in absolute terms* about the changes taking place in the labour process or about their effect on the Fordist model's profitability crisis. What, for instance, happens to the apparent growth in productivity or the fall in the capital coefficient? Despite all the weaknesses one would expect to find in this kind of statistics, CEPII's 1984 report does provide

Table 7
Per Capita Levels of Productivity in Manufacturing Branches:
1980. Base 100 = USA

	France	W. Germany	UK	Japan
Metal-working branches	62	64	28	122
of which:				
Steel and metal	70	91	38	137
Mechanical engineering	71	65	27	117
Electrical and electronics	50	40	26	135
Vehicles and transport*				
equipment	55	55	21	94
Non-metal working				
branches	73	70	47	59
of which:				
Building materials	71	76	38	47
Textiles	64	69	46	48
Wood, paper and misc.	63	67	42	66
Chemicals	78	79	46	101
Food and agriculture	76	48	54	43
Manufacturing industry	69	67	38	90

*Relative changes occur very rapidly in this branch. In 1981, Japan overtook the USA, reaching a relative level of 101.

Source: CEPII, 'Dualité, change et contraintes extérieures dans cinq économies dominantes', *Economie Prospective Internationale*, 13-14, 1983.

us with some indications.[4]

In the period 1973-79, annual growth rates of productivity in manufacturing in all countries were between one and three points lower than they had been in the period 1960-73 (in the USA, productivity rose by little more than one per cent). These rates were not to return to that level, although certain countries did enjoy a slight acceleration in 1979-83. Even so, they rose to only 2.5 per cent in the USA and to only 7 per cent in Japan. Over the same period, fixed capital in Japanese manufacturing industry grew by almost 6 per cent annually, whereas employment in manufacturing rose by 1.5 per cent per year until 1979, and then fell by 1 per cent per year from 1979 to 1981. The technical composition of capital thus rose considerably, but so did productivity; the capital coefficient[5] for manufacturing industry, which had risen by 1.3 per cent per year between 1963 and 1973, *fell* by 2 per cent per year between 1974 and 1982.

Once again, it seems that Japan really had found a way out of the profitability crisis. On the other hand, the 'reduction' of the organic composition of Japanese industry may have been the effect of an intersectorial redistribution towards lighter industries like electronics (and if it is the case, it cannot have a lasting effect). This did not happen anywhere else: the capital coefficient continued to rise in the UK (+4 per cent per year in 1974-82), in France (+2 per cent) and in the USA (+1.4 per cent). In Germany, it continued to rise but did so more slowly (+0.3 per cent).

As a result, the rate of return[6] in Japanese manufacturing industry started to rise again, slowly, in the middle of the decade (but it had fallen by half in the period 1970-75), whereas in the USA it continued to fall by 2.7 per cent per year until 1982 (2.1 per cent for all industries). It fell by 3 per cent in West Germany and France, and by 5 per cent in the UK. Whilst something new was obviously happening in the midst of the crisis (witness Japan), the 'social-democratic' phase had done nothing to reverse the underlying tendencies which had caused it.

Compulsory World Keynesianism?

After this brief glance into the heart of the crisis in Fordism, we are in a better position to understand the conditions that gave rise to the 'miraculous' success of peripheral Fordism. It will help if we go back to the conditions, described in Chapter 3, that led to the relative failure of early import-substitution policies. We can ignore internal causes, except, perhaps, the weakness of the home market. The point is that the peripheral sub-Fordism of the fifties was unable to insert itself competitively into the world market for manufactures because the extremely rapid success of Fordist production methods in the centre had resulted in a productivity gap. Wage differentials, which were to become very great after twenty years of growth in the centre, did not *yet* compensate for that. Finally, it was impossible to finance the purchase of capital goods because the terms of trade were worsening for economies relying upon primary exports.

By the end of the sixties, these restrictions had been partly lifted. Initially, the NICs turned to the foreign market (primarily the North), beginning with those branches which required little investment: this was 'primitive Taylorization'. In the seventies, this strategy encountered an unhoped-for conjuncture. First, productivity slowed considerably in the North, but in the first NICs productivity began to accelerate as Taylorist and Fordist methods became more widespread. They began to 'catch up' at a historically unprecedented rate. Secondly, in the North, 'social-democratic' crisis management meant that the purchasing power of wages continued to rise; in the South, repression kept purchasing power down and in some cases reduced it to below the levels it had reached under populist regimes at the end of the import-substitution period.

The NICs thus became increasingly competitive (as compared with the centre) as their unit wage costs fell, but this did not lead to any reduction in demand as the expanding markets of the centre opened up.

But this was not all. Investments have to be financed. The rise in oil rents totally reversed the terms of trade, and that provided some countries with a solution. Mexico, however, was in fact the only oil-exporter NIC. The other oil exporters were buying 'final' goods (including warplanes) or fully-equipped factories which did not go into production immediately. What is more important, they were investing their money abroad or in private banks.[8] The increase in oil rents was initially another burden for the vast majority of candidates as NICs, which were either investing or had already begun to make the transition from primitive Taylorization to peripheral Fordism.

As we have seen, direct investment on the part of multinational companies also provided a partial solution. The third source of finance came from oil rents themselves, as they were 'recycled' to the non-oil NICs by multinational banks. The extraordinary complacency ('benign neglect') with which the USA used its own currency to pay for its trade deficit allowed the OPEC countries to accumulate a considerable surplus in petrodollars, most of it available for deposit in banks in America or the Middle East. The USA in fact had a trade deficit both with OPEC and with certain developed countries (Japan and West Germany). As Japan and Germany therefore had a net surplus, they could begin to issue loans in their own currencies. It was therefore definitely the issue of dollars which increased the amount of money available on the world market. For the sake of convenience the term 'petrodollars' is used to describe this money, but it would be more accurate to speak of xenodollars or even xeno-currencies, as the yen and the mark are playing an increasingly important role.

Now there are no restrictions on the use that can be made of xenodollars. They provide the banks with liquid assets in the form of a universally accepted currency. By 'monetizing' American deficits and pseudo-validating both sustained growth and OPEC surpluses, they provide the basis for a new international credit issue. A bank operating in the Euro-market, or rather the 'xeno-market' (a financial market which is not regulated by the system that issued the currency in which it is dealing) can take the gamble of lending more xenodollars than it holds in reserve because all the loans made by the world banking system are eventually deposited within the system itself. As bankers say, 'credits make deposits.'

The only obstacle preventing an *individual* bank from opening new credits is the need to anticipate the balance between the credits flowing back and the withdrawals its own depositors can be expected to make at any given moment. By issuing *private* credit money it prevalidates the real growth stimulated by the loans it makes. The original xenodollars it holds (those issued by the American monetary system itself) function as a safety device. In other words, it requires a certain coefficient of pseudo-validation to underwrite its own prevalidations. But there is no specific way of regulating the ratio of the international credit money supply (payable in dollars) to its base – the cumulative American deficit owed to the banks.[9] Such regulation is possible only in a national framework.

After the first oil price shock, international banks oper-

ating on the xenomarkets found that they had a liquidity surplus; they were holding a large amount of the central
currency issued by the central country, and they began to
look for borrowers.[10] They found them, both in the deficit
countries in the North (but not in the USA) and especially in
the NICs. Credit was extended to the NICs because the banks
believed that they could industrialize successfully. In other
words, the banks prevalidated values-in-process that had
been invested in the logic of peripheral Fordism. As we now
know, the banks' expectations were unreasonably high. But
the loans they advanced did make a major contribution to
the establishment of peripheral Fordism as a *real* component element in world accumulation.

Not only did the NICs sell their products to surplus countries, which was equivalent to making real payments and to
wiping out a corresponding share of their debts for good.
They also bought capital goods from the centre. They
thus helped to validate the expected upturn in accumulation
which provided the basis for the credits granted to central
countries (primarily the USA). Only one condition remained
to be met: if the world banking system's prevalidation of the
success of peripheral Fordism was to become a truly world
prevalidation, the NICs had to repay their debts by selling
their products. Not immediately (that is, after all, the principle behind credit), but eventually. And it was not unreasonable to believe that they would do so, the criterion being
the belief that their 'exports/debt service' ratio would
improve within a few years.

The international debt economy was, then, based upon
two assumptions. In terms of the creation of a mass of international money (xenocredits), it was assumed that capital
investment in peripheral Fordism would prove profitable. In
terms of the creation of an international money base
(primary xenodollars), it was assumed that central Fordism
would weather its balance of payments crisis. Like any
assumption as to the success of a regime of accumulation,
these were self-fulfilling prophecies.

To sum up. During the first phase of crisis management
(1973-79), the world configuration was as follows:

˙In the OECD countries, and especially in the USA, growth
was led by consumption, which was slowing down but not

decreasing; productivity gains were low, and investment was slowing down.

˙These countries paid for their imports on credit, and this led to the proliferation of an international credit money (xenodollars) based upon American national credit money.

˙Liquid assets lent by surplus banks (OPEC and Japan) to certain countries in the South (NICs) allowed the latter to buy machinery from OECD on credit.

˙The NICs hoped to be able to repay their debts by selling their manufactures to OECD and OPEC countries. This seemed reasonable for two reasons: first, productivity was rising very rapidly in these 'new' countries (whereas it was slowing down in the North), and their hourly wage costs were five to ten times lower; secondly the world market was expanding as a result of 'social-democratic' management of the crisis.

Given this ephemeral and extremely fragile configuration, the NICs were able to reach annual growth rates of about 10 per cent, which is not bad during a major crisis! Moreover, their demand for capital goods from the North more than compensated for job losses in the old industrial countries caused by their increased competitiveness in the consumer goods sector. Thanks to a strange ruse of history, we find here an echo of the virtuous USA–Europe–Japan configuration of the fifties. In a sense, the rise in oil rents, which had been financed by the monetization of America's deficit and then recycled to the NICs by private banks, acted as a '*compulsory Marshall Plan for the Third World*'.

It must, however, be stressed that both private recycling and the peripheral Fordist regime itself are extremely fragile mechanisms. The model was highly dependent upon the growth of world demand, and it applied to only a limited number of countries in the South. It also destabilized their internal structures. Moreover, *private banks* could not *regulate* the regime in any stable fashion.

Insofar as it was based upon a pure credit money issued by banks which assumed that the regime could be completed, this model displays some of the features of monopolistic regulation. But insofar as it was based solely upon a private banking system, without any central institution to regulate the volume of pseudo-validation and the liquidity coefficient, it had more in common with the proliferation of private domestic credit during the boom periods of nineteenth-century competitive regulation. It presupposed that everything would be fine in terms of demand, that there would never be any clearing problem, that credits and withdrawals, and repayments and deposits would balance out, and that there would never be a frantic search to find 'real' money or a currency that was universally accepted as valid.

The absence of a safety device invalidated these assumptions. The absence of regulation (in the American sense of 'rule-making') led to an accelerated triangular trade between the deficit countries of the North, the surplus countries of the North and OPEC, and the NICs. It allowed and stimulated both the investment of world labour in capitalist wage relations, and the rise of peripheral Fordism. In that sense, Charles-Albert Michalet is quite right when he sardonically comments that, 'The absence of any regulation in the American sense of the term in the Eurobanking system ensured the regulation of world capitalism in the French sense.'[11]

The crisis in regulation, in other words the monetarist shock, was to be devastating. But before we turn to that, we have to look at the increasing instability in the NICs and, more generally, within the Third World as a whole.

The Clouds Begin to Gather

Summarizing, much less pursuing, Carlos Ominami's courageous attempt to make a case by case (or type by type) analysis of crises is out of the question here.[12] We will therefore simply evoke the most specific difficulties inherent in the logic of peripheral Fordism.

Internal Factors

Without wishing to curry favour from Alfred Sauvy, we have to begin by mentioning the major factor in the crisis affecting virtually the whole of the Third World: the population explosion.

i) Demographic Tensions

For a long time, the anti-imperialist left dismissed this problem out of hand because it clung to an angelic conception of an ideal schema of reproduction: more mouths to feed meant more arms to feed them. Which is perfectly true ... given a permanent regime which ensures that the annual growth of the active population remains proportional to the growth of stock of means of production and to the growth of total production. But the population explosion in the Third World is not the statistical expression of a permanent regime. On the contrary, it represents a *demographic transition* from the old regime (lots of children and lots of premature deaths) to a 'new' regime (few children and greater life expectancy).[13]

It has been argued that it was the stabilization of the Fordist regime which normalized the size of the family in the North (two children, so that they could fit into the back of the car and would do well at school). But this complex and long-term phenomenon, which began very early in the advanced industrial countries, by no means coincided with the appearance of new medical techniques, new norms of hygiene and changes in life style in the Third World. These factors affected only a small proportion of the population of the Third World, and the old demographic regime is still dominant. It is true that the transition has now begun and that the apparently exponential growth in the population has begun to level out.[14] For the moment, improved hygiene is leading to a decrease in infantile and adult mortality, resulting in a *temporary* but substantial increase in the economic burden placed on the active population or, to put it more accurately, in the *dependency rate* (the ratio between children and old people, and the total population between the ages of fifteen and sixty-five). The rise in the dependency rate must be subtracted from growth of productivity of those at work. It reduces the surplus available for improving living standards as a whole. What is more important, it also reduces the product that would otherwise be available for accumulation.

This phenomenon is partially responsible for the stagnation affecting the overwhelming majority of low or middle-income countries. It does not, however, excuse their failure to implement agrarian reforms which would allow the 'under-employed' to live, provide a living for their families, and save. Nor does it excuse their indulgence in 'Pharaonic' projects which waste savings and credits, but which create few jobs. But it is a real phenomenon, including some NICs, from Mexico to Algeria.[15]

ii) The Difficulties of Peripheral Fordism (Continued)

It is against this already difficult background that the logic of peripheral Fordism compounds both the difficulties of Fordism itself and those of peripheral countries.

In terms of the labour process, the problems of the early import-substitution policies re-emerge in a more or less attenuated form. It is difficult to achieve the productivity levels which are the norm in the centre, though wage differentials compensate for that to a large extent. As new heavy industries emerge, the cost of importing investment goods rises. Increased protectionism in the centre and the appearance of more sophisticated new technologies sometimes lead to a process of reverse relocation. Low capital-intensity technologies located in the periphery meet with increasingly fierce competition from highly automated technologies, which are of necessity located in level-1 and -2 spaces. This is very clear in the case of the textile industry, where mass production is now often more profitable in the centre, and as an emergent trend in the electronics industry.[16]

In terms of demand, with slow growth in the centre (cars being a typical example), the main market for mass production lies in the growth of wage income in the periphery. But although wage-earning has become widespread, wages themselves are held back by the need to compete both with the centre and other peripheral countries. As the economic burden on the active population increases, wages have to be distributed within the extended family, and consumption is therefore restricted to the most elementary items. Furthermore, unplanned urbanization and the destruction of subsistence agriculture mean that many middle-income countries can no longer feed themselves. Foodstuffs have to be imported, and this leads to a vicious circle: everything (land, capital) is devoted to the export sector, and less and less is available to promote self-sufficiency in food.

iii) Hegemonic Crisis

Perhaps the greatest problem, however, is that it is difficult to represent the interests of those groups who benefit from peripheral Fordism as coinciding with the 'interests of the people as a whole' for any length of time. As we saw in the previous chapter, 'overall socio-political regulation' can rapidly degenerate into a 'chaos of social relations'.

On the one hand, authoritarian structures are required to sustain very high rates of exploitation in the export sectors – rates of exploitation which vary considerably from near-slavery in the agricultural export sector, to bloody Taylorization in the sweat shops of the textile industry, to quasi-Fordist norms in heavy industry. On the other hand, the rise of the urban middle classes and of independent trade unionism in the factories leads to a demand for democratization, particularly as authoritarian management of the economy increases the likelihood of political and financial scandals. Either the demand for democratization is repressed, and repression destabilizes the regime (Korea, Poland), or it explodes in uncontrollable fashion, particularly when the rejection of the dictatorship becomes identified with a rejection of 'inhuman' modernization (Iran). Alternatively, the demand for democratization can be met to some extent. But in that case it remains precarious and opens the floodgates to working-class demands, and thus destroys the competitiveness of export-substitution (Portugal).

Chaos of social relations, which both democracies and dictatorships find difficult to manage, is probably the major obstacle to the transition of which the apologists of capitalist development dream: an economic sequence of 'primitive Taylorization ... peripheral Fordism ... autonomous Fordism ...' leading quite naturally to the sequence 'dictatorship ... liberalization ... (social-) democratization'. This sequence may be conceivable in a country where peripheral Fordism itself is based upon an earlier agrarian reform, or where social polarization is not too great (and this is one of South

Korea's advantages). But many middle-income countries have 'exclusionary' regimes of accumulation,[17] with the old oligarchy, the internal bourgeoisie and the new middle classes at one extreme, and the proletarian masses at the other (and they are 'proletarian' in the etymological sense of the word: their only contribution to the wealth of the nation is the production of an immense reserve army of children who are available for wage-labour as and when required).

Careful! The term 'exclusionary' may give rise to confusion. It is *purely descriptive*, and refers to the multiple effects of multiple causes: the degeneration of relations between town and countryside in the articulation of modes of production, the reduction of wages – in either absolute or relative terms – in accordance with the logic of 'primitive Taylorization', and so on. On the other hand, the transition to peripheral Fordism usually leads, in absolute and often in relative terms, to increased purchasing power for wage-earners and workers who are caught up in its logic (but not necessarily for women workers in textile industries, and definitely not for agricultural wage-earners).

Thus, the 'first wave of Asian NICS' which emerged in the seventies did not have 'exclusionary' regimes of accumulation, whereas the 'second wave' (Malaysia, etc.) may well do so. In all the second-wave countries, home consumption is rising more slowly than GDP. Whereas between 1975 and 1980 real wages rose by 73 per cent in South Korea faster than productivity) and by 32 per cent in Hong Kong, they fell by 20 per cent and 30 per cent in Thailand and the Philippines respectively.[18]

There is a further point of comparison. In the mid-seventies in South Korea, the central group representing 60 per cent of the population appropriated 50 per cent of all revenue; the poorest 20 per cent appropriated 5 per cent, and the richest 20 per cent appropriated 45 per cent. At that time, Taiwan was much more egalitarian, with the central group appropriating 52 per cent, and the richest 20 per cent, 39 per cent. But even in the early seventies, Brazil was far more exclusionary: 32 per cent for the central group, 66 per cent for the richest 20 per cent ... and 2 per cent for the poorest 20 per cent. And matters are getting worse: between 1960 and 1980, the share of the richest 1 per cent rose from

12 to 17 per cent; that of the richest 5 per cent rose from 28 to 38 per cent, and that of the poorest 50 per cent fell from 18 to 13 per cent.[19] In the 'centre' of Brazil (the Southeast), however, urban working-class households are beginning to buy consumer durables[20] (but not cars, which are reserved for the middle strata). Working-class households earning the equivalent of double the minimum wage represent a particularly dynamic market for consumer durables.[21]

The situation in Brazil is all the more serious in that the polarization of the national state along an inverted North–South axis in accordance with the 'old' international division of labour implies a certain *complementarity* between very low wages in the Northeast, middle-class standards of living and the employment of workers in the Southeast. To produce the alcohol needed to run four cars, the family of an agricultural labourer earning the equivalent of $1.25 a day had to be deprived of its two hectares of land. This means that it is impossible to satisfy the democratic aspirations of the population as a whole without threatening the obvious privileges enjoyed by the middle classes, and even certain of the interests of the urban working class: with the risk of splitting the democratic front in two and reverting to dictatorship.[22] The country's size and its federal nature make it obviously easier to manage the 'chaos of social relations' within democratic forms. But in the medium term, the possibility to sustain the existence of 'a Switzerland surrounded by Biafras' (to use a Brazilian image) seems to go against the universalist principles of democratic political forms. Witness the growing instability of Indian democracy; the centrifugal forces at work within it may well take on an ethnic or religious coloration, but they are based upon one of the most exclusive regimes of accumulation imaginable.

Even in a relatively non-exclusionary country like South Korea, all is not well. It was before the great monetarist shock that the country experienced economic recession for the first time (−5.7 per cent), just after Iran and at the same time as Poland. Excessive wage increases had of course made South Korea less able to compete with the rest of Asia, and the second oil shock led to increased external constraints. The use of domestic credit to finance a considerable level of investment which would take a long time to show any return resulted in a fearful inflation rate (though it was much lower than Latin America's). On top of that, there was a bad harvest.[23] But it was mainly the assassination of Park and hopes for democratization which sparked off the student and worker insurrections centred on Kwangju. Tanks were used to put down the insurrections, and the Chun dictatorship restored competitiveness by imposing savage wage cuts and devaluation. Paradoxically, South Korea was then placed in a better position to ride out the coming storm.

Rising Debts

A country which wishes to accumulate capital should not be automatically criticized for contracting debts. Credit means the prevalidation of values-in-process which, it is hoped, will complete the full cycle of valorization and realization. It is not unreasonable to buy machinery on credit, provided that you can use it and are likely to be able to sell the product. European and Japanese reconstruction was based upon credit, and that succeeded spectacularly. Under Reagan, the USA has broken all records for debts.[24] Its creditors think that that will work too.

It is when debts become cumulative that the problems begin. This is a sign that the society in question has not used its credit to invest in production that can be validated on the world market. It has either consumed the credit in nonproductive ways or has invested in labour which will not be validated on the world market. The same considerations apply to direct investments, but then it is the foreign investor who takes the risk. The problem of rising debts has been carefully studied by a number of expert authors using such sources as the World Bank, the IMF, the Bank for International Settlements and the OECD, and I will not bore the reader by going through it all again.[25] A few comments are, however, required.

It must first be stressed that there are many different types of debt in the Third World. This is to a large extent a reflection of the great variety of concrete regimes of accumulation to be found within the field marked out by the various logics defined in Chapter 4. Some countries, like

India, have relatively few debts, whilst others, the more industrialized countries, have enormous debts.

But even within the latter group, debts are put to very different uses. We have already mentioned the Newly De-industrializing Countries like Chile and Argentina, where the military, acting on the advice of the Chicago Boys, forced domestic industry into a recession and the middle classes into a credit-based consumer society, and imported arms. Others (the real NICS) embarked upon the adventure of Fordist industrialization. Throughout the seventies, that model of industrialization usually produced a deficit. Increasing oil rents did have a serious effect, but the major deficit in the trade in manufactures with the centre was more important.[26] This initial trade deficit was not necessarily serious to the extent that some of the accumulation on credit has been reserved for export activities.

This brings us to our final criterion: the ratio of debt-servicing to exports. This brings out the difference between Brazil and South Korea. Because it was so exclusionary and therefore made the middle classes richer, the Brazilian regime generated a structural flow of imports by buying luxury goods or the means to produce them. The cost of financing Pharaonic projects also has to be taken into account.[27] The South Korean regime, which was ultimately able to ensure the population a similar, but more evenly distributed standard of living based upon local production, devoted much of the money it borrowed to developing its export capacity. Thus, its ratio of outstanding publicly guaranteed debts to GDP was twice that in Brazil (32 per cent, as against 16). Brazil's trade balance was also healthier. But that did not mean that its economic situation was any healthier, because the use Brazil made of its debts was not designed to finance repayments. Moreover, Brazil relied more heavily than South Korea upon short-term bank loans (which, as we shall see, are more expensive). The ratio of debt-servicing to exports was therefore much higher: between 1970 and 1980, it rose from 12.5 to 40 per cent, whereas in South Korea it fell from 19.5 to 13 per cent.

It has to be remembered that the fact that a given regime of accumulation is exclusionary does not in itself explain why it contracts debts. The notion of an 'exclusionary regime' is, I emphasize, purely descriptive. It is neither a necessary (witness South Korea, or even Argentina) nor a sufficient condition. India has used the polarization of incomes to its own advantage by harnessing domestic savings to finance industrialization. In the period between 1960 and 1981, its investment rate rose from 17 to 32 per cent of GDP, but in 1981 the ratio of outstanding debts to GDP (11 per cent) and the ratio of debt-servicing to both GDP (0.6 per cent) and exports (8.5 per cent) fell. They are now amongst the lowest in the world.

A second point also needs to be made. Even though national political regimes are to some extent responsible for the debt strategies they adopt, they have no control over *the nature of the credits made available to them.* Credit creation is conditioned by the refusal (or inability) of the hegemonic powers to organize debt-recycling by creating a world credit-money which is both explicitly regulated and development-orientated. The relative decline in the mass of government loans as private banks take over the role of lending has had a serious effect as banks lend in the long or medium-term, but have to recycle and increase their short-term deposits.[28]

The banks tried to escape this difficulty by inventing the heresy of *variable loan rates.* The interest rate payable over the duration of the loan varies, depending on how much it costs the bank to refinance it on the international financial market. Previously, loans had been to dividends what share-cropping is to farming. It was accepted that, as bank capital was not involved in all the problems of valorizing capital, the banks would be content with a fixed income. Their income was fixed in advance, and was below the expected average rate of profit. It was accepted that the borrower would pocket the difference as a reward for his managerial skills. By introducing variable rates, plus a commission for 'risk countries', the banks make the borrower pay not only for the difficulties she has in valorizing capital, but also for the difficulties they have in procuring money once they have granted her the loan.

As a result, interest rates rose throughout the decade, and the period over which loans were granted became shorter and shorter.[29] An increasing proportion of new loans was used to pay interest on old debts and to renew the principal ('roll over'). In 1979, debt-servicing by non-OPEC developing countries (roughly equally divided between interest and principal) outstripped new long-term credits (Table 8). As they now had a definite trade deficit because of the second oil shock, they had to make up the shortfall by contracting short-term loans at the very time when interest rates, or the cost of loans, were rising very rapidly. By now, debts were feeding on debts, and the debt problem had become partly autonomous from the financing of peripheral Fordism.

Table 8 does reveal, however, that a *ray of hope* existed. The ratio of debt-service to exports did not rise constantly (as we have seen, it fell sharply in South Korea). The fluctuations reflected both the erratic repayment schedule and export successes, but the fact that the ratio fell in both 1976 and 1980 suggested that it might eventually stabilize and then decline. That would have been an indication of peripheral Fordism's success as an international regime. But that slender hope was soon to be dashed by the great monetarist shock.

A Pointless Catastrophe: The Monetarist Shock

Promoting the expansion of peripheral Fordism and sustained by its growth, central Fordism weathered its own

Table 8
Non-Oil Developing Countries: Ebb and Flow of Long-Term Debts

	1974	1975	1976	1977	1978	1979	1980	1981
Total new debt ($bn)	23.3	26.5	29.4	40.2	56	50.1	77.3	55.1
Interest and principal ($bn)	17.5	21.4	23.8	30.3	43.7	60.5	75.2	96.4
Debt service as % of exports of goods and services	11.2	13.5	12.8	13.8	17	18.3	18.2	20.8

Source: D. Llewellyn, 'Avoiding an International Banking Crisis', *National Westminster Bank Quarterly Review*, August 1982.

crisis, which had been latent since the end of the sixties and which became obvious with the catalysing effect of the first oil shock. It was able to do so by maintaining forms of monopolistic regulation. Despite de-industrialization, the sustained or even rising purchasing power of the mass of wage-earners, combined with the increase in jobs in the tertiary sector and indirect wages, prevented a cumulative fall in demand and production. At the same time, the international banking system 'monetized debts', mainly by recycling OPEC dollars, and offered credit against deposits of petrodollars. This made it possible to stave off the devalorization of crisis-stricken capitals and to finance new investment in the expectation that expanded intensive accumulation would resume on a world scale. We have already seen that the development of peripheral Fordism was based upon this assumption and that, as is normal in any regime of accumulation, it was to some extent a self-fulfilling prophecy.

From the Second Oil Shock to the Monetarist Shock

After six years of social-democratic crisis management and after the absorption of the first oil shock into world inflation, the purchasing power of oil exports in terms of manufactures from the centre was similar to what it had been at the end of the Korean war, when Fordism entered its phase of rapid growth. The political crisis provoked by the Iranian people's gut rejection of 'bloody Fordization' and Iraq's attempt to exploit the crisis by attacking Iran at the time when it was being torn apart by the Islamic revolution now led to tension on the oil market. OPEC took advantage of the situation to return the real level of oil rents to $34 per barrel. The old rent question reared its head again. Could the rise be absorbed, as in 1973? No, but it is not easy to understand why not. This time, everything was very different. It was as though the ruling classes no longer believed – or could no longer believe – in Keynesianism.

Future historians will discuss at length the chain of events which led from the second oil shock to the monetarist shock of 1981. Objective constraints were now greater than they had been during the first shock, and Keynesianism had less room to manoeuvre. France and the UK were faced with the threat of a trade deficit, and the USA, West Germany and Japan had cumulative national debts.[30] Besides, financial flows between the industrial economies had led to an increased concentration of international capital. Most of these flows related to mergers and takeovers of competing firms, and represented what Madeuf, Michalet and Ominami call 'investments without accumulation'.[31] As the industrial economies became increasingly complementary, there was less room for autonomous Keynesian policies: the 'European stagnation configuration' had become more widespread and more serious.

Perhaps more important, was the fact that the world's elites, the business men and the politicians behind the Tri-lateral Commission had ceased to believe in international Keynesianism. The regime's shortcomings were obvious. While the safety net of monopolistic regulation prevented a depression in the North, it was also an obstacle to redeployment towards new norms of production and consumption because of the rigidity it imposed upon the labour force and upon the allocation of capital between branches. Moreover, international credit money, like any credit money, was based upon the assumption that the regime of accumulation would re-establish itself, that the country issuing that money (the USA) could supply unconditionally competitive goods to the value of the monetary signs it had issued, and that the debtor countries of peripheral Fordism would find enough markets in the North to be able to repay their debts.

Towards the end of the seventies, it became clear that these assumptions were not founded. Growth was still mediocre, productivity was still slowing down, and per capita capital was still increasing. The dollar was coming under increasing pressure and its international purchasing power was falling. Like so many admissions of defeat, governments came into power based upon monetarist, or simply 'less Keynesian', coalitions: the Conservative victory in Britain, Volcker's arrival at the Fed and then Reagan's arrival in the White House, the liberal hegemony in West Germany's centre-left coalition, and the full application of Barreism after the defeat of the French left in 1978. A recrudescence of neo-classical liberalism filled the vacuum in alternative policy. Market forces alone would ensure the survival of those firms which were using the techniques of the future, and would eliminate the relics of the past. Market force alone would ensure the compatability of economic behaviour.[32]

By 1980, the change was very clear. West Germany and France had forced their wage-earners to adjust to the oil shock by accepting lower wage settlements, which had reduced their industrial output by 5 per cent.[33] Britain had already opted for monetarism in 1979, a point to which we will return below. Volcker's Fed attempted to apply the same policies, with the same results (a fall of 7%).

Although minor, this first monetarist shock had serious effects. Not least in that it gave American voters, and especially workers, the impression that Carter had presided over a recession. This is not the case. Overall industrial growth was very strong under Carter, but during Reagan's first term of office it fell to zero.[34] Furthermore, this first monetarist shock led to a sudden rise in interest rates and set off a chain of bankruptcies in countries caught up in the logic of peripheral Fordism. The most obvious example is Poland, which had already been hit by a political crisis.

Japan was the only country to enjoy any growth in industrial output during the second oil shock. By gambling on protectionism and the efficiency of its export apparatus, it increased its output by 10 per cent. It allowed its currency to fall sharply, seized the dynamic markets of the OPEC countries and launched a new export drive aimed at conquering the rest of the world. But even Japanese growth was halted by the great monetarist shock of 1981.

The use of Keynesian policies at home and abroad in previous years had fuelled inflation and, by causing the dollar to fall in an increasingly worrying way, had ultimately destabilized the world economy. Obviously, this could not go on. Tighter controls over nominal prices and wages would of course have slowed down inflation, and an international agreement on the regulation of off-shore financial circuits would no doubt have prevented the banks from unconditionally prevalidating the most extravagant investment plans. Until such time as wage relations were restructured

Graph 3
Industrial Output Since 1974

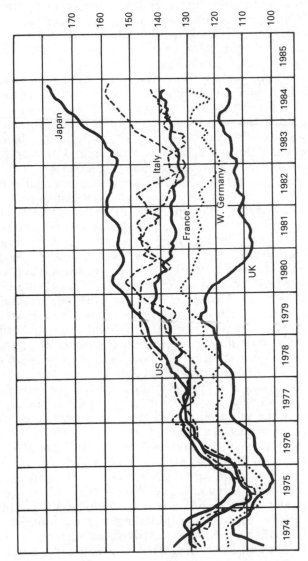

Source: INSEE, *Tendances de la conjuncture.*

in the centre and industry was restructured in a controlled way, it seemed not unreasonable to at least maintain the level of wage-earners' purchasing power, even if it meant reducing the working week so as to put an end to rising unemployment, the assumption being that maintaining purchasing power would provide a way out of the crisis by facilitating the introduction of new social techniques of production. Nor was it unreasonable to assume that a selective renewal of the credits granted to the South would promote growth in peripheral Fordism and thus help the world market to stabilize and then improve.

Monetarism[35] is basically a refusal to subscribe to either of these assumptions, a decision to open up the crisis, to challenge the distribution of value-added between capital and wages, and to refuse credit to insolvent capitals and consumers. All this was done in the name of a mythical 'cure', as though destroying the safety nets which prevented the Fordist regime of growth from collapsing would set free a new regime, as though the 'invisible hand of the market' had already shaped a new model which needed only to be set free of Keynesianism. In a curious way, one is reminded of the vulgar Marxist dogma that the productive forces have only to 'break the outmoded fetters of the old relations of production.'[36]

The attack on wage income in the UK and then the USA (where the attack was concentrated on cutting the revenue distributed by the welfare state) was the first element of this policy. The second, which gave the offensive its name, meant putting an end to pseudovalidation by slowing down the rate at which the American Federal Reserve issued official money in the hope that the inevitable rise in interest rates would decrease the demand for prevalidation and therefore slow down the creation of private credit money. The regulation of international money creation depends simply, but crucially, upon its base (the xenodollars, or US currency held by non-residents) and upon interest rates on the US market. And that international credit-money (primarily petrodollars which had been lent, multiplied and re-lent) was the very thing that was financing both growth in the NICs and the rejection of austerity in central countries with a negative trade balance.

As cures go, it was certainly drastic. Within eighteen months, Thatcherism had wiped out all the industrial growth achieved under Callaghan's Labour government (−15 per cent), and within three quarter-years, Reaganism had wiped out the growth achieved under Carter (−10 per cent). The perverse mechanisms of 'competitive stagnation' wiped out what growth was left in the centre, even in social-democratic countries like Mitterrand's France[37] and even in the most competitive exporter (Japan).

Central Monetarism Strangles Peripheral Fordism

Within a few months, the general recession led to a fall in demand, both in volume and price terms, for raw materials, including oil. As a result, OPEC surpluses dried up, but the soaring dollar, doped up by the rise in interest rates, gave no price respite to oil-importers and at the same time deepened the recession in the USA.

A crisis in the NICs was now inevitable. On the one hand, their foreign markets (which were mainly in the North and OPEC) were contracting, and therefore depressing sales of manufactures and raw materials and even the price of raw materials. At the same time they had to reimburse the loans which had financed their investments at a time when oil prices were still rising (for those which were not oil-exporters). As we have seen, since 1980 all the NICs had been relying upon short-term credits to reimburse long-term debts. And it was at this very moment that OPEC surpluses dried up, that the USA began to show a trade surplus.[38] Interest rates were rising, and excess world liquidity was giving way to a shortage of capital: xenodollars were becoming scarce and expensive. Such was the new configuration imposed by American policy.

The crisis had reached dramatic proportions, and for the first time it began to resemble the depressive spiral of the 1930s, even though monopolistic regulation did not collapse under the impact of monetarism. For three successive years (1980-82), there was no growth in the North, and for the first time growth was halted also in the South, including the NICs. International trade, which had still been growing by 5 to

6 per cent at the end of the seventies, stagnated in 1980 and 1981, and actually fell by 2.5 per cent in 1982. In 1982, per capita income declined in the Middle East and Latin America – something which had previously been experienced only in Africa. World demand, both internal and external, was very sluggish, yet in 1982 Third World countries had to repay long-term loans worth $80 billion (most of it from industrial exporters). If short-term credits are also taken into account, the total was probably closer to $200 billion.

All those countries which had banked upon reexporting to repay their debts – and they ranged from Poland to Mexico – and those which, like Pinochet's Chile (the country with the largest per capita debt) were buying a middle-class consensus on credit, suspended payment. As we can see from Graph 4 (overleaf), the trap had closed on peripheral Fordism. Perhaps the gamble had been too risky, but it was also true that the rules of the game had been changed. And as is usual in an international regime of accumulation, a crisis affecting one partner (in this case the NICs) had repercussions for the other (the North). The recession in the North deepened, particularly in countries which exported a lot to OPEC and the NICs.[39] Those involved in major projects fared even worse.[40]

'What of the second oil shock?', one might ask. Was it not that rather than the monetarist shock which ruined the 'new industrialization'? It certainly had an effect, particularly in inducing the central governments to turn toward monetarism. But it should be noted that the first oil shock had been a powerful stimulus to the generalization of new industrialization, and that Mexico and Venezuela ought to have benefited from the second shock. As it happens, they did not.

What exactly happened? According to Cline's famous report,[41] the increase in non-oil countries' debts between 1973 and 1982 breaks down as follows: 1) oil prices rising faster than US inflation: 260 billion; 2) real interest rates in 1981 and 1982 rising faster than the average for 1961-80: 40 billion; 3) deteriorating terms of trade and loss of exports (volume) because of the 1981-82 world recession: 100 billion; 4) 'others': 80 billion. External factors account for four fifths of the increase in debt. More than half that figure

Diagram 1
Financial Strangulation of Peripheral Fordism

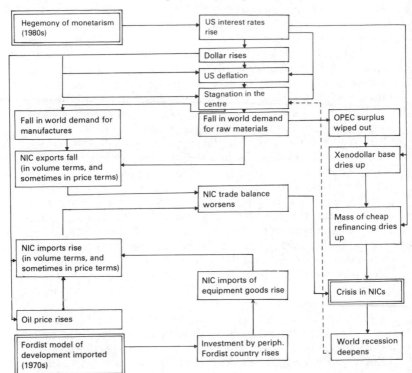

can be seen as a result of the monetarist crisis. Everything else was 'the Arabs' fault'.

This is of course an accountant's way of breaking down the figures, and the results are open to debate. The increase in oil rents simply meant that part of the South had asserted its rights over world production.[42] Most of the increase was recycled to non-oil exporting NICs, and it gave them the right to buy capital goods, provided that they repaid their debts by selling. They did not always use this right to their best advantage, but without it they could have done virtually nothing. They were only too willing to repay their debts by selling to the oil countries (and on other markets).

The *OECD Observer* (January 1983) also blames the breakdown on the second oil shock, but the figures it gives suggest that this interpretation must be qualified (Table 9 overleaf). It was in fact in the years *before* the shock that the debts of the non-oil developing countries increased most rapidly. It was in 1980 that interest charges shot up (the first monetarist offensive). It was in 1981 that the price of their exports collapsed, and it was in 1982 that the volume growth of their exports came to an end.

According to the World Bank's 1983 *Report*, the terms of trade of middle-income oil-importers (unit export values divided by unit import values) deteriorated by 10.7 per cent between 1979 and 1982 and by 9.7 per cent during the first oil shock period of 1973-76. The variation is similar in both periods. But the purchasing power of exports (the above figure multiplied by the growth in export volume) rose by only 2.5 per cent, as against 4.5 per cent during the first shock. The difference between the two shocks is that the second was 'managed' in such a way as to produce a contraction, and not merely a shift, in effective world demand.

The remarkable thing is that the purchasing power of exports rose at all. The strangulation of these countries took place at the level of the current balance of payments rather than at the level of trade itself. According to the same report, variations in relative prices were much greater at this level. The 'real' Eurodollar interest rate (i.e. the three-month rate deflated by the export prices of all exporting countries, including OPEC) – which expresses relative nominal changes in the cost of the capital borrowed and the export prices used to pay for it – was zero in 1970-72. It fell to −30 per cent in 1974 (because of the rising price of oil), hovered around zero again in 1975-78, fell to −10 per cent in 1979,[43] and then climbed back to +20 per cent in 1981 and 1982.

Finally, it will be recalled that the price of oil rose to $34 a barrel at a time when the dollar was highly depreciated, and that the price rise was largely a reaction to that depreciation. The rise of the dollar increased unit oil rents considerably, but the fact that the dollar rose was the result of the Fed's monetarist policies.

Whatever the responsibility of the second oil shock for the disruption of world trade, and whatever hypotheses can

Table 9
Relative Trends in Interest, Debts and Exports of Non-OPEC, Non-OECD Developing Countries

	1970-1973	1973-1978	1979	1980	1981	1982[1] est.
Interest payments and exports: annual % change						
– Gross interest payments	20	27	40	48	31	25
Exports						
– Receipts	23	19	28	25	5	−6
– Prices	12	13	18	17	−5	−8
– Volumes	10	6	9	8	10	3
Nominal interest cost %						
– Current cost of floating interest debt	8	9	12	15	17	17
Average cost of total outstanding debt						
– NICs	7	19	10	12	14	15
– Middle-income countries	4	5	6	8	8	10
– Low-income countries	3	3	3	4	4	5
Outstanding debt: annual % change						
– NICs	22	26	18	16	19	17
– Middle-income countries	8	21	21	17	16	16
– Low-income countries	17	21	15	13	10	16

1) Estimated, assumes constant rates of exchange.

Source: *OECD Observer* 120, January 1983.

be put forward as to what would have happened if the oil shock had not been followed by a monetarist shock, the fact remains that monetarist policies translated the oil price rise into a lasting world recession, and that they are largely responsible for the financial crisis in the Third World.

Recoveries and Scars

13 August 1982. Like a thunderbolt from a sky heavy with
clouds, the 'event' which everyone thought would signal a
world financial crash finally happened: a major Third World
debtor defaulted. Mexico, which owed $80 billion, $60
billion of them to Western banks, declared that it was
suspending payment. A host of all the major borrowers, and
dozens of small ones, immediately demanded the renegotiation of their debts.

The expected disaster did not happen. A summer on the
brink gave way to a calm autumn. Nothing, of course, had
been resolved. Month after month, the three biggest debts
were renegotiated with considerable difficulty (and smaller
ones were renegotiated behind the scenes). Payments fell
due, were postponed and then fell due again. Even by the
beginning of 1985, nothing had been resolved. The debate
goes on. How do we find a way out? And who is to blame?
The two questions are of course related. Everyone knows
that the Third World debts (plus interest) will never be
repaid in full. The question is: to what extent will they be
cancelled (and therefore be paid for by the lenders), and to
what extent will they be *postponed* (and paid for by the
borrowers, who will also have to pay commissions and
premiums)? The debate as to who is responsible revolves
around two arguments. Either the banks had lent too liber-
ally, or Third World countries had taken on unreasonable
debt burdens and had then squandered the money.[44]

As we have seen, both parties have to bear some responsibility, but there is also a third guilty party: the American
administration's monetarist policy. And when that policy
was reversed in the summer of 1982, the crisis, which had
reached panic proportions, temporarily subsided.

We will look first at the modalities of the reversal of
policy, and then at the new configuration which began to
take shape at the end of 1982. We can then go back to the
wretched fate of the borrowers ... and their creditors.

Sanity Prevails

I have analysed elsewhere the way in which monetarism was jettisoned after having taken the world to the edge of the brink.[45] The 'experts' had in fact begun to see its limitations in the first half of 1982: the Fed's policy of restricting the pseudo-validation of credits and of limiting the money supply had created a hierarchy of values-in-process. It was quite acceptable for 'large' industrial values and even small banks to go bankrupt. Major banks and states were a different matter altogether. The world financial system, which had become a monetary system, could not be allowed to collapse.

But with the collapse of Drysdale Government Securities in May 1982, it became difficult to make such distinctions between credits (or fictive capitals), as Chase Manhattan lost a quarter of a billion dollars. In June, it was the turn of Banco Ambrosiano as the Italian central bank refused to cover its losses. Midland Bank lost half a million. In July, it was the turn of Penn Square. Continental Illinois never recovered.

The problem was the same when it came to states. Why declare Poland bankrupt by refusing to renew credits it could never reimburse? Doing so might well have 'punished' General Jaruzelski, but it would have been a disastrous operation for the big banks: it would have meant declaring that credits which had been prevalidated would no longer be validated. The big banks would have been forced to admit that they could not recover their loans and to write them off as losses. It was easier to 'pretend' and to go on as before. Particularly as a new threat was looming in Latin America.

This time the threat was very serious. The debts involved were enormous and highly concentrated. And the banks had to take full responsibility: they had acted as 'private regulators', as institutional forms for financial mediation. The three biggest debtors (Brazil, Mexico and Venezuela −30 per cent of the total owed to the banks) owed Citicorp 180 per cent of its own total assets, Chase Manhattan 183 per cent, Hanover 174 per cent, and Bank of America 148 per cent (on average the figure was between $5 and $8 billion per bank).

There was only one solution. Pseudo-validation had to begin again. New official currency had to be issued and the Fed's guarantee had to be extended to private debts (which amounts to the same thing). At the end of July, that is, before Mexico went bankrupt, the Fed announced a reversal of policy.[46] Within five months (July–December), the interest rate fell from 205. to 15.5 per cent on Treasury Bills and from 19 to 12.5 per cent on Federal Funds. These figures are, however, deceptive, as they have to be revised downwards to take inflation into account.[47] The real short-term interest rate fell from 8.5 to 2.5 per cent.

The money supply, which had been rising by 4.5 per cent for one year (in line with Friedman's recommendations), rose at an annual rate of 13.3 per cent during three quarter-years (up to June 1983). At the same time, US representatives ordered both the IMF and the Bank for International Settlements to organize a last-ditch attempt to bail out the bankrupt countries. American banks injected $40 billion into the Euromarket.

On the debtors' side, whereas Mexico agreed, after a change of presidents, to accept IMF discipline, Brazil, which had promised an improvement, declared in December 1982 that it was no longer willing to pay (in 1982 debt-service had reached a level equivalent to Brazil's total exports). It then signed a letter of intent in January, but in May and August 1983 the IMF complained that its terms had not been implemented. A new letter of intent was signed in September, and so on. Using the tactics of threatening a unilateral moratorium, introducing an austerity policy, and then immediately rescinding it when it provoked insurrections in the towns, Brazil wrested one credit after another out of the IMF and BIS. Each one gave the green light for the renewal of credits from private banks. Delfin Neto, the minister for the economy, described this as 'pushing debts with your stomach'.

On a broader scale, on 1 August 1983 the *IMF Bulletin* estimated the total debts renegotiated by these three countries, plus Poland and Argentina, at $75 billion. Another $25 billion had been renegotiated by a dozen other countries. In the previous twenty-five years, only thirteen such agreements had involved commercial banks, the most recent having been for $3 billion in 1979 (Turkey) and $4.8 billion in 1982 (Poland).

The whole nature of debt-renegotiation had obviously changed. It was no longer a matter of making short-term adjustments for individual countries. It was a matter of admitting, in one way or another, that a large amount of international credit-money was not pledged against anything (but that the world banking system would collapse if that came out in profit-and-loss accounts), or that it was as effectively frozen as the capital of a 'direct' shareholder in peripheral Fordism.[48]

The USA: The 'Brazil' of the Eighties?

The reversal of American policy produced a new world configuration, the third since the official beginning of the crisis. One might have been forgiven for thinking that it would be similar to the 'internal Keynesianism plus lax external policies' configuration of the Carter era, and I myself thought so. Matters were in fact much more complicated than that.

Once monetarism had been relegated to the background, the other element in Reagan's policy came to the fore: the 'supply side'. The argument is microeconomic: profitability has to rise in order to stimulate enterprise. We know that this is not a false argument, as the origins of the crisis in Fordism do lie in the fall in profitability. But increased profitability is not an answer in itself (hence the tragic recession of 1981-82). Final demand also has to rise. And how can demand grow if profitability is restored by cutting wages and welfare payments, and if credit becomes increasingly scarce? The Fed's volte face removed the latter obstacle and provided a partial solution.

The concrete application of supply-side policies removed a further obstacle by cutting taxes. The effect of general tax cuts began to be felt in the 1982-83 fiscal year. The main beneficiary was the business world: the period over which expenses could be written off against tax was extended, and 10 per cent tax credits were introduced for new investments. In other words, profitability was restored by reducing the State's share of surplus-value. But the question of demand could only be resolved if the cuts applied to *all* tax-payers and if State spending, and especially defence spending, *rose*. The supply-side policy therefore began to look like a Kennedy-style recovery: tax cuts + defence spending + lax monetary policies. The only victims were the poor. Those who paid no income tax gained no benefit from tax cuts, but welfare programmes established by Johnson were cut drastically.[49]

The recovery was spectacular, the economy growing at the same rate as during the 1975-77 recovery. But when it stopped in summer 1984, it had not yet caught up the trend of the late 70s. And if we look more closely, it becomes apparent that this was not a truly Fordist-based Keynesian recovery. It did not affect the entire population. On the contrary, it led to social polarization and to a break with mono-polistic regulation.

The income of managerial staff and wage-earners in expanding sectors (mainly military electronics) rose very rapidly. Company income rose too, and investment increased faster than during the 1975-77 recovery. Meanwhile, the traditional working class accepted lower wage bargains (though the fall in inflation meant that wages fell less than might have been expected, and in some cases purchasing-power actually rose). The purchasing-power of the average wage remained, however, at 1962 levels. As the economy got under way again, millions of young people and women came into the commodity sector. Most of them took part-time jobs which had previously been within the province of domestic labour (fast food, janitoring).[50] Finally, the thirty-five million people living below the poverty line became even poorer. Homelessness and vagrancy increased in the midst of an economic recovery.

This was, in short, a New Deal in reverse. The model was 'exclusionary', or at least had a polarizing effect, but the economy was forging ahead. The model therefore had the enthusiastic support of the middle classes. This is the first bizarre similarity with Brazil in the seventies. Let us take this provocative idea a little further, bearing in mind that even in 1982, at the darkest hour of the recession, the USA was still the greatest power in the world, that it had the most advanced technology in the most important branches, and that it had the highest average level of productivity in the world.

The second similarity with the 'Brazilian miracle' is that everyone is buying on credit. The state had cut taxes and was spending as never before. Its deficit rose from $61 billion in 1980 to $174 billion in 1984. Companies, seeing that profitability was rising, were investing hand over fist: the cumulative gap between profits and net investments reached $210 billion in the period 1981-84. Individuals, seeing that prosperity had returned after four years of recession and stagnation, began to buy houses and equipment goods again. House purchases alone exceeded by $36 billion domestic savings during the two-year recovery period. The result was a large trade deficit: $48 billion in 1983 and $123 billion in 1984. And as no one was saving, the entire deficit had to be financed by borrowing abroad. Reagan's USA, like Geisel's Brazil, contracted foreign debts in order to buy capital goods and consumer durables.[51]

The third similarity with Brazil marks the difference between the Reagan period and the Carter period. The USA was no longer paying its debts by issuing money as and when needed; it was paying with money borrowed from abroad, even if it was paying in dollars. This requires some explanation. By mid-1983, Paul Volcker, the pragmatic monetarist head of the Fed, had decided that irresponsible pseudo-validation had been going on long enough. Monetary policy became tighter again. Real short-term interest rates rose inexorably, climbing to 6 per cent by mid-1983 and putting an end to economic recovery in the summer of 1984. They then fell back to 4 per cent, under the pressure of the supporters of supply-side policies. Thanks to defence spending, the recovery got a second chance. But it has to be remembered that between 1973 and 1980, real short-term rates were negative. Real long-term rates (debentures) never fell, and since the beginning of 1982 they had been hovering at just over 8 per cent; this is twice the level of the historical tendency within capitalism.[52] They were, moreover, three and half points higher than the Japanese, German and French rates.

The USA was buying capital goods and consumer durables by contracting large debts with its suppliers. An 'inverted

Marshall Plan' was being implemented. European and Japanese trade surpluses flooded into the USA, attracted by the high rate of return in a low risk country, and by US power and growth. The flow did not, however, consist of dollars which had been accepted and re-lent, but of dollars which had to be bought before they could be lent. And the Federal Bank was issuing few dollars. This was the basic difference with the Carter period: as the USA's debts increased, it had to draw more heavily on a supply of xenodollars which was itself dwindling because Third World debts were not flowing back into the banks. The more US currency was sought after, the more it appreciated. This had two side-effects. High real interest rates were charged on loans which must be repaid eventually. At the same time, American industry and agriculture became less and less competitive.

A headlong rush to borrow money began. The USA had to borrow to service both its debts and its trade deficit. In the summer of 1984, taxes on interest paid to non-residents were abolished in order to make US bonds more attractive. In international organizations, the USA argued the case for freedom in financial activities; If it could have done so, it would have borrowed old ladies' savings. The situation is highly unstable. When it becomes obvious that the USA will have to pay out more than it could obtain from the world capital market, the dollar will fall, and the xenodollars invested in the country will take flight.[53]

It is, however, true to say that, like Geisel's Brazil, the USA used the dollars it borrowed. The USA had not yet been dethroned from its position at the centre of the world economy. And yet (new aberration or bold attempt?) it borrowed technology and capital from its rivals so as to reinforce its position. And as with Brazil, the big question – indeed the only question – was 'What did they do with the loans?'

There is no point in criticizing the USA for contracting debts. Federal debts of course represented 44.7 per cent of GDP in 1984, as against 34.8 per cent in 1981. But these debts have represented 51 per cent of GDP in 1964 ... and even 125 per cent of GDP in 1945. Borrowing in order to modernize and to acquire an export capacity may well be a sensible policy. But is that what is in fact happening?

Opinions are sharply divided. Some critics, like Toinet, argue that the USA is in decline and living beyond its means, and that by contracting debts, it is simply putting off the day of reckoning. Others claim that the USA is about to make the breakthrough to the post-crisis regime of accumulation of the future.[54] Although the first argument is probably closer to the truth, it has yet to be proved. Marie-France Toinet bases her claims on the falling profit and investment levels of the period 1973-79, whereas Philippe Lefournier is arguing on the basis of a rise in profits and investment over the two-year period of recovery (1983-84).

As in Brazil (or rather, as in Chile and Argentina), much of the capital transferred to the USA is obviously squandered in defence spending, while the high dollar is an inducement to import luxuries.[55] The polarizing nature of the regime of accumulation means that it is probably not socially stable in the medium term, and it is far from certain that it is stable in macroeconomic terms. But industry is being transformed as the strong dollar encourages specialization in 'grey matter' industry and allows traditional industries to re-equip cheaply. The motor industry, the most Fordist of all, is also being transformed along the lines described earlier in this chapter. Chrysler is negotiating wage cuts and specializing in the top of the range. Ford is gambling on relocation (building Escorts in Brazil and selling them in northern Europe), whilst General Motors, in association with Japanese companies, is trying to master new automated processes.[56]

Although information technology continues to flourish, all the other branches of US industry appear to be losing ground as a result of competition from Japan, Italy and Germany. Overall labour relations have regressed in face of brutal employer 'take backs'.[57] The average age of plant is considerably less than it once was, and plant is now newer than it is in Japan (but this development largely occurred under Carter). But capital intensity continues to increase. Despite the short-term effect of the sharp reduction in the labour force during the recession, total productivity and even manufacturing productivity do not seem to have emerged from the torpor into which they have been plunged for over a decade. If the United States is indeed the 'Brazil of the eighties', the 'miracle' may well lead to a rude awakening.

The Third Configuration

It remains for us to take stock of the new configuration produced by this rather dubious miracle. It is highly contradictory. The USA is both absorbing world surplus-value and providing an outlet for that same surplus-value. In other words, the USA is promoting an export-led recovery in other countries and at the same time preventing an investment-led recovery; it is, that is, appropriating world surplus in kind. All this is being done on credit, which suggests that we will see a fourth configuration when the dollar falls and when the USA has to export to repay its debts. However, sufficient unto the day is the evil thereof.

Local regimes of accumulation do of course diffract the present configuration to a large extent. Very schematically: Japan is both exporting and investing, while Europe exports, but with slowing investment and overall stagnation.[58] The Third World is more fragmented than ever. Some countries are exporting, but not accumulating, or accumulating less than before. Others are exporting and de-accumulating. Still others have gone under. We will come back to these points.

For the moment, we will restrict the discussion to the countries of the 'centre'. Japanese productivity and profitability continue to rise. Like the USA in the fifties, Japan is now the world's biggest creditor.[59] It is in a position to lend to its clients (including the USA), who can therefore buy superior Japanese goods. Its expansion is great enough to allow profits to be ploughed back, despite the high public deficit. If problems of socio-political regulation do not destroy the consensus, and if its foreign markets grow fast enough to prevent South Korea from compromising its export trade, Japan may have found a way out of the general crisis in Fordism. But unlike the USA in the fifties, it will not show the rest of the world the way.

Europe, in contrast, is now totally paralysed by its obsolete institutional forms. Without going into details as to how wage relations have changed in each country,[60] mention should be made of the absurd constraints imposed by EEC institutions on each separate country. As Jacques Delors contritely put it at a forum organized by *L'Expansion* in January

1984, 'For several years to come, our growth rate will have to be 1 per cent lower than everyone else's.' In fact there is no corrective mechanism, other than competitive stagnation, to compensate for the trade deficit accumulated by any country that grows more quickly than its partners. In the absence of any political consensus as to how to bring about a concerted recovery, expansion will have to be directed towards countries outside the EEC. Whilst the USA attracts European exports (though the threat of protectionism is becoming more open), Europe's other big markets (the Eastern bloc, the Middle East, Africa and Latin America) are shrinking, as they too adopt an austerity policy.[61] Even more so than Japan, Europe is unable to retain its trade surpluses, which are absorbed into loans to America. There is therefore little accumulation in Europe.

In Which it is Shown that Becoming Poor is Neither a Necessary nor a Sufficient Condition for Paying One's Debts

One major pole imports and monopolizes credit, a second exports, and the third is stagnating. It is within the interstices of this new configuration, which limited growth in world trade to 2 per cent in 1983 and 8 per cent in 1984, that peripheral Fordism has to adjust. But it is not enough to describe the configuration in terms of variations in trade flows. The stocks of the productive forces, debt levels and other factors change from one configuration to another. The massive rise in debt levels due to the monetarist shock (second configuration) is still one of the Third World's great liabilities. And the third configuration leaves them few new credits; credit has taken flight for the USA.

And so, the countries of the Third World pay, come what may. The poorer they become, and the more they owe, the more they pay. The logic of the Shylocks of the world market is implacable: a dollar costs a pound of flesh. Between 1980 and 1983, per capita income fell by 6.8 per cent in the Third World as a whole. It fell by one third in western Asia, by 10 per cent in Africa and Latin America, but in east Asia it rose by 10 per cent. Debt repayments involve a huge transfer of resources from South to North,[62] and the effects are all the more serious in that the demographic transition has yet to be completed. On top of that, the Third World has to cope with natural disasters and the 'bloody providence'[63] that have such devastating effects when social conditions degenerate. The Sahel and Northeast Brazil are ravaged by famine. What Marguerite Duras calls the 'absolute evil' of leprosy is on the increase and is leaving the hideous imprint of social relations on the bodies of human beings.

Disgust, shame and outrage are not enough. We have to understand, and that means going back to the implacable logic of economics. For the purposes of this book, we can restrict the discussion to the avatars of peripheral Fordism.

It is not difficult to understand how debt repayments reduce the share of GDP available for consumption and investment within a given country, or how they determine the use that can be made of domestic product. But why do they also seem to reduce the *total product*, or at least per capita revenue? The connection between debt repayments and impoverishment is not as clear as it might be. If I earn 5000 francs a month and have to pay back 1000 francs, I have only 4000 francs to spend. But, due to debt repayment, it is as if my income falls to 4500 francs and that I am left 3,500 francs to spend ...

We have to start again. When people pay, they are certainly paying for something, namely the reimbursement of their debts. Debt-servicing, expressed as a percentage of exports, peaked in 1982 and then began to fall (except in Africa and the Middle East, which have nothing to sell). Taking the non-oil developing countries as a whole, debt-servicing fell from 25 to 20 per cent in 1983. In Latin America, it fell from 55 to 45 per cent in 1984, much to the delight of the IMF.

Why the improvement? First, when countries cannot pay, they do not pay, and, as we shall see, the international banking system can do nothing about it. Second, as imports fall very sharply, the trade balance improves. In Latin America, imports fell by a startling amount: almost one third. And that is the main condition the IMF imposes in exchange for rescheduling: 'economic adjustment'.

The IMF should not be turned into a scapegoat, even if, at

the level of domestic politics, it is sometimes convenient to make it take the blame for 'austerity' and at the same time, everyone – including the left – admits in private that the irresponsibility of the local leaders made austerity inevitable.[64] Besides, the underlying *principle* behind such an institution is beneficial, if not essential, and in a better world order, it would have a greater role to play. Private regulation by the multinational banks led to catastrophe, which simply goes to show that it is impossible to manage credit-money in a completely fragmented system. In the first configuration, all the banks lent at the same time; in the second and third, they would have refused the NICs new credits, had it not been for the IMF. A single institutional form cannot at the same time create credit-money on the basis of private gambles and ensure that all those gambles are coherent.[65] It could not, of course, do anything about the money supply, but it could encourage or discourage prevalidation.

The whole problem centres upon how the IMF, or more precisely the team of orthodox technocrats which make it up, plays its role. The IMF claims that other institutions such as the World Bank are responsible for development, and that its own policy is therefore simple: short-term adjustment. In concrete terms this means: 1) cutting public spending, wages and domestic credit so as to hold back the volume of growth, and therefore imports; 2) real devaluation (higher than the rate of inflation) to discourage imports and encourage exports.

A further question now arises: does IMF policy explain the relationship between debt repayments and impoverishment? Do increased repayments lead to a pointless reduction in total output (including repayments, or in other words exports)? The simple answer is 'yes'.

It is immediately obvious that the first set of measures are by definition in contradiction with growth. They are in fact equivalent to leaving existing capital fallow, particularly as local activity is directed towards the home market. In the medium term, these measures can mean only one thing: 'gunboat diplomacy'.[66] 'You may no longer produce for yourselves; you have to produce for us.' This is a short-sighted policy, even for the advanced capitalist world; as we have seen, the advanced countries profited greatly from the NIC miracle of the 1970s. And for the people concerned, it is quite disastrous.

The basic hypothesis behind the policy of using stagnation to achieve adjustment implies a constant elasticity ratio between imports and domestic product. Assuming that hypothesis, and taking into account various other hypotheses as to the growth of foreign markets and as to the share of those markets that various countries might hope to win, CEPII has attempted to calculate what would happen if the policy were successful, if, that is, the interest was repaid and the balance of payments did improve.[67] The results are very instructive. Assuming a reasonable world growth and assuming that the countries of the South simply stopped their debts increasing (or balanced their current payment account, including interest) in 1985, per capita GDP would remain stationary for a whole decade in Southern Europe, Mexico and North Africa. It would fall by 3 per cent *per year* in Brazil and by 2 per cent in the rest of Africa. In the rapidly developing regions of Asia, it would rise by only 3 per cent.

Only a *fall* in the import coefficient can provide a way out, for not everyone can win a share of the market at the same time. 'But', says the IMF, 'that is precisely the aim of the other side of our policy: devaluation.' Elsewhere I discuss at length the benefits of devaluation (I take the case of France, but the same considerations apply to the USA, Japan and Italy).[68] There are two preconditions for a successful devaluation.

It must be real, in other words it must not be immediately swallowed up by domestic inflation. In many 'dollarized' countries,[69] this precondition cannot be met. Many incomes are directly indexed to the dollar, and the result is a vicious circle of devaluation and inflation which leads eventually to hyperinflation. Even the possibility of being 'better indexed' than others to the dominant foreign currency can lead to a massive redistribution of income.[70] It is possible that this will happen in Brazil. Devaluation failed to keep pace with inflation between 1980 and 1982, and in 1983 the rate of devaluation was 25 per cent above the inflation rate![71] Who gains? Those who can invest in financial assets. Who loses? Wage-earners, whose wages are adjusted every six months. As prices triple in a year, they lose 42 per cent of their purchasing-power within six months. Yet again, the short-term policies of the IMF, which always insists that wage-earners are responsible for inflation, whereas they are in fact the 'worst-indexed',[72] not only work against the people but lead to a general recession. To quote Talleyrand, 'If there is one thing worse than a crime, it is a mistake'.

The second precondition depends upon the 'price elasticity' of foreign trade. If real devaluation is to have any positive effect, 'substitutions' (goods which can be produced and exported as easily as they can be imported) must outweigh 'complementarities' (goods which have to be imported if the rest of the economy is to function). But 'complementarities' are by definition dominant in a subordinate country within the international division of labour. Reducing imports therefore means reducing accumulation and leaving existing plant idle (for lack of spare parts, etc.). The application of the econometric tests devised by Gylfason and Risager to a sample of developed and developing countries confirms this diagnosis.[73] In industrialized countries, devaluation has a favourable effect on both the external account and domestic output; in developing countries, it has a favourable effect on the external account (though this is not true of Argentina, for the reasons we looked at earlier), but it also reduces domestic output.

In their dealings with the IMF, NICs therefore do all they can to limit the short-term adjustments they have to make if they are to be given credit, and behind the scenes they apply the only reasonable policy: they go on investing so as to modify the import-export structures of their economies. They do not, however, all have the same room to manoeuvre.

At one extreme, we have South Korea, which was already very export-orientated at the time of the 1980 crisis. The adjustments introduced after the military coup d'état (wage-cuts, devaluation) had therefore only a minor effect on domestic growth and made up for the ground that had been lost in terms of competitiveness. South Korea and the other Asian NICs (including the 'second-wave' countries) were the main beneficiaries of the new configuration. They were bound up with the expanding pole (Japan) and had an insatiable market for their exports (the USA). They also had huge markets with few debts close to hand in India and China. Now that it was no longer under IMF tutelage, South Korea systematically went ahead with its import-substitution policy and adapted its export sector to more lucrative activities. The share of traditional labour-intensive industries in exports fell from 53 to 39 per cent; steel rose from 4 to 10 per cent, ships from 6 to 15 per cent, and electronics from 9 to 12.5 per cent. The country could even afford the luxury of a recovery on the home market.[74]

At the other extreme, we have Argentina. The ships and planes purchased with the money borrowed by the dictatorship are at the bottom of the sea off the Falklands. The country does not have the plant to adjust to exports, as the IMF insists it must do. Argentinian democrats have only one card left in their hand: a political rejection of IMF policy. 'Let's not talk about what we owe. Let's talk about what we can pay, given that our national income must go on rising. We suggest that no more than 15 per cent of our exports should be devoted to debt-servicing.' This is the position defended by Aldo Ferrer, amongst others.[75]

In between the two extremes, we have Brazil. The IMF's deflationary policy cost Brazil dear. One third of all workers in the São Paulo area lost their jobs. The area of land devoted to foodcrops shrunk, and that devoted to export crops grew. Poverty spread from the countryside into the cities.[76] But the results are there. In 1981 Brazil was already a surplus country and in 1984, it had a trade surplus of $13 billion (the IMF had asked for a surplus of $9 billion). But the IMF is still not happy: the results could not really be attributed to the effects of the policies it had dictated, and besides, those policies had not been fully implemented. Brazil has begun to reap the expensive harvest of Geisel's dictatorial developmentalism. In four years, the oil bill was cut by half, thanks to the discovery of the Campos field and to the use of substitutes to fuel such as alcohol from sugar. Financial strangulation encourages import-substitution, and the reduction in export credits discourages the import of luxuries. If, as Castro sardonically notes, IMF policy had been applied during the first oil shock, Brazil would not have been able to adjust so well to the second.[77]

A policy which adjusts the exploitation of workers to the

need to support middle-class consumption habits is obviously open to criticism. So is the environmental damage done in such a short period, on the edges of Amazonia, the planet's 'lung'. But Brazil has shown that orthodox policies are not the only policies. Import-substitution has regained a certain prestige, and it has been proved that there is an alternative to the IMF's policy of 'accelerated insertion into world trade'. Brazil has yet to embark upon a second stage, which involves the internal transformation of norms of distribution and consumption, but that is a different story.

Even though reduced purchasing-power or import-substitution may have led to a fall in imports,[78] and even though the world recovery or falling prices may have led to increased exports, it remains true to say that adjustment policies are not enough to solve the debt problem. Latin America's overall balance of trade produced a record surplus in 1984 (Mexico and Brazil: $13 billion; Venezuela: $8.5 billion; Argentina: $4.5 billion), but the price was heavy: a recession in the second configuration and slow growth in the third. The surpluses remain roughly equivalent to the interest paid. The commercial tigers of East Asia are still deficit countries, and a twofold threat is hanging over them. Firstly, there is the threat that they will no longer be regarded as 'developing countries' and that they will lose their right to cheap credit. Then there is the threat that pro-tectionist barriers will be used against them. In Latin America, the debt problem remains intact. It may be getting worse for the Asian NICs.[79]

Making the Creditors Pay?

No one would dream of blaming the directors of Electricité de France for borrowing 170 billion francs (i.e. $17 billion; Mexico borrowed $80 billion) in order to acquire a surplus nuclear capacity. The loans were raised in the expectation of industrial growth, but the subsequent crisis, aggravated by the deflationary policies adopted by the governments of the main industrial countries, has proved that the underlying assumption was unfounded. Is not the same thing true of most Third World debts?

There is no denying that some Third World ruling classes did wantonly misuse their credits. It is sometimes said that the owners of wealth in the South showed a lack of civic virtue by placing the private wealth they had acquired in the South in the banks of the North.[80] In 1982, $11 billion were 'recycled backwards' in this way. But this phenomenon has mainly been confined to oil-exporters like Mexico and Venezuela; after all, rent does have its own socio-logic. There is also talk of the voracious appetites of the middle classes, of property speculation, and so on. But it is well known that these factors apply primarily to countries which had a 'monetarist' regime in the seventies – and above all to model 'Newly Deindustrializing Countries' like Chile and Argentina, where the government choked to death a national industry which had been built up by decades of import-substitution.[81]

No, what has to be explained is the dramatic fate of countries which really did play the investment game, gambled on a genuine supply-side policy of import-substitution and export-promotion, and staked their past loans against the 'promise of future work'. Quite apart from the fact that humankind must display solidarity with the least developed countries, we have to ask whether imposing such an intolerable burden of repayments on the countries of peripheral Fordism can ever be justified. We also have to raise the issue of how far new democracies like Argentina and Brazil can be held responsible for the debts that dictators contracted with the blessing of the North.

A number of Third World countries are now in the position in which the French steel industry recently found itself (and the nuclear industry may soon find itself). Some credits were of course squandered, but the main point is that these countries did invest too. They invested in a development model which is highly debatable in social and cultural terms, but the world financial community persuaded, or even forced them, to adopt it. The IMF had been urging them to adopt an export-orientated model for ten years. They therefore brought their internal regimes of accumulation into line with the international logic of peripheral Fordism.

The model is now in crisis, both in internal and external

terms. One reason for this is that it appears now there is no outlet for the new investment. When this happens to an individual firm, the remaining flesh is usually stripped off by the receiver and distributed amongst the priority creditors. Alternatively, its debts can be socialized by means of subsidies or injections of credit, or it can be nationalized. This is quite normal in the case of a major firm, and a fortiori an entire branch.

There are of course those who support the first course: 'It is no good saying it is "politically unrealistic"', writes *The Banker*, 'revolutions too are part of the adjustment process. A country can turn itself upside down and kill many of its own people, but it will still have to keep its foreign spending within its revenue if it has no access to loans or grants and no reserves.'[82]

Most of the international financial community probably has a more moderate version of this plan in mind: to negotiate (for a commission) a rescheduling of debt-service, so that as much as possible can be salvaged and reinvested elsewhere (which, in the third configuration, means the USA). The rescheduling policies associated with the Rohatyn and Zombanakis plans do have the merit of avoiding the mindless catastrophism of the monetarist Shylocks, whose stupidity is now widely recognized, but they also have the effect of making the popular masses of the South pay in instalments for the mistakes committed by the governments of the North between 1979 and 1982.

This is in fact more or less what is happening. The Third World is repaying its debts, at a huge price, and it is being given time. But this simply slows down the rate at which its debts accumulate. Is there any alternative? Yes: refuse to pay the whole debt and 'socialize' the banks' losses.

If the debtor countries stand together, they have the ability to enforce such a policy. The argument is rather similar to that of Mutually Assured Destruction. A country which repudiates its debts does of course run the risk of terrible retaliation: assets held abroad can be frozen, it can be refused new credits, and so on. But as Ominami points out, the cost of reimbursement is now almost as high as the cost of repudiation.[83] Conversely, a coalition of several big debtors would have a terrifying weapon at their disposal:

they would survive a blockade, but the banks would not survive repudiation. Banks are now central to the creation of money, and chaos would spread from the South to the North. The 'debtors' club' which began to take shape during the Cartagena Conference of 21-22 June 1984 provides the framework for a general renegotiation, which could include a moratorium and the repudiation of some debts.

Naturally enough, the creditors have seen the danger and have adopted a clever 'divide and rule' policy. On 7 September 1984, the IMF and Mexico signed an agreement spreading debts which fell due between 1985 and 1991 over a period of fourteen years. Those falling due between 1982 and 1984 were to be spread over a twelve-year period. In exchange, Mexico made itself a ward of the IMF. But within a matter of months, the IMF was already objecting to the policies Mexico had implemented. It was not possible to extend the agreement to other debtor countries. The question of overall renegotiation remains unresolved.

What arguments can the debtors put forward? The legal arguments themselves are far from negligible. Many countries agree in their common law that the creditors and those who sell on credit have to take some responsibility.[84] At the international level, Kniper points out that there are precedents and even cites the argument Sack put forward in 1927: 'If a despotic power contracts a debt which does not serve the needs or interests of the State, but which strengthens its rule or helps it to oppress a rebellious population, that debt is a bad debt as far as the whole population of the State is concerned. This debt places the nation under no obligation. It is the regime's debt, a private debt, and when the regime falls, it is cancelled.'[85]

Such jurisprudence is particularly applicable to the arms bills run up by dictatorships which have subsequently collapsed. Given the present climate of liberalism and supply-side policies, it might even encourage the internal bourgeoisies to overthrow more dictatorships!

But there is also an overwhelming economic argument, which is clearly set out by Frank and Jedlicki.[86] If the South did in fact reimburse its debts, it would be a terrible deflationary blow to the North. Assuming a hypothetical debt of $600 billion,[87] and given the present state of the South's trade deficit, Jedlicki shows that with an interest rate of 10 per cent and repayments spread over ten years, the South would have to generate an annual trade surplus of $128 billion. That is equivalent to America's deficit for 1984. Then there is the possibility that the USA might one day decide to balance its accounts ... or (horror of horrors!) to repay its own debts.

Elsenhans is quite right to point out that the world economy is undergoing a crisis of under-consumption, or a Keynesian-style crisis, and that demand from the popular masses of the South is inadequate.[88] Peripheral Fordism has failed to become a world Fordism. We have, however, already seen that this is not the root cause of the crisis in the centre. The first configuration of the seventies offset the Keynesian component of the crisis in the centre, and under social-democratic crisis management, growth was restricted by the fall in profitability. The simultaneous impact of 'competitive stagnation' policies (which Coussy aptly describes as a 'composition fallacy'[89]) and of America's monetarist policies did, however, force the world into a configuration characterized by a Keynesian-style 'deficit in growth'.

When a similar situation arose in the thirties, the Great Powers simply ignored the war reparations owed by Germany and forgot about Russian Bonds. The world financial system did not collapse. It was the small rentiers (many of them French) who suffered by losing their nesteggs. But how, in an epoch of pure credit-money, can the hole in the accounts of the big banks be filled? The unprecedented rise in interest rates suggests that Keynes's vision of 'the euthenasia of the rentier' is more remote than ever.

On the contrary, rentier capital is acquiring a 'historically unprecedented oppressive power'. Chesnais sees this as confirmation of Marx's ironic comments: 'If we depreciated credit-money (to say nothing of taking away its monetary properties, but that is only an imaginary possibility), all existing relations would be revolutionized. The value of commodities is therefore sacrificed to preserve the mythical and autonomous existence of a value incarnated by money. Being a monetary value, it is only safe so long as money is safe. And so, to save a few millions, many millions of commodities are sacrificed. This phenomenon is inevitable in the capitalist system of production, and it is one the system's beauties.'[90] No doubt Third World producers who sell their products cheaply to pay their debts are the first to appreciate its beauty.

But matters are more complex than this. The rise in interest rates also incorporates the devalorization of debts that cannot be recovered. This is one way of socializing the destruction of values-in-process in a monopolistic mode of regulation which operates with pure credit-money.[91] In other words, those who pay their debts pay dearly, but others do not pay their debts at all. The European banks, and especially the French nationalized banks,[92] have already written off their assets in Poland and other debtor countries. Increasingly, US banks are being forced to follow suit because of the regulations pertaining to 'non-performing' loans.[93] A market in bad debts has developed,[94] and this has similar effects on the banks' assets. The devalorization of credit-money pledged against a bankrupt logic of accumulation is already being socialized on a world scale. It would be better to organize the process by bailing out the bankrupt economies and allowing them, if possible, to adopt a new regime.

One solution which would prevent the banks from going bankrupt and which would not impair their ability to lend would be a compensation fund drawn from taxation in the developed capitalist countries. There is an economic rationale for such a generous initiative, but its political credibility is to say the least doubtful. The obvious point of reference is the Marshall Plan. In the course of four successive years, the USA transferred 1 per cent of its GDP to Europe, most of it in the form of gifts. If the OECD applied the same policy to the South, it would release $400 billion, and that would cover more than half the South's debts.[95] A tax of 1 per cent is not a lot to pay for such a result, but public opinion is far from convinced that such is the case.

Given the present impasse, the most reasonable solution is to go on as usual, to pseudovalidate and to monetize debts in the hope that many of the most unwise investments will eventually find an outlet, and that the devalorization of the rest will be absorbed by a slight rise in world inflation. In concrete terms, this could happen in several ways.

1) The Fed's monetarist policies could be relaxed. At the

moment (end of 1985), they mean that credit flows towards the country that needs them least: the United States.

2) Another powerful and therefore credible credit pole could be created alongside Japan. It could then grant cheap or interest-free loans to the Third World, as happened in the seventies. One immediately thinks of Europe's ECU, but it is difficult to see how Europe would accept to create a currency that would immediately fall against the dollar or the yen. If Europe was to gain anything from this, the currency in question should be convertible only against EEC products or against those of an ad hoc EEC–Third World partnership. At the moment, such a partnership seems politically unlikely.

3) The least utopian solution would be to distribute a new international credit-money to Third World countries free of charge (their bad debts would first have to be written off, and the amount distributed would be determined by their needs and legitimate debts). This could, for instance, take the form of Special Drawing Rights. The IMF is gradually coming round to this position by 'arguing discretely for an all-round liquidity increase'.[96] At the same time, it is asking the biggest debtors to make the sharpest adjustments (and this still works to the detriment of the home market). This is a highly contradictory position. In the absence of a vigorous upturn in world demand, an export-orientated adjustment will simply intensify the NICs structural profile that led to the crisis of 1981-82. Wiping out the deficit caused by the monetarist shock (by the monetization of debts) would be meaningful only if it did not reproduce the earlier model, if, that is, it provides the NICs with the opportunity to adopt a development model which is less tied to the dying convulsions of central Fordism, which is geared to making more sparing use of imported goods, to forms of production which make greater use of local resources and to a regime of accumulation that is less dependent upon the vagaries of foreign markets. But all this presupposes both changes in the international economic order and internal social transformations that go far beyond the monetary level.

Conclusion

'The sequence of traditional forms of dependency tends now to be further complicated by a return to old forms of dependency. If we wish to evaluate the degree to which a Third World country is dependent, we now have to study it over a longer period than before and we have to be careful not to see belated manifestations of dependency as indications of non-dependency.'[97] Coussy's judicious comments should not be taken as an invitation to revive the dogma of the 'dialectic' of dependency. We must not make the same mistake as the hero of *The Name of the Rose*, who thought that the Beast would commit its next murder in the stables because the curses of the Apocalypse suggested that the next crime would have something to do with the Horse.

The financial crisis in peripheral Fordism is not the unavoidable materialization of a destiny that has been written in the stars ever since the establishment of the old division of labour. In the seventies, that division was really challenged by a conjuncture determined by the desires of concrete social groups. The new configuration therefore took different modalities in different areas in what had once been the periphery. The changes in the world configuration which have brought peripheral Fordism to crisis were at least to some extent themselves the result of readily identifiable policies, and it cannot be said that they were particularly profitable, even for the ruling classes in the dominant countries.

The historian, and the economist turned historian, are quite justified in stating their findings, even if they are valid only in the short term. They may find that certain countries are financially dependent. But their findings relate to results, and not to immanent causes. It is by analysing immediate causes that nations and social groups learn why they are trapped and how to free themselves. But they will not all find that conditions are always in their favour.

Conclusion

After this too rapid and partial survey of the new economic geography of the world, the reader will, I trust, be convinced of the need to beg the duckbill's pardon, even if its viability is problematic. There is therefore no need to reiterate the methodological considerations of our first chapter. But I would like to outline a few political considerations. Not as to whether or not we should reject or support the strategies of bloody Taylorization or peripheral Fordism in order to break with underdevelopment: that is a matter for militant workers, peasants and intellectuals in the countries concerned. But as to the attitude that militant trade unionists and intellectuals in the former imperialist metropolis should take towards the NICs, whose manufactures are now beginning to compete with the centre. It seems to me, speaking as a European, that the preceding analysis allows us to advance the following conclusions.

The 'old division of labour' has proved to be less rigid than we thought. Whilst capitalism in the industrial countries still needs a labour force and raw materials from poor and rural countries, it certainly no longer needs to keep the outside world in a state of industrial non-development in order to flood it with its products. Since the Second World War, Fordism, which is an intensive regime of accumulation centred upon mass consumption in the developed capitalist countries, has developed its own markets. The relative failure of early import-substitution policies cannot be ascribed to an imperialist desire to block competition from new producers. It reflects the temporary inability of the countries in question to insert themselves into the virtuous circle of intensive accumulation.

It was when the weaknesses of its regime became apparent that central capitalism had to look once more to the periphery for help, not in the shape of markets, but in the shape of low-cost production. This coincided with the local ruling classes' ambition to impose a new form of industrialization on their countries. A new division of labour was superimposed upon the old, but it did not replace it. Branch circuits and production were distributed across countries with different degrees of skills and with different wage-levels.

Insofar as this process simply involved the relocation of productive segments of labour-intensive industries, the market was still primarily in the developed countries. Bloody Taylorization improved the living standards of its peripheral victims to only a very minor extent. But as peripheral Fordism developed, the world regime of accumulation, which was being squeezed in the centre, found a last opportunity to expand. Real industrial growth in certain countries in the South provided the North with outlets for its advanced technology and capital goods. In exchange, the South supplied cheap consumer goods and components. This did not really reduce the central industries' market, as the extension of the wage system and the rising purchasing-power of the middle classes in the NICs helped to increase world demand.

It was not the increase in oil rents, which simply redistributed surplus-value on a world scale, that put an end to this final phase of growth of the 1970s, which had been moderate in the centre, rapid in some countries, and negative as far as the broad rural masses were concerned. Nor was it competition from cheap commodities produced by exploiting workers in the periphery. On the whole, the competition was marginal, and the creation of jobs in the North for workers producing capital goods for the South more than compensated for its effects.[1] Even so, growth would have been faster if the living standards of the masses in the South had risen more rapidly.[2] The damage was done by the choices made by the ruling classes and conservative majorities in certain central countries, and especially by the choices made in the dominant economy, the USA. They resolved to break what little growth was left by making their wage-earners pay for the crisis and by wrecking the international credit system.

If there is any hope of 'economic recovery' in the old industrial countries, and in Europe in particular, it lies in co-operation with the South, and not in driving out the new competitors who have emerged from the old periphery. The fetters on mass purchasing power in the Third World have increasingly become the constraints on wage bargaining power in the Centre. The only agents who have an absolute interest in perpetuating nineteenth-century conditions of exploitation in the countries of bloody Taylorization, apart from remnant local oligarchies, are firms which have relocated the most labour-intensive segments of their production processes. Starvation wages and near slavery cannot provide a market for world output, but undercut wage levels in central Fordism and restrict metropolitan demand as a secondary consequence. In the absence of a selective protectionism based on compliance with minimal standards of social welfare and trade-union rights, the countries of the centre reward the dominant classes of the Third World and their multinational allies who most excel in repression and super-exploitation. Under these conditions 'free trade' means bringing world norms of exploitation into line with the norms of the most underprivileged sectors of the global proletariat.

Although there is a grain of truth in the old argument that the superexploitation of Third World labour does result in cheaper consumer goods and food products for the workers of the advanced capitalist societies, this is far less significant than the manifold ways in which the pillage of immiserated labour-power in the South is used to bludgeon the workers of the North. A clear declaration, preferably at the European level, to the effect that exports will no longer be accepted from countries which do not respect the human rights of labour would not only prevent some old industries from being relocated on the periphery, but would also put pressure on authoritarian regimes to choose between improving the living standards of 'their' working masses and being excluded from their major export markets. Conversely, joint development agreements with Third World countries which respected international labour conventions (as established, for instance, by the ILO) would allow all parties to benefit from the industrialization of the periphery. But that presupposes a general moratorium and cancellation of a large part of the Third World's debt.

We should not expect miracles. Plans for 'world Keynesianism' (as in the more recent version of the Brandt Report) or 'a Marshall Plan for the Third World' would come up against the general constraints of the crisis of central Fordism. Moreover we should not romanticize Fordism in its metropolitan heydays. The boom of the 1960s was scarcely paradise, and youth and large sections of the less skilled working class dramatically rejected the social implications of the Fordist model well before it had begun to run out of economic steam. The acid rains came to remind us that ecological debts contracted by reckless, unplanned accumulation must, sooner or later, be reimbursed with interest. Indeed, anyone who has experienced the living nightmare of Cubatão (São Paulo's port and industrial satellite) knows that peripheral Fordism carries with it an ecological debt that is still graver and harder to cure than the financial debt.

In discussing options that might allow peripheral Fordism to move towards new variants of social democracy, I do not at all intend to suggest that a Third World repetition of the North's road to developed Fordism is the only, or the best, solution for the world as a whole. That road is, in any case, probably not open for the 'least advanced countries', or for the overwhelming majority of 'intermediate economies'. I merely wish to underline the responsibility of the centre for the harsh conditions of exploitation and the economic blockages encountered by the 'new industrial countries'. It is possible to reject this model of development, in the name of social, cultural or ecological arguments. That is up to the peoples in question to decide. But the policy now being pursued by the central governments and international agencies effectively shunts the growth of new peripheral industries onto the most predatory, exploitative and degrading tracks.

International solidarity with the peoples of the Third World must involve a struggle against everything which blocks their national growth – even in a Fordist–capitalist sense – or which steers it to barbaric forms of primitive Taylorization. At the same time an attempt must be made, in equality and partnership, to find progressive exits from the crisis of Fordism, at the technological level as well as in social relations. For the proposals to 'adapt' technology will be rejected – often wrongly, it should be said – if they appear as modernist surrogates handed down with condescension to countries incapable of paying the price of 'real' modernity. The search will continue for new productive forms which, in North and South alike, break from alienation vis-à-vis the machine, and for new forms of collective organization that break with the tyranny of competition. In this common endeavour, starting from different situations, the workers of North and South, progressive economists, sociologists and technicians may carry the world towards a more just and humane future.

A necessary first step will be to overcome that apologetic discourse, unfortunately shared by Marxists like Arghiri Emmanuel and Bill Warren, which sees the 'progress' of capital across the globe, whatever its social and cultural cost, as the motor of technological 'progress' and the necessary route to the 'unification of humanity' and socialism.

As we have seen, the deformed development of market and wage relations in the Third World – from primitive Taylorization to peripheral Fordism – does not point inevitably to a radiant future. But even if it did, what right would anyone have to forbid dominated peoples and exploited classes to rebel while they are awaiting this glorious tomorrow? For the liberal discourse of a Rostow and the Marxist discourse of a Warren both lead to the *political* conclusion that 'populist' attempts to resist imperialism and mis-development are either 'inappropriate' or 'ineffective', a mere barrier to the development of the productive forces that capitalism is called upon to assure. It would be 'moralism' to condemn this growth model in the name of the injustices and human agony that it brings in its wake. True scientists can have but one aim: the growth of the productive forces, and the 'unification of humanity'! From such noble heights how petty must seem the struggles of workers and peasants, how trivial the rebellion of women in the home, the factory or the reaim of prostitution! And how astonishing it must seem that such a powerful mind as Karl Marx's should have wasted time organizing the nascent workers' movement, and in supporting the Irish national liberation movement even against the English labour organizations.

And yet, those who believe in capitalist horror as the midwife of socialism can justly lay claim to one aspect of Marx's work (his veritable fascination with the historical march of capitalism 'through blood and filth') and, above all, to Marx's descendants. I am referring to that mechanistic, economist, productivist and ultimately cynical Marxism of the Second and Third Internationals which still sees the 'development of the productive forces' as the index of historical progress. For that Marxism, flesh-and-blood generations are but sacrificial lambs to the God of Progress, in the name of a heavenly future to which our valley of tears will eventually lead. This vision represents no more than an internalization by the workers' movement of the positivist myths of the nineteenth-century Euro-centrist bourgeoisie. Every revolutionary practice – from Lenin through Gramsci (who hailed the 'revolution against *Capital*') to Mao Zedong – has had to break with this 'left' version of productivist mythology, which has been used to justify all the social-democratic capitulations, and all the abominations of Stalinism.

This is what people have in mind when they talk of a 'crisis of Marxism'. The disgust which it arouses has turned a growing number of workers, feminists and ecologists away from any reference to Marxism, both in the East and the West. In many parts of the Third World (e.g., Iran and Egypt) the identification of such Marxism with the bourgeois project of unconditional industrialization has deflected the masses and revolutionary intellectuals from Marxism and other secular ideologies, shifting their revolt towards reactionary clericalist ideologies.

To reconstruct the idea of progress, to weigh the cultural, ecological and social costs and advantages of what is presented as 'progress' – this is without doubt one of the chief responsibilities facing intellectuals in both North and South. It is certainly not up to Northern intellectuals to impose a new dogma that simply inverts the old progressivist-productivist credo. But nor is it the task of their Southern counterparts to blame all their country's difficulties on the ravages of technological, financial or cultural 'dependence'. I hope to have shown that no external destiny, no general law of capitalism dictates a nation's place within an ineluctable division of labour – unless, of course, one means by 'external destiny' the weight of the past inscribed in the social structure; unless one means the internalization of norms from a model of development which, having appeared to succeed elsewhere, has entered into crisis while leaving the ecological bill to be paid. In this sense, the only 'coercive law' is deliberate acceptance of the rules of free trade, of the free play of market forces. For, even though it be 'on the basis of given conditions inherited from the past', it is still people who make their own history.

Notes

Introduction

1. Noam Chomsky, *Language and Responsibility*, Hassocks 1979, pp. 175-176.
2. Walt Whitman Rostow, *The Stages of Economic Growth, A Non-Communist Manifesto*, Cambridge 1960.
3. For a summary showing the links between these currents, see G. Palma, 'Dependency: A Formal Theory of Underdevelopment, or A Methodology for the Analysis of the Concrete Situation of Underdevelopment', *World Development*, vol. 6, nos. 6-7, July-August 1978.
4. The terms are taken from Bill Warren, *Imperialism, Pioneer of Capitalism*, Verso, London 1980. Arghiri Emmanuel takes a similar position in his recent *Appropriate Technology or Underdeveloped Technology?*, trans. T.E.A. Benjamin, Chichester 1982. For a critique of Warren, see Alain Lipietz, 'Marx or Rostow?', *New Left Review* 132, March-April 1982, pp. 48-58.
5. C. Palloix, *De la socialisation*, Paris 1981.
6. André Gunder Frank, 'Asia's Exclusive Models', *Far East Economic Review*, 25 June 1982, p. 22. The initials NIC will be used here to refer to a purely empirical group of countries which have recently become industrialized and which are major exporters of manufactured goods.
7. For a savage picture of this stalemate, see Carlos Ominami, 'Aperçu critique des théories du développement en Amérique Latine', *Revue Tiers-Monde*, no. 80, October 1979. For a critique from a rather different viewpoint, see P. Salama and P. Tissier, *L'Industrialisation dans le sous-développement*, Paris 1982.
8. Pierre Bourdieu, *Leçons de sociologie*, Paris 1980.
9. The results of my work were presented at a number of international conferences and seminars. Particular thanks are due to Gustave Massiah, Ricardo Hausmann, Carlos Ominami and Patrick Tissier for

introducing me to so many problems and so much data, and for the rigorous but friendly manner in which they criticized my original statements.

The original papers I refer to are as follows: 'Towards Global Fordism?', *New Left Review* 132, March-April 1982 (presented to the Symposium International de Sfax, April 1981); 'De la nouvelle division internationale du travail', *Espaces et Sociétés*, 44, 1984 (presented at the Modena Colloquium, 'Problèmes de la reprise européenne et nouvelle division internationale du travail', November 1982); 'Imperialism or the Beast of the Apocalypse', trans. M.-P. Allum, *Capital and Class*, no. 22, Spring 1984 (presented to the Ottawa Conference on 'Canada and the New International Division of Labour', January 1983); 'Sur les fordismes périphériques de l'Europe du Sud', *Poli ké Peripheria* (Salonika), no. 7, 1983 (presented to the Conference on 'European Integration: Urban and Regional Problems', Naxos, November 1983); 'Le Fordisme périphérique étranglé par le monétarisme central', *Amérique Latine*, no. 16, December 1983 (presented to the Conference on 'Vers un nouvel ordre mondial?', Paris, October 1983); 'La Mondialisation de la crise générale du fordisme: 1967-1984', *Les Temps modernes*, November 1984 (presented at the Conference on 'Development in the 1980s: Canada in the Western Hemisphere, Kingston, May 1984).

10. For an analysis of these state capitalisms from a kindred problematic, see Charles Bettelheim, *Les Luttes de classes en URSS. Troisième Période*, Paris 1982; B. Chavance, *Le Systéme économique soviétique*, Paris 1983; D. Leborgne and Alain Lipietz, 'Est, Ouest: deux modes de régulation du capitalisme', *Reflets et perspectives de la vie économique* no. 4, October 1983. In more general terms, see the November 1983 issue of the same journal.

11. The 'happy few' will have recognized the words of William de Baskerville, the hero of Umberto Eco's novel *The Name of the Rose*, trans. William Weaver, London 1983, p. 492. This 'nominalist' position is basic to Eco's semiotics, and he expresses similar views in the opening pages of his theoretical essay *La Strutture assente*, Milan 1980 (the title in itself is significant). Eco's remarks are not far removed from the distinction Louis Althusser makes between the 'real concrete' and the 'concrete in thought' in his reading of Marxist methodology in *For Marx*, trans Ben Brewster, London 1969.

1. Questions of Method

1. Warren, *Imperialism*.
2. Karel Kosik, *Dialectics of the Concrete: A Study on Problems of Man and World*, Dordrecht 1976.
3. Karl Marx, *The Holy Family*, Marx/Engels, *Collected Works*, vol 4, London 1975, p. 58.
4. Cited, Dognin, *Les 'Sentiers escarpés' de Karl Marx*, Paris 1977.
5. Marx, 'A la redaction de *Otetchestvennie Zapiski*' (1874), Marx/

Engels, *Gesamtausgabe* (MEGA), Band 25, Berlin 1985, p. 117.
6. Frederick Engels, letter of 12 March 1895 to Conrad Schmidt, Marx/ Engels, *Selected Correspondence*, Moscow 1965, p. 484.
7. For a more detailed discussion, see Alain Lipietz, 'Réflexion autour d'une fable', Working Paper CEPREMAP, Paris 1985.
8. Charles-Albert Michalet, *Le Capitalisme mondial*, Paris 1976.
9. Fernando Henrique Cardoso and Enzo Faletto, *Dependency and Development in Latin America*, trans. Marjory Mattingly Urquidi, Berkeley and London 1979, p. 15.
10. Karl Marx, *Capital*, vol. 1, Harmondsworth 1976, p. 476.
11. Michel Aglietta, *A Theory of Economic Regulation: The US Experience*, trans. David Ferbach, New Left Books, London 1979; CEPREMAP, *Approches de l'inflation: l'exemple français*, Rapport au CORDES par J.P. Benassy, R. Boyer, R.M. Gelpi, A. Lipietz, J. Mistral, J. Munoz, C. Ominami, Paris 1977 (mimeo); CEPREMAP, 'Redéploiement industriel et espace économique', Rapport à la DATAR de J. Lafont, D. Leborgne, A. Lipietz, *Travaux et recherches de prospective*, no. 85, 1980; R. Boyer and J. Mistral, *Accumulation, inflation et crise*, Paris 1978, new enlarged edn., Paris 1983; Alain Lipietz, *Crise et inflation, pourquoi?* Paris 1979; Alain Lipietz, *The Enchanted World*, Verso, London 1985; B. Mazier, Basle, Vidal, *Quand les crises durent*, Paris 1984; Boyer et al, *Capitalismes, fin de siècle*, Paris 1985.
12. Bourdieu, *Leçons de sociologies*.
13. Benjamin Coriat, *L'Atelier et le chronomètre*, Paris 1979.
14. Concepts are malleable things. One might say that an economy is in major crisis when its mode of regulation can no longer ensure the stability of its regime of accumulation. But the world still goes on, even during a crisis (and it has been going on since 1973). There is, then, nothing to prevent us talking about a 'crisis regime' in the same way that other writers speak of 'dependent development'. The important point is knowing when to throw away worn out concepts.
15. I outline a critical survey of how these theories came into conflict in the early seventies in *Le Capital et son espace*, Paris 1977. I leave it to the reader to decide whether or not I then took the good advice I am giving here.
16. Fernando Henrique Cardoso, "Théorie de la dépendence" ou analyse concréte des situations de dépendence?', *L'Homme et la société*, nos. 33-34, 1974.
17. Cited, Palma, 'Dependency …'.
18. Apart from the young Lenin's canonical work on *The Development of Capitalism in Russia*, *Collected Works*, vol. 3, Moscow 1960, which Louis Althusser used to say one should read before looking at any theoretical Marxist texts, the first contemporary works to make an explicit analysis of dominated countries in terms of specific regimes of accumulation and successive modes of regulation were Carlos Ominami, *Croissance et stagnation au Chile: éléments pour l'étude de la regulation dans une écomonie sous-développés*, Thesis Paris X, 1980, and Ricardo Hausman, *State Landed Property, Oil Rent and Accumulation in the Venezuelan Economy*, PhD Thesis, Cornell University, 1981. Studies by the same authors of their respective countries

can be found in Boyer et al, *Capitalismes* ... We will see later how some authors from the Dependency school have evolved in a similar direction. See in particular, the recent works of J.M. Cardoso de Mello and Fernando Henrique Cardoso.

19. As we shall see, the connection between the two aspects has a variety of effects, not all of them negative, on the working population of both the NICS and the industrialized West. But while there may exist some peculiar groups of the West which profit from the famine in the Sahel, it would, however, be wrong to say that the states of the South are starving because their wealth is being plundered.

20. Similarly, modern physics tends to refer to the 'locality' principle (according to which distant influences can only work via a local modification of the field) rather than to the Newtonian principle of 'forces acting at a distance' (a principle which has somewhat mystical origins).

21. There are of course regional social formations, and, following A. Rist, I describe them in terms of 'regional armatures' in my *Le Capital et son espace*. Regional social formations are capable of generating their own internal dynamics and of negotiating with the state so as to ensure the preconditions for stability in their local compromises. Arguments which apply to small centralized countries like France certainly also apply to continental federations like India or Brazil.

22. André Gunder Frank, *Dependent Accumulation and Underdevelopment*, London 1978, p. 82.

23. Charles-Albert Michalet, M. Delapierre, B. Madeuf, Carlos Ominami, *Nationalisation et internationalisation. Stratégie des multinationales françaises dans la crise*, Paris 1983.

24. I. Wallerstein, *The Modern World System*, New York 1974-80; Fernand Braudel, *The Mediterranean and the Mediterranean World System in the Age of Philip II*, trans. Siân Reynolds, 2 vols., London, 1972, 1973.

25. In my early work on space ('Approches théoriques des transformations de l'espace française', *Espace et société* November 1975), I noted the variety, variability and relative independence of the topographies and 'spatialities' characteristic of various socio-economic relations and their articulations. At the same time, I relied upon a schema (regional armature/national social formation/multinational bloc) which was not dissimilar to the 'world economy' which Fernand Braudel uses in his *Capitalism and Material Life* (trans. Miriam Kochan, London 1973.) Unfortunately Braudel's admirers do not always display his caution and subtlety. The typical configuration of a world economy centred upon nineteenth-century England seemed, then, to provide a universal schema to which all future concrete situations had to conform, except perhaps during wars of succession.

Rather than looking for the famous 'centre' that is supposed to exist somewhere between Japan and California, might it not be preferable to abandon Wallerstein and to go back to Braudel's *The Mediterranean*, or even to the 'age without Rome', when early capitalism's only backbone was a network of fairs in Champagne? Those who delight in prophecy would do well to meditate upon the following statement from the *Neue Rheinische Zeitung*: 'The Pacific Ocean will have the same role the Atlantic has now and the Mediterranean had in antiquity and in the Middle Ages – that of the great water highway of world commerce; and the Atlantic will decline to the status of an inland sea, like the Mediterranean nowadays.' Marx/Engels, 'Review', 31 January 1850, *Collected Works*, vol. 10, London 1978, p. 226.

26. In more general terms still, the whole of Latin America can be described as 'underdeveloped', along with Africa and Asia. But if an Argentinian thinks he has discovered underdevelopment when he reaches Mexico, what must a Malian think when he arrives in Buenos-Aires?

27. L. Boltanski, *Les Cadres*, Paris 1982.

2. The Fortunes and Misfortunes of the Central Regime of Accumulation: Fordism

1. Cf. Chapter I, note 11.
2. The latter can be further broken down into relations of 'property' and 'ownership'. Cf, my *Crise et inflation* . . ., and *The Enchanted World*.
3. The 'transformation problem' is notoriously delicate. Statisticians studying 'conditions of profitability' are right not to linger over it. See *The Enchanted World*.
4. See, for example, H. Bertrand, 'Le régime central d'accumulation de l'après-guerre et sa crise', *Critiques de l'économie politique*, nos. 7-8, April 1979.
5. The notion of the articulation of modes of production was introduced by P.P. Rey in his 'Sur l'articulation des modes de production', in *Les Alliances de classe*, Paris 1969, in which he discusses 'centre-periphery relations'. The articulation of modes of production can go through several stages (external articulation, integration . . .), and the concept thus allows us to further refine our analysis of regimes of accumulation. For an analysis of the articulation between small-scale agricultural commodity production and capitalism in the economic history of France, see Alain Lipietz, *Le Capital et son espace*.
6. C. Palloix, *Les Firmes multinationales et le procès d'industrialisation*. Paris 1973.
7. R. Boyer, 'La Crise actuelle: une mise en perspective historique', *Critiques de l'économie politique*', nos. 7-8, April 1979.
8. Relative surplus-value increases when the value of the commodities which establish norms of consumption falls because productivity has risen (the purchasing-power of wages remaining constant).
9. Coriat, *L'Atelier et le chronomètre*.
10. CEPREMAP, *Redéploiement industriel* . . .
11. These concepts are statistical rather than theoretical. 'Apparent productivity' refers to the quantity of use-values produced per unit of concrete labour time in a given branch. It includes both changes in intensity and productivity increases in the strict sense of the term, though it is in fact difficult to distinguish between these two elements. 'Per capita volume of capital' is roughly equivalent to the Marxist con-

cept of 'technical composition', which is difficult to quantify. See Alain Lipietz, *Crise et inflation*, and 'Derrière la crise: la tendance à la baisse du taux de profit', *Revue économique*, 2, March 1982 (to be translated in *Review of Radical Political Economics*).

12. A. Granou, Y. Baron, B. Billaudot, *Croissance et crise*, Paris 1979.
13. For an algebraic and statistical description of this model, see Lipietz, 'Derrière la crise.'
14. A discussion of how monopolistic regulation encouraged intensive capital accumulation is beyond the scope of this book. See *The Enchanted World*.
15. Michel Aglietta and A. Brender, *Métamorphoses de la société salariale*, Paris 1984.
16. Official definition of money supply (and, as we shall see, of the 'monetary base') are, of course, rather more technical. For a fuller theoretical analysis, see *The Enchanted World*.
17. It will be recalled that I am not dealing here with the 'centralized economies' of Eastern Europe and Asia.
18. G. Arrighiri, 'Une Crise d'hégémonie', in *Crise, quelle crise?*
19. Europe is discussed here as though it were a bloc, but the member states of the EEC can be shown to coexist within a configuration of 'virtuous complementarity'. Very schematically, West Germany acts as a workshop producing equipment goods for France and Italy which, in return, sell Germany consumer goods. Mechanisms for adjustment are provided by prices (the changing exchange rate) and by volume (moderate 'cooling off' plans).
20. We can speak of a 'World Economy', provided that we do not take the term to mean a true 'pyramid'. The reader has, however, been alerted to the need for scepticism in the use of concepts, and will realize that any term can be used to describe a 'configuration'.
21. Why use only this industrial indicator to measure accumulation? Because it is both the most reliable and the most homogeneous. And because GNP (or GDP, which amounts to much the same thing) has no obvious meaning. It is precisely 'gross' (and therefore includes the cost of using fixed capital as well as value-added, which means that an increase in GNP can mean mechanization without growth) and measures primarily the intensity of commodity and wage exchanges. This leads to some well known paradoxes. Two young mothers who pay each other for baby sitting 'create GDP'; but if each looks after her own baby, or if the sitter is not paid, no GDP is created. If a man marries his housekeeper, GDP falls. This is no laughing matter. In both France and the USA, the number of hours of domestic labour performed by women was in the seventies greater than the number of hours worked by wage-earners. The transfer of domestic labour to the tertiary market sector in the developed capitalist countries during the crisis led to major changes in the regime of accumulation, but not necessarily to the emergence of a stable regime. And yet it certainly did lead to a rise in GDP. (The fluctuations to be observed in the USA in 1981-84 also show that this labour can rapidly be transferred back to the domestic sector). This phenomenon is even more marked in underdeveloped countries where the domestic economy is being destroyed, even

though the extent to which social relations have been monetized tends to be under-estimated because of the informal nature of much of the commodity economy.

22. CEPII, *Economie mondiale: la montée des tensions*, Paris 1983.

23. See especially, CEPII, 'Dualité, change et contraintes extérieures dans cinq économies dominantes', *Economie prospective internationale*, nos. 13-14, 1983. Amongst other things, this article discusses the different conditions under which surplus productivity is divided between the manufacturing sector, which is internationalized, and the tertiary sector, which is protected.

24. R. Boyer, 'Déterminants et évolution probable de la productivité et de l'emploi: un essai de synthèse des travaux récents', CEPREMAP, *Couverture orange*, no. 7922, 1979 (mimeo).

25. For this whole discussion see Alain Lipietz, 'Derrière la crise', and the comparative international statistics given in C. Lapierre-Donzel, 'Le Partage des revenus, la formation du profit: comparaison entre les cinq grandes économies', *Statistiques et études financières*, Série orange, no. 44, 1980.

26. *The Enchanted World*.

27. Coriat, *L'Atelier et le chronomètre*.

28. Recent works on what lies beyond Fordism are based upon this more basic consideration. See *Emploi-Formation*, no. 8, 1984 and *Sociologie du travail*, no. 4, 1984.

29. CEPII, 'Dualité, change ...'.

30. When the gold pool was abolished in 1968, the dollar became a world currency; it had to be accepted in final payments, and could no longer be exchanged for a 'more real' currency like gold. On 15 August 1971, all reference to gold was officially dropped, and from March 1973 the dollar was left to find its own parity against all other currencies. The Jamaica agreement of January 1976 made this change official.

31. It will be recalled that in 'classic economic thought' there are two views as to the meaning of an increase in ground rent. According to Ricardo, it reduces capitalists' profits. But as we shall see, oil rents were recycled into investments. According to Malthus, on the other hand, it leads to an increased effective demand for 'luxury' goods. He was correct about the rise on oil rents; warplanes are the modern equivalent to carriages. The 'oil shock' in itself did not, then, cause the crisis; at most, it brought out the latent contradictions.

3. The Old Division of Labour, or What Did Capitalism Want With the Periphery?

1. We have, then, to be very careful when we use long-term statistical data to assess the importance of foreign trade with the periphery for what are *now* central countries. Quite apart from the fact that French and Russian agriculture and handicraft production were largely 'outside' capitalism in those countries during the nineteenth century, one could say that a large part of what is now industrial Europe (and of

Russia, until 1917) was then part of British capitalism's periphery.

2. V.I. Lenin, 'A Characterization of Economic Romanticism', *Collected Works*, vol. 2, Moscow 1960.

3. Lenin, *The Development of Capitalism* ...

4. V.I. Lenin, 'Once More on the Theory of Realization', *Collected Works*, vol. 4, Moscow 1960.

5. Rosa Luxemburg, *The Accumulation of Capital*, London 1951.

6. Lenin, *The Development of Capitalism* ..., p. 594

7. Rey, 'De l'articulation ...'.

8. C. Palloix, *L'Economie mondiale capitaliste*, Paris 1972.

9. Samir Amin, *Unequal Development: An Essay on the Social Formations of Peripheral Capitalism*, trans. Brian Pearce, Hassocks 1972.

10. Amin explicitly refuses to dissolve these social formations into the transnational articulation of all the modes of production in the world. He stresses that they are relatively autonomous, but from the outset he does articulate them with a 'world capitalist system'.

11. The English cut off Indian weavers' thumbs so as to be able to flood India with textiles from Manchester. One hundred and fifty years later, they were setting their descendents to work and flooding the high streets of the North with cheap clothes.

12. See, for example, Arghiri Emmanuel, *Unequal Exchange: A Study in the Imperialism of Trade*, London 1972, Bettelheim's 'Theoretical Comments' in Appendix 1, and the ensuing debates. Very schematically, 'unequal exchange in the broad sense' occurs when the transfer of value results from price mechanisms (because of the mechanisms of the equalization of the rate of profit, or because the industrial producers of the North and the agricultural producers of the South do not have the same 'market power'). 'Unequal exchange in the narrow sense' occurs when the transfer results from high wage differentials (why the differential should be appropriated by capitalists in the North rather than by the ruling classes in the South remains somewhat unclear). There are two difficulties with this debate. Firstly, is there such a thing as an international value which can be transferred? And, secondly, does not the productivity gap between North and South compensate for wage differentials and thus equalize the value of labour power? It is easier to answer these questions at the level of inter-regional relations. See Lipietz, *Le Capital et son espace*.

   Afficionados of mainstream mathematic economics will find a very interesting transposition of this debate in the *Journal of Development Economics*. See especially G. Chichilnisky, 'North–South Trade and Export-Led Policies', *Journal*, vol. 15, 1984, pp. 131-160.

13. In 1984, Antenne 2 broadcast the famous *Vive la crise!* (scripted by Michel Albert and presented by Yves Montand), in which we were told that we owed our past prosperity to the colonies, and that the crisis resulted from the end of the subjugation of the Third World. Not even the Third Worldists were happy with that argument. The productivity of French workers has been rising at an annual rate of 5 to 6 per cent for the past twenty years. The Centre d'Etude de l'Impérialisme estimates that the value transferred from the South was equivalent to 4 per cent of GDP in 1972. The transfer therefore cannot have had any great

effect, even if some of it was clawed back by rising oil rents in 1973. See, CEDETIM, *L'Impérialisme français*, Paris 1978.

14. S. Latouche, L'Impérialisme précède le développement du capitalisme, *Les Temps modernes*, no. 434, September 1984.
15. Braudel, *Capitalism and Material Life*; André Gunder Frank, *World Accumulation, 1492-1789*, London 1978.
16. Amin, *Unequal Development*.
17. The metaphoric 'application' of the thermodynamics of dissipative structures to society was popularized by I. Prigogine and I. Stengers, *La Nouvelle Alliance*, Paris 1979. In the foreword to *Crise et inflation*, I happily borrowed metaphors of this kind from Prigogine's early work, and I even saw them as illustrating dialectical materialism. Since then, the debate has shifted considerably. Thom and Prigogine, whom I regarded as theoreticians of the discontinuous and of global non-determinism, now disagree as to the statute of 'attractors' (stable equilibria). It is, however, clear that all the formalized models inspired by Thom and Prigogine are highly determinist, even if they include cases of a continuity of causes generating a discontinuity of effects. Thom now has the courage to admit this and takes a determinist stance, whereas Prigogine denies it, as he wishes to defend indeterm-inism. See, *Le Débat*, nos. 3 and 6, 1980. For my part, I do not think it is by 'determinism' that capitalism finds one or another solution to its contradictions; in each case, the solution is a real 'discovery'. Within the reified world of the history of capitalism, however, it does no great harm to behave as though what happened had to happen, or to show that what happened did solve a problem of historical dynamics raised a a particular time by the structural constraints of social relations. Which is not to say that it was the only solution.
18. Latouche, 'L'Impérialisme ...'.
19. Lenin, *The Development of Capitalism*, p. 25.
20. Ibid., p. 65.
21. François Partant, *La Fin du dèveloppement*, Paris 1983.
22. V.I. Lenin, 'Imperialism, The Highest Stage of Capitalism', *Collected Works*, vol. 22, Moscow 1964, p. 241.
23. For broad historical studies of Chile and Venezuela using these methodological conceptions, see Carlos Ominami, *Croissance et stag-nation au Chili: éléments pour l'étude de la régulation dans une économie sous-développée*, Thesis, Université de Paris X, 1980 (mimeo); Hausman, *State Landed Property* ...; Ricardo Hausman and G. Marquez, 'Accumulation et crise dans une économie pétrolière: le cas vénézuélian. Crise du bon côté du choc pétrolier', in Boyer et al, *La Régulation* ... Venezuela is of particular interest in that it is an OPEC country; the crisis in import-substitution therefore cannot be explained in terms of 'deteriorating terms of trade'.
24. It is because the market became 'monopolistic' so early in Chile that the phenomenon of 'stagflation' appeared so rapidly. The countries of the centre did not experience this until later.
25. It is therefore not enough to say that import-substitution failed to gen-erate mass production 'because the market was too small'. At a deeper level, there was a contradiction between the logic of trade and the

industrial logic of mass production. See Hausman, *La Productividad....*

26. That is, the ratio of the unit volume price of Southern exports to Northern exports. Cf T.H. Nguyen, 'Trends in Terms of Trade, *Journal of Economic Studies*, vol. 8, no. 2, 1981. Nguyen even supplies statistics on price effects drawn from the countless studies devoted to the question. The example of Venezuela shows, however, that even though the terms of trade improved between 1972 and 1980 (thanks to the rising price of oil), the rising volume of imports of equipment goods was enough to strangle import-substitution.

27. J. Mistral, 'La Diffusion internationale inégale de l'accumulation intensive et ses crises', in J.L. Reiffers, ed., *Economie et finance internationale*, Paris 1982.

28. Boltanski, *Les Cadres*.

29. Joao Manuel Cardoso de Mello, *O Capitalism tardio*, São Paolo 1982.

30. M.C. Tavares, *Auge y declinacion del proceso de substitacion de importaciones en Brasil*, cited, Cardoso de Mello, *O Capitalismo tardio*.

31. A summary of the debates betwen the evolutionists (the Rostowians), the *dessarollistas* (ECLA) and the dependency theorists will be found in Ominami, 'Aperçu critique ...'. F.H. Cardoso and J. Serra, 'Les Mésaventures de la dialectique en Amérique Latine', *Amérique Latine*, 1, 1978 gives a clear account of the reasons for the break between Cardoso (and the Campinas school) and the dependency theorists (as personified by Ruy Mauro Marini). See also Marini's stinging reply in his 'Les Raisons de la nouvelle idéologie du développement', *Amérique Latine*, 2, 1978.

32. In some cases they were of course '*gorillas*' and 'puppets'. In both Chile and Argentina, the 'monetarist' policies of the military juntas did lead to a real deindustrialization. But this did not happen in Brazil. American historians have made the French realize that there is a certain continuity between the development policies of Vichy and those of Mendès-France, De Gaulle and Mitterrand. Perhaps we will one day have to look at the possible continuity between those of Kubitschek, Geisel and Sarney in Brazil.

4. Towards Global Fordism?

1. The theory of 'branch circuits' was originally developed with reference to inter-regional relations in France. See Lipietz, *Le Capital et son espace*, and 'La Dimension régionale du développement tertiaire', *Travaux et recherches de prospective*, 75, 1978. By starting with the *endogenous* dynamics of regions dominated by different modes of production and different hegemonic blocs, it was possible to identify a sequence of stages within the inter-regional articulation of modes of production. The final stage involves the establishment of Fordist branch circuits; in the case of France, most of them prove to be centred on the Paris area. For similar studies of Italy and Ireland, see M. Dunford, 'Integration and Unequal Development: The Case of Southern

Italy', in A. Scott and M. Storper eds., *Production, Work, Territory: The Geographical Anatomy of Industrial Capitalism*, London 1985; D. Perrons, 'Unequal Integration in Global Fordism', ibid.

2. E.P. Thompson, *The Making of the English Working Class*, London 1963.

3. De Gaudemar, *La Mobilisation générale*, Paris 1979; *L'Ordre et la production*, Paris 1982.

4. Salama and Tissier, *L'Industrialisation dans le sous-développement*.

5. L.K. Mytelka, 'Direct Foreign Investment and Technical Choice in the Ivorian Textile and Wood Industries', *Vierteljahnes berichte*, 83, 1981.

6. The distinction between 'promotion of traditional exports', 'import-substitution' and 'export-substitution' was popularized by M. Myint, *Southeast Asia's Economy. Development Policies in the 1970s*, Harmondsworth 1972.

7. If we agree to use the term 'regime of accumulation' to refer to the *overall* transformations in both conditions of production and conditions of consumption within a national social formation, we can refer to sub-sets within those transformations as *components, elements of the regime* or *logics*. If, for instance, we take the case of postwar France, we see that a closer examination reveals that its Fordist regime was highly specific. In fact, until the late 1960s, the development of Department 1 was greatly accelerated by the speed with which Department 2 was brought into line with the Fordist norms imported from the USA (cf. Bertrand, 'Le Régime central d'accumulation ...'). This logic of 'transition to Fordism' was not so dissimilar to the logic of what we will term 'peripheral Fordism'. The logic of integration of small-scale agricultural commodity production accelerated the process still further (cf. Lipietz, *Le Capital et son espace*). Within Department 2 itself, a distinction should be made between the *endogenous logic* of the motor industry, where rising productivity supported rising demand and vice versa, and the *exogenous logic* of the construction industry, where rising demand was stimulated by the monetary transfer of surplus productivity originating in manufacturing industry. Cf. CEPREMAP, 'Redéploiement industriel ...'.

8. See Patrick Tissier, 'L'Industrialisation dans huits pays asiatiques depuis la fin de la seconde guerre mondiale', and 'Conditions de travail et zones franches d'exportation dans quelques pays d'Asie', *Critiques de l'économie politique*, 14, January 1981; A. Gauthier, *Les Pays-Ateliers d'Etrême-Orient*, Montréal (France) 1982. As we shall see, the four Far Eastern NICS can no longer really be described as 'workshop countries'. On the other hand, the free zones of the 'Four' and of other Asian countries remain a real 'Gulag Archipelago'. Both Gauthier and Tissier describe the atrocious conditions of exploitation to be found in the zones.

9. P. Salama, 'Recherches d'une gestion libre de la force de travail et divisions internationales du travail', *Critiques de l'économie politique*, 13, October 1980.

10. Salama, 'Recherches ...', P. Tissier, 'L'Industrialisation ...'; 'Conditions de travail ...'; G. Mathias, 'Transfert de technique et transfert des théroies: du "dualisme" du marché du travail aux nouvelles formes de

résistance ouvrière en Amérique Latine', *Critiques du l'économie politique*, 14, January 1981.

11. Textile factories in Hong Kong employ an average of twenty people, and are crammed into the floors of tower blocks. Two thirds of all Taiwanese textile factories employ less than ten people. The garments they produce are sold under the labels of 'central' companies. It is almost as though the whole of Sentier had been relocated (Sentier is Paris's garment area, and it employs a host of illegal and super-exploited immigrants).

12. Salama, 'Recherche d'une gestion …'.

13. In 1978, labourers in the four Asian NICs earned an average of between £100 and £150 per month. In the centre, labourers earned between £500 and £900, but worked half as many hours per year. Indirect wages, which are almost non-existent in the NICs, also have to be taken into account.

14. In 1982, the EEC placed strict restrictions on rising textile imports from both the 'Multi-Fibre Agreement' countries and the Mediterranean 'Preferential Agreements' zone. Imports from the Asian NICs were actually cut; the measures affected 45 per cent of all jobs in the Hong Kong textiles industry. The NICs reacted to the threat by accelerating their industrial diversification, by turning to markets in the South, or by reaching sub-contracting agreements with the 'preferential' countries. Cf C. Marty, 'Les Arrangements concernant le commerce international des Textiles', *Revue de la concurrence et de la consommation*, 3ième trimestre 1982.

15. It should, however, be noted that, whereas ECLA's 1951 model of import-substitution was designed to construct an intensive regime of accumulation centred upon the production of equipment goods, the 'peripheral Fordist' model is explicitly predicated upon the assumption that mass consumption outlets can be increased either by winning a share of the world market or by stimulating home demand.

16. I. Ramonet, 'Le Mexique sous le choc', *Le Monde diplomatique*, December 1982.

17. R. Benabou, 'La Corée du Sud ou l'industrialisation planifiée', *Economie prospective internationale*, 10, August 1982.

18. 1981 has been chosen as a reference point because it was then that the effects of the crisis in the centre began to be felt in the NICs.

19. To be more specific, average per capita income in India was $240 per month in 1981. This is equivalent to seven francs per day. This obviously means that two thirds of the population live in poverty, and that the 'new poor' of Europe cannot even begin to imagine their misery. But it also means that they depend for their survival on sectors which are barely touched by money relations. Cf. note 21 below.

20. For most rapidly industrializing countries, 1981 was a high point. The 'monetarist shock', which is discussed in Chapter 6, still lay in the future. In South Korea, however, it was in 1981 that the first recession occurred. The figures given are for 1982, when the recovery began.

21. Cf. Chapter 2, note 21. Growth of GDP is not simply an effect of the growth of the *real* product. Insofar as it is a measure of *commodity* production, it also takes into account changes in the ratio between the

'commodity or even capitalist-economy' and the 'natural economy'. If communal life in an African village breaks up as a result of colonization and if, whilst most of its inhabitants are reduced to begging in shanty towns, some of them being reduced to wage-earning, GDP per head rises considerably, even if production techniques remain unchanged. The extension of the wage system is probably in fact the main driving force behind the rise in GDP throughout the Third World.

Insofar as it is a measure of *gross* product, it also takes in changes in the ratio between 'net product' and 'amortization of fixed capital'. If, given constant labour productivity, peasants or artisans who used to work with their hands or with rudimentary tools are set to work on expensive but badly-used machines, GDP will again rise. The mechanization of the Third World is probably the second most important factor in its growth. The corollary of mechanization is the need to buy equipment goods, and the volume of equipment goods needed rises out of all proportion to the net product.

22. The manufacturing sector is defined as all industry, less mining (and therefore oil), construction, energy and other public services. It is, then, the sector which obeys most strictly the capitalist logic of producing commodities which compete on the world market. Growth in the manufacturing is measured here in volume terms; this index is not affected by the distortions noted above in GDP measurement.

23. Kenya's growth has been the subject of intense debate amongst Anglo-Saxon economists. It is worth noting that the World Bank's *Report on World Development* for 1984 reclassifies Kenya as a 'low-income country'.

24. This is not necessarily true of ship-building, which is a great NIC speciality (Portugal, Yugoslavia, Brazil, South Korea, etc.). Work organization in the NICS (in South Korea, for instance) sometimes involves principles which go beyond Taylorism (quality-control groups, etc.).

25. On changes in world agricultural structures, see R. Green and C. Viau, 'Echanges agro-alimentaires: le poids de la CEE et des Etats-Unis', *Economie prospective internationale*, 1984; A. Mounier, 'Le "Péril blanc". Les Agriculteurs des pays riches: une menace pour le Tiers-Monde', *Agricultures en question*, 6, 1984; L. Tubiana, 'Le Commerce mondiale des produits agricoles: de la régulation globale au fractionnement des marchés', *Economie et société*, vol. 19, no. 6, June 1984.

26. Taking developing countries as a whole (UN classification), the construction industry achieved an annual growth rate of over 9 per cent between 1968 and 1979. In the developed countries, the growth rate fell to below 1 per cent over the same period.

27. For a critique of 'mimetic bias' and an account of how suppliers pressurize the ruling classes of developing countries (including those of China and Tanzania) into buying heavy technology 'because' it is the most modern, see *Revue Tiers-Monde*, no. 100, October-December 1984.

28. A whole range of intermediate situations does of course exist. At one extreme, high-pollution industries are quite simply relocated to, say, Puerto-Rico. At the other, basic industries can be created by 'climbing

the technological ladder', as in South Korea. For studies of the problems involved in running fully-equipped factories in Algeria, and of their inefficiency, see R. Linhart, 'Le "Transfert de technologie" et ses contradictions: quelques aspects de l'industrialisation algérienne', *Revue française d'administration publique*, no. 4, October 1977; C. Palloix, 'Un Essai sur la formation de la classe ouvrière algérienne (1936-1978), *Revue Tiers-Monde*, no. 83, July 1980. Brazil, an NIC in which 'import-substitution' plays an important role, distinguished itself in the field of 'upstream-substitution'; the dictatorship indulged in costly 'Pharaonic projects', but it is Brazilian democracy that has been left to pick up the bill.

29. M. Arbella, 'Les Migrations de travailleurs d'Asie du Sud et du Sud-Est: questions de politique générale', *Revue Internationale du travail*, July 1984.

30. Lemperière, 'La Restructuration des échanges commerciaux', *Economie et société*, vol. 19, no. 6, June 1984.

31. Tubiana, 'Le Commerce mondial ...'. To give a caricatural example: Volkswagen of Brasil produces both cars that can run on alcohol for the home market and Beetles for the world market. It also recently acquired 100,000 hectares of land for export-oriented ranching.

32. See K. Vergopolous, 'Les Politiques de transnationalisation des aliments', *Amérique Latine*, July 1984; J.P. Bertrand, C. Laurent and V. Leclercq, *Le Monde du soja*, Paris 1984. It is becoming apparent that the new-style agro-export orientation adopted by some countries in the South has catastrophic effects on their ability to feed themselves. There is no mechanical connection between cause and effect, but it is mediated via the land question, as small-holdings once reserved for food crops are taken over for cash crops. Cf. Linhart's excellent *Le Sucre et la faim*, Paris 1984 (Linhart also describes the effects of the existence of 'centre-periphery' relations inside Brazil itself) and Coriat, *Alcohol*, Paris 1982.

33. It can also take the form of an 'intra-tertiary' division. China, for instance, now translates software from one language to another for Californian firms on a sub-contracting basis.

34. A new sub-contracting Level-2 industry is now rising from the ruins of Britain's old industries. It is dominated by American and Japanese electronics, machine-tools and by the motor industry. The 'wafer' industry in Scotland's Silicon Glen is a typical example. ('Wafers' are blocks of silicon used to make 'chips').

35. A wealth of statistics drawn from UN, World Bank, OECD and IMF sources, and from CEPII's CHELEM data bank will be found in P. Judet, R. Chaponière and A. Gaule, 'Les Nouveaux Pays Industriels dans l'évolution du commerce mondial', *Monde en développement*, no. 39, 1982; Lempeière, 'La Restructuration ...', and Carlos Ominami, *Les Transformations dans la crise des rapports Nord-Sud*, Thesis, Université de Paris-X, 1984.

Most of the statistics we will be using make no distinction between the state-capitalist countries of Eastern Europe and the rest of the 'North'. The state-capitalist countries have in fact only a minor share of world trade; their share of trade with the South is small and *falls* over the period under consideration here. Between 1973 and 1982, Eastern-bloc imports fell from 9.9 to 9.4 per cent of world trade; Eastern-bloc exports fell from 10 to 9.4 per cent. Eastern-bloc imports from non-o PEC developing countries rose from 0.8 to 1 per cent at a time when o- PEC exports rose from 11.9 to 14.2 per cent of world trade; exports to OPEC countries rose from 1 to 1.2 per cent at a time when OPEC imports rose from 14.5 to 17 per cent of world trade.

36. Palloix makes this claim with an enthusiasm which could well have been devoted to better causes in his *De la socialisation*. According to Palloix, equipment goods exported to the developing countries are simply delivered and absorbed 'like any other commodity'. They will not function as fixed capital, because there is no 'collective social worker' trained to use them. On the other hand, the debts contracted by the countries involved have to be paid for in primary goods, or with emigrant labour. Thus, it is always the 'old division of labour', with primary goods being exchanged for manufactures! The fact that these manufactures have a theoretical use-value as means of production does nothing to alter the situation, according to Palloix: in macroeconomic terms, there is no difference between them and arms! This is an attractive argument, and it does contain a grain of truth. We have used similar arguments with reference to the difficulties involved in 'transfers of technology' and to the poor productivity of fully-equipped factories. But the reader must surely now agree than Palloix's position relies upon an unwarranted extrapolation.

37. In some level-2 activities they are also competing within the North itself. South Korea's shipyards are now the second biggest in the world, and South Korea will soon be competing with Japan for sales of video recorders. Brazil is exporting executive aircraft to the USA (which represents one third of the world market for thirty-seater aircraft) and selling Xingus to the French military. The USA now has to protect itself against Brazilian cast iron and steel tubes, and has even bought a rolling mill from Brazil's Vilares. All these developments are as yet marginal, but they do indicate the limitations of certain theorizations of the 'new international division of labour'.

38. IFRI, *Rapport Annuel mondial sur le système économique et les stratégies*, Paris 1982; P. Judet, *Les Nouveaux Pays Industriels*, Paris 1982.

39. Gauthier, *Les Pays ateliers*.

40. A number of papers presented at the American Economic Association's 1982 Conference were devoted to the issue of the development of an *endogenous* technology in peripheral Fordist countries. See *Journal of Development Economics*, vol. 16, nos. 1-2, September 1984. These papers show that industrial growth in the NICs would have been impossible were it not for technological research into the adaptation of imported technologies. As a result of this research, the productivity of direct workers rose steadily. The presence of 'level-1' activities is essential if even a peripheral Fordism is to develop. The extent to which such activities are successful varies, but the need for local output to compete on the world market acts as a stimulus (this did not happen with early import-substitution policies). At a later stage, they can be exported or 'transferred' to less developed countries.

41. Benabou, 'La Corée du Sud ...'.
42. See, however, Ominami's remarkable, but by definition debatable attempt to provide such a typology in his *La Transformation dans la crise* ... Ominami identifies five model regimes in the South, and then discusses the *different* dynamics which led to the crisis within them.
43. Nicos Poulantzas, *La Crise des dictatures*, Paris 1975.
44. F. Frobel, J. Heinrichs and O. Kreyes, *The New International Division of Labour*, Cambridge and Paris 1980; D. Ernst ed., *The New International Division of Labour, Technology and Underdevelopment: Consequences for the Third World*, Frankfurt 1980.
45. A remarkable summary of these debates will be found in *Revue d'économie industrielle*, no. 14, 4ième trimestre 1980 (special issue on 'Vers une nouvelle division internationale du travail?'). W. Andreff's contribution represents a variant on the new orthodoxy, whilst Bernadette Madeuf takes a more qualified view. J.L. Reiffers stresses the *local* 'societal' changes that have to take place if the new international division of labour is to be established, and J.P. Angelier shows the limitations of the policy of simply relocating productive segments (and that this policy was being abandoned by 1975). In their contributions, J. Brasseul, P. Judet and A. Benachenchou stress the importance of state strategies in Brazil, Korea and Algeria respectively.
46. The following account is based upon the tireless efforts of research workers at the Centre d'Etudes et de Recherches sur les Entreprises Multinationales, and upon their numerous publications: Bernadette Madeuf and Carlos Ominami, 'Crise et investissement international', *Revue économique*, 5, 1983; Madeuf and Ominami, 'Nouvelle DIT et keynesianisme planétaire: la fin des illusions', *Economie appliquée*, vol. 19, no. 6, June 1984; Madeuf and Ominami, 'L'Accumulation internationale dans les années 1975-1980', *Espaces et sociétes*, no. 44, January 1984; Charles-Albert Michalet, M. Delapierre, Bernadette Madeuf and Carlos Ominami, *Nationalisation et internationalisation*; Ominami, *Les Transformations dans la crise* ....
47. The investment of minimal amounts of new money is not the multinationals' only contribution to the formation of fixed capital, as both they and local firms can obtain money by borrowing either on the spot or on the world market. See D. de Laubier, 'Les Investissements internationaux: quels changements pour les années 1980?', *Economie prospective internationale*, no 12, 1982.
48. C. Oman, *New Forms of Investment in Developing Countries*, Paris 1981.
49. *Fortune*'s 'top 500' list for 1980 (companies are ranked in order of income) includes 32 Third World companies. Of the top one hundred, eight are Third World companies; they are all oil companies, with the exception of Korea's Hyundai. South Korean foreign investment reached $235 billion in 1980.
50. Michalet, *Le Capitalisme mondial*.
51. Michalet et al, *Nationalisation et internationalisation*. North American companies explain their direct investments in similar terms. D. Nayyar, 'Transnational Corporations and Manufactured Exports from Poor Countries', *The Economics Journal*, March 1978, shows that in

almost all countries, us multinationals have less than an 8 per cent
share in exports of manufactures. However, his data only goes up to
1974.
52. Madeuf and Ominami, '*Nouvelle DIT* ...'.
53. In the case of the 'new inter-*regional* division of labour', it would be
correct to say that it is primarily determined by the internal division of
labour within branches and branch-circuits (within firms, and between
firms and sub-contractors). A Thomson assembly plant in a town in the
west of France has no particular relationship with the regional market.
See *Le Capital et son espace.*
54. CEPREMAP, *Redéploiement industriel....* See R. Prud'homme, 'Les
Investissements des multinationales de l'automobile dans le Tiers-
Monde', *Revue d'économie industrielle,* no. 29, 3ième trimestre 1984.
55. J. Perrin, *Les Tranferts de technologie,* Paris 1983.
56. I.e. the super-profits an individual capitalist can make by using more
productive technology, provided that wage-norms do not vary. The
extra surplus-value is absorbed by falling prices or rising wages. Under
peripheral Fordism or primitive Taylorization, it is divided in varying
proportions between: rising profits for exporter firms (in the South),
higher margins for importers (in the North), increased purchasing
power for end clients (in the North), and increased purchasing-power
for producers (in the South).
57. C. Palloix, 'L'Economie de crédit international', in *La France et le Tiers-
Monde,* Grenoble 1979.
58. Ibid., cf. CEPII, 'Vers des limites financières à la croissance'; de J.C.
Barthélemy, D. Besnainou, A. Brender, P. Ewenczyk, *Economie prospective internationale,* no. 3, 1980; C.-A. Michalet, 'La Dimension
monétaire et financière du capitalisme mondial', in *Les Eurocrédits: un
instrument du système bancaire pour le financement international,*
Paris 1981.
59. It might be objected that they had no choice, but China and Albania
completely refused to adopt this strategy. India did not fully adopt it.
The main point, and we will return to this, is that not all ruling classes
'chose' to borrow the same things.
60. OECD, *Endettement extérieur des pays en développement. Etude 1983,*
Paris 1984.
61. In the case of export credits, the bank also prevalidates the output of
the export company. As credits are usually guaranteed by a state institution in the exporter State (Coface in the case of France), we could
even say that the commodities exported are pseudovalidated. In other
words, it has found a 'provisionally definitive' social validation.
62. More complex combinations are also possible. See H. Hirata and J.
Humphrey, 'Economic Crisis and the Sexual Division of Labour: The
Case of Brazil', *Capital and Class,* no 24, Winter 1985.

5. Peripheral Fordism in Southern Europe

1. Poulantzas, *La Crise des dictatures.*

2. Initially, the internal bourgeoisie gambled on the possibility that the dictatorships would change from within; this seemed most likely to happen in Spain and Portugal, which had the oldest dictatorships and were, moreover, originally supported by a very different social bloc. This was the political meaning of the shift from Opus Dei to Arias Navarro, from Salazar to Caetano.

3. It is significant that, in an interview with *Libération* (22 February 1985), South Korean opposition leader Kim Dae-Jung also referred to the West German model.

4. For France, see the works already cited; for Italy, see the writings of the *operaista* current (Panzieri, Tronti, Negri ...).

5. Cf. Braudel, *Capitalism and Material Life*; Wallerstein, *The Modern World-System*.

6. It will be recalled that when Gramsci advanced the notion of 'Fordism', he linked it with 'Americanism'.

7. CEPREMAP, *Redéploiement industriel*; Alain Lipietz, *L'audace et l'enlisement*, Paris 1984.

8. France, Japan and Italy had an advantage over the future NICs in that they were old industrial powers (during the 'war of the English succession', France and Japan had even challenged the hegemonic ambitions of Germany and the USA respectively). And as their elites had lost the Second World War, they found themselves under the leadership of 'developmentalist' technocrats who were themselves American-influenced. For a possible explanation of the differences between Italian and Portuguese fascism, with comments on the difficulties facing the dictatorships in postwar Greece and Turkey, see G. Arrighi, 'From Fascism to Democratic Socialism: Logic and Limits of a Transition', in G. Arrighi, ed., *Semiperipheral Development: The Politics of Southern Europe in the Twentieth Century*. Beverley Hills 1985.

9. Braudel, *The Mediterranean; Capitalism*.

10. Emigration from Greece during this dark period strengthened the *Koiné*, the transnational community which is scattered throughout the Atlantic world and the Middle East. The *Koiné* was subsequently to prove a source of strength.

11. On the development of heavy engineering in Portugal, see F. Patriarca, 'Taylor no Purghatorio. O Trabahlo Operaio na Metalmecanica Pesada', *nalise Social*, no. 2, 1985.

12. It should be recalled that, in terms of the 'old' international division of labour, Portugal was *also* a metropolis with a colonial empire.

13. The only countries in which 'textiles and clothing' have a higher share of exports than in Greece (17 per cent) are Portugal (27), Bangladesh (49), Pakistan (37) and India (22), Tunisia (18), Korea (29) and Hong Kong (17). Bangladesh, Pakistan and India export relatively little; Tunisia, South Korea and Hong Kong export over 39 per cent of their GDP.

14. Cf. Table 4. The following comments are partly based upon the more detailed account given by F. Freire de Souza in his remarkable *Contrainte extérieure et régulation macroéconomique dans les economies semi-industrialisées; le cas de Portugal*, Thesis, Université de Paris-I, 1983 (mimeo).

15. Similarly, it will also buy different amounts at different times. 'International value' is to spatial disparities what 'volume' is to diachronic developments. The 'theory of indices', however, is much more complex. See 'Comparaison en valeurs réelles des agrégats du Systéme Européen de Comptabilité', *Eurostat* (Luxemburg), 1977.
16. This does not simply mean that Portugal's position in the inter-European division of labour had deteriorated. The loss of a colonial empire also has to be taken into account. When it lost its empire, Portugal also lost a guaranteed market for itᵤ 'bottom of the range, and middle-range' manufactures.
17. The fact that the ratios remain constant over both sub-periods masks the fact that real wages rose rapidly after 25 April 1974 ... and the fact that they were 'normalized' after 25 November 1975.
18. Greek unit wage costs were also increased by political events, and were rectified by devaluation a year later. Expressed in 'international currency', they rose by 13 per cent in 1974, when the colonels were overthrown, and by 11 per cent in 1982, when PASOK came to power. See *Economie européenne* (Luxemburg), No 5, March 1983.
19. Freire de Souza, *Contrainte extérieure* ...
20. Portugal's inter-regional structure resembles the old inter-regional division of labour, but the uneven distribution of forms of exploitation does not mean that we have to retheorize supposedly explanatory 'centre-periphery' relations within the Nation-State. As J. Ferrao and C. Jensen-Butler point out in their 'The Centre-Periphery Model and Industrial Development in Portugal', *Environment and Planning*, vol. 2, 1984, observable structures are the result and not the cause of development. This is of course always the case.

6. From the Configuration of Success to Crises in Peripheral Fordism

1. For this notion of transformation within the world configuration, see Michel Aglietta, 'Capitalism in the Eighties', *New Left Review*, no. 136, November–December 1982.
2. Lipietz, *The Enchanted World*.
3. In both countries, the level of manufacturing productivity is lower than in the USA, but in terms of wage purchasing-power, they are catching up. But as CEPII, 'Dualité, change ...' points out, it is well known that productivity gains in American industry (which were in any case slight during this period) were eroded by rapid growth in the sheltered tertiary sector. Even though the dollar was under-valued, Europe could therefore compete reasonably well.
4. CEPII, '*Economie mondial 1980-1990* ....
5. This is, it will be recalled, the best available index of organic composition. It indicates the ratio of value-added to fixed capital, both expressed in volume terms. If, then, productivity gains in both Departments are broadly similar, changes in the capital coefficient will be very similar to changes in the value ratio between value-added and

fixed capital. It does not, of course, take into account the changing cost of circulating capital.

6. This is a rough index of the rate of profit, and indicates the ratio between the gross before tax corporate profit and the gross stock of capital. The figures are taken from *Perspectives de l'OCDE*, December 1984.

7. The case of Venezuela is extremely interesting in that it provides the only example of an early import-substitution policy being followed up as a result of the terms of trade being reversed. The fact that it bene-fitted from the oil shock and was still hit by the crisis shows that the terms of trade were not the main problem. Cf. Hausmann, *State Landed Property ...*', and Hausman and Marquez, 'Accumulation et crise ...'.

8. According to A. Aroyo and M. Fouet, 'Les Petrodollars, une réserve liquide en voie d'assèchement', *Observations et diagnostiques économiques*, no. 10, January 1985, the accumulated mass of petro-dollars was distributed as follows at the end of 1981: contributions to international organizations: 5 per cent; direct loans to developing countries 15 per cent; investment in OECD countries: (shares and especially US government securities): 40%; liquid bank deposits: 40 per cent.

9. For a theoretical analysis of the 'multiplier' (or rather the 'divisor') effect of the ratio of the total new credits a bank can issue to the total amount of 'official' currency (in this case dollars) it holds, see *The Enchanted World*. A very good introduction to the concrete mech-anisms of the international credit economy will be found in P. Arnaud, *La Dette du Tiers Monde*, Paris 1984.

     Some authors claim that the Euro-market has no real multiplier effect. If that were the case, primary Eurodollars would provide the only supply of finance (though it would still be a considerable supply). This position is, however, rather dubious in that there is no equivalent within the Euromarket to the regulation of liquid coefficients which applies within national monetary spaces. The liquidity of Eurobanks is a matter for their own judgement as to their ability to mobilize dollars to cover their commitments. The only limitation imposed upon them is the rate of interest at which the American Federal Reserve System itself lends dollars. For this whole debate, see IFRI, *Rapport Annuel mondial 1982 ...*, and F. Chesnais, 'Quelques Remarques sur le contexte mon-dial de la dette des pays en développement et la nature du capital prêté', *Revue Tiers-Monde*, no. 99, July 1984.

     Regardless of whether or not they had a multiplier effect, oil rents were certainly re-lent (and even over-lent) and therefore stimulated world demand, perhaps to an unreasonable extent. Emmanuel's claim to the effect that the increase in oil rents had a deflationary effect in his 'L'Endettement ...' is all the more astonishing in that in his earlier *Le Profit et les crises*, (Paris, 1976) he explains crises in terms of under-consumption, and in that he is by no means unaware of Malthus's argument that rent increases have a positive effect. As he himself puts it, the increase in oil rents not only stimulated 'ability to buy', but also encouraged a 'desire to buy' and even 'over-trading'.

10. For an account of the astonishing 'international surplus liquidity' phase

which followed the first oil shock, see 'Recyclers' Recession', *The Economist*, 7 August 1982. Between 1974 and 1978, total new loans issued by the major western banks rose from $280 billion to $900 billion. Bankers were literally laying siege to potential borrowers.

11. Michalet, 'La Dimension monétaire ...'.
12. Ominami, *Les Transformations dans la crise*.
13. For a remarkably clear historical analysis, see the World Bank's, *Report on World Development*, 1984.
14. There is a fairly close correlation between rising income and a decline in the mortality rate. The correlation between rising income and the fall in the birth rate is not so marked, as the effect of political and cultural factors (birth control, etc.) is less clear. China, for instance, has been able to reduce its fertility rate considerably, but in Algeria the rate remains both constant and very high.
15. In the developed industrial countries, what demographers term the 'dependency rate' varied from between 50 to 60 per cent in the period 1960-80. In West Germany, it reached a low of 47 per cent in 1960; since then, it has increased as the working population has become older. In both the USA and France, it is falling as the active population becomes younger. In the NICS, there appears to be a correlation between economic success and the dependency rate. Between 1960 and 1980, the dependency rate fell from 80 to 45 per cent in Hong Kong and Singapore, from 86 to 60 per cent in Korea, from 86 to 72 per cent in Brazil, from 96 to 93 per cent in Mexico, and rose from 91 to 104 per cent in Algeria.
16. For an assessment of 'volatility' in US subsidiaries producing semiconductors which have relocated to NICS, and of the effect of wage increases and political risks, see Flamm, 'The Volatility of Off-Shore Investment', *Journal of Development Economics*, no. 16, 1984. Although relocation can be achieved rapidly and cheaply, it appears to be weakly affected by moderate wage rises.
17. M. Ikonicoff, 'Technologie et modèle de consommation dans le Tiers-Monde', *Revue économique*, no. 4, July 1973; P. Salama, 'Endettement et disette urbaine', *Espaces et sociétés*, no. 44, July 1984.
18. J.R. Chaponnière, 'La République de Corée', *Notes et études documentaires*, no 4667-4668, May 1982.
19. J. Brasseul, 'Internationalisation de l'industrie brésillienne depuis 1964', *Notes et études documentaires*, nos. 4675-4676, July 1982.
20. Wells, 'The Diffusion of Durables in Brazil and Its Implications for Recent Controversies Concerning Brazilian Development', *Cambridge Journal of Economics*, vol. 1, no. 3, 1977.
21. Very schematically, a *fichado* (registered) sugar-cane worker can earn a minimum wage of a dollar a day (the fluctuations depend upon the date of indexation) during the six-months harvest period. An urban worker who is employed throughout the year and who earns twice the minimum wage is four times better off. A worker in a car factory can earn up to the equivalent of six minimum wages. Those who earn the equivalent of fifty minimum wages are referred to as 'the middle classes'. One can only speculate as to the meaning of 'the upper classes' ....

22. The splits can even extend to within the working class; significantly the Workers' Party (which is based upon the new proto-Fordist workers of the São Paolo area) has difficulty in finding support amongst the peasantry. This was also one of the major problems facing the Portuguese Revolution.

23. Chaponnière, 'La République de Corée'.

24. As Claude Julien points out in his 'L'Empire du dollar', *Le Monde diplomatique*, February 1985, 'The USA has one twelfth the population of the Third World, and seven times its debts.' In more general terms, Emmunuel notes in his 'L'endettement' that future 'centres' always start by contracting debts with old centres. Holland borrowed from northern Italy; England borrowed from Holland (which accounted for three fifths of its national debt in the eighteenth century); and the USA borrowed from England in the second half of the nineteenth century. At that time, the US debt/GDP ratio was higher than that of modern Brazil or Mexico.

25. Clear analyses can be found in P. Arnaud, 'Le Dollar et la dette du Tiers-Monde', *Revue Tiers-Monde*, no. 99, July 1984 and Ominami, *Les Transformations . . . .*

26. In 1973 and 1977, Brazil had no balance of trade problem. In 1982, it had a trade surplus of $1.2 billion. In other years, the deficit was roughly $2 billion. South Korea had a constant deficit during this period (again of some $2 billion).

27. M. Santos Filho, 'Le Financement du projet de Carajas et le secteur des biens de production au Brésil', *Revue Tiers-Monde*, no. 99, July 1984.

28. It is, however, true that the conditions attached to cheap IMF loans induced some countries – particularly those which want to develop a home market – to turn systematically to the banks.

29. The apparent rate of interest (the annual rate payable on the total debt) for fixed-rate debts was 4.5 per cent in 1972. It rose to 6 per cent in 1980 (and therefore rose less than the rate of inflation). The rate for variable rate debts rose from 8.3 per cent to 12.3 in 1979 and to 15.5 in 1980 (the year of the first monetarist shock). It reached 17.4 per cent in 1981. Figures from OECD, *L'Endettement extérieur . . . .*

30. J. Le Dem and J. Pisani-Ferry, 'Crise et politiques économiques dans les grandes économies industrielles: permanence et changement', *Critiques de l'économie politique*, nos. 26-27, January 1984.

31. Bernadette Madeuf, Charles-Albert Michaelt and Carlos Ominami, 'D'Une Crise internationale à une crise mondiale', *Critiques de l'économie politiques*, no 26-27, January 1984.

32. For a remarkable description of the volatility of orthodoxy in the higher spheres of the international economics intelligentsia by an OECD 'super-expert', see S. Marris, 'Apprendrons-nous jamais à gérer l'économie mondiale?', *Economie prospective internationale*, no. 19, 3ième trimestre 1984.

33. The general downturn, which began in 1979 in the USA and which affected virtually all countries during the 1980 recession, allowed the USA to master its current balance of payments (−$12 billion in 1977 and 1978: +$2.6 billion in 1979; +$6.6 billion in 1980 – despite the oil shock). Germany and France limit their deficits in 1980 (−$8.3 billion

and −$2.5 respectively). Japan, which was, as we shall see, pursuing a policy of expansion, had a surplus of $17 billion in 1978, but a deficit of $8 billion in 1980 and $10 billion in 1981.

34. M.F. Toinet, 'Coûteuse "reprise", persistant déclin', *Le Monde diplomatique*, January 1985.
35. For a fuller analysis of monetarism, see *The Enchanted World*.
36. The 'theory of productive forces' is a vulgar version of historical materialism, though it can be found in certain texts by Marx himself (such as the 1859 'Preface' to *A Contribution to The Critique of Political Economy*). In the sixties and seventies, it came under heavy criticism from the French Althusserians, the Italian *operaista* current and from English and American 'radicals'. Both Marxists and radicals adopted the view that it is social relations that determine forms of production, or that there is at least a non-mechanical dialectical relationship between the two.

The same could be said of relations between regimes of accumulation and modes of regulation, or of those between models of industrialization and industrial relations. Curiously enough, it is now non-Marxist writers and politicians who talk about new industrial revolutions which obey only their technological logic and who claim that social relations will either have to adapt to them or be dissolved (one thinks, for instance, of the 'revolutions' in electronics, computers, biological engineering ...).

37. Lipietz, *L'Audace ou l'enlisement*.
38. The USA had a trade surplus for three years, thanks to the recession: $2.6 billion in 1979, $6.6 billion in 1980 and $10.7 billion in 1981. Symmetrically, and despite the second oil shock, the OPEC countries had to dig deeper into their reserves. By 1981, they were already drawing heavily on reserves held in bank deposits outside the USA: $35 billion were withdrawn. Cf. Aroyo and Fouet, 'Les Pétrodollars ...'.
39. By using existing macroeconomic models of the world economy (LINK, EUROLINK, INTERLINK and COMET III), Lenormand and Vallet attempt to quantify certain aspects of this chain of events in their article, 'Les Responsabilités de la politique monétaire américaine dans les difficultés économiques mondiales', *Economie prospective internationale*, 1984. In the EEC, for example, American monetary policies resulted in a 3 per cent fall in economic activity between 1979 and 1982. This can be broken down as follows: contraction of the US market: −0.5 per cent; rising interest rates: −2.1 per cent; worsening conditions in the developing countries: −0.6 per cent.
40. Lemperière, 'Les Difficultés de la construction et des grands travaux: symptôme de la crise dans le Tiers-Monde', *Revue Tiers-Monde*, no. 99, July 1984.
41. W.R. Cline, *International Debt and the Stability of the World Economy*, Washington 1983.
42. Hausmann, *State Landed Property*.
43. This too was due to oil, and it obviously had negative effects on non-oil-exporting NICs. It was, however, simply one factor amongst others, and it was not necessarily the determining factor. The long-term terms of trade of 'major developing countries exporting manufactures'

deteriorated by 1.1 per cent per year between 1967 and 1976. In 1977, they improved by 5 per cent, but in both 1978 and 1981 they deteriorated by 3.3 and 3.4 per cent respectively (the dates mean that this was not because of the oil shock). During the oil shock, they deteriorated by 2.8 per cent in 1979 and by 6.8 per cent in 1980. See the IMF's *Report* for 1984.

44. Significantly, *The Economist* (30 April 1983) used the sub-heading 'An Orgy of Credit' to describe banking trends in the seventies; another article on Latin America ('Where the Money Went') lays great stress on the squandering of credits.

45. *The Enchanted World.*

46. For a more detailed analysis of changes in American monetary policy and of its mechanisms, see V. Coudert, 'Une Dynamique des taux d'intérêts élevés aux Etats-Unis', *Economie prospective internationale*, premier trimestre 1984.

47. This may be debatable in terms of the long-term rates, but the revision of the short-term rates is perfectly justified. The figures used here are taken from *Bulletin du Centre d'Information sur l'Epargne et le Crédit*, no. 69, January 1985.

48. As this book is devoted to peripheral Fordism, only countries caught up in its logic are discussed here. The debt crisis did, however, effect virtually all Third World countries, regardless of their regimes of accumulation. Venezuela, Chile and Argentina (which are not involved in the logic of peripheral Fordism, and which had very high debts in both relative and absolute terms) were badly hit, as were 'small' countries like Bolivia, which have very high debts but which make little impact on the banks. There is no point in going into the painful details of renegotiation here, as the information available will be out of date when this book appears. A partial account (of the renegotiation of Latin America's debts in 1984) will be found in *Problèmes d'Amérique Latine, Notes et études documentaires*, no. 4768, 1984.

49. The share of the Federal Budget devoted to defence spending rose from 25 to 36 per cent (the level at which it stood at the end of the war in Vietnam) between 1981 and 1986. Welfare spending fell from 10.3 to 7.7 per cent, and other transfers fell from 8.3 to 4.3 per cent. Once again, I refer to industrial output (Graph 3). I have already given my reasons for doing so: what significance are we to attach to a rise in GDP which is due to more people taking jobs as janitors? It will be noted that the GDP curve is in fact very similar to the industrial output curve, with recessions being smoothed out. It is as though nonproductive activity in the commodity sector automatically compensated for the recessions. Research into the statistical effects of contemporary forms of capitalist regulation would no doubt produce fascinating results.

50. The USA created 5.8 million jobs between December 1982 and August 1984. But the share of the manufacturing sector fell in both absolute and relative terms (−21 per cent). The average working week in the tertiary sector is now less than thirty-two hours. Half the jobs created were in the domestic service sector. Wage-earners working for only a few hours per week either began to take jobs which had previously

been within the domestic sector (fast food) or which redistributed income which had already been distributed (janitoring). I leave the task of establishing the status of these activities to theoreticians working on non-productive labour, but I would point out that it is not dissimilar to that of semi-formal labour in Brazil.

51. In 1984, the cumulative public sector debt reached $1,573 billion. Household debts totalled $1,832 billion, and company debts reached $2,589 billion.

52. From the nineteenth century onwards, rates hovered at between 2 and 4 per cent. I analyse the underlying reasons for the rise, which is characteristic of a crisis in monopolistic regulation, in my *The Enchanted World*. How can anyone contract debts when interest rates are so high? Interest on house purchases is of course tax-deductible, and businesses are ploughing more of their profits back into investment, but one can only assume that the agents involved believe that inflation is likely to take off again in the medium term. Inflation has of course fallen considerably as a result of stagnating unit wage costs and because the rising dollar implies 'falling inflation rates' through importations. (Cf. CEPII, *Economie mondiale* ...). This implies too that the price of American products rises very quickly on the world market.

53. By 1984, credit was already widely distrusted in the USA. Continental Illinois collapsed completely and was effectively nationalized by an injection of $7.5 billion from the federal guarantee system. Other banks are also in difficulty as their loans to the Third World, and to American farmers, the American construction industry and the energy sector are not flowing back. Their losses on these loans are now almost equivalent to their net income, and the net income of the three biggest banks is itself falling. The total sums involved in non-performing loans (which become bad debts when debt-servicing is suspended) is thirty to forty times greater. On 11 May 1984, dealers who had bought $5 millions in treasury bonds realized that they could not find buyers, and had to unload the bonds as cheaply as possible. In 1985, failures of local banks and thrift institutions continued to increase.

54. Marie-France Toinet, 'Coûteuse "reprise"'; Philippe Lefournier, 'Pourquoi Reagan a réussi: parce qu'il est aux Etats-Unis', *L'Expansion*, no. 297, 19 October 1984.

55. See 'The Rewards of the Dollar's Rise – and the Risks', *The Financial Times*, 24 September 1984.

56. Benjamin Coriat, 'L'Automobile, le dollar et la réindustrialisation', *L'Economie en question*, no. 30, premier trimestre 1985.

57. Differences between the present crisis and the period 1930-45 mean that capitalism may well be able to emerge from the crisis by moving 'to the right'. It is, however, unlikely that growth based upon non-productive labour and upon the polarization of skills (as opposed to the mobilization of *all* skills) can provide a real way out of the crisis in Fordism, even for capitalism. See Lipietz, *L'Audace ou l'enlisement*.

58. See Graph 3. Taking 1970 as a base of 100, by mid-1984, Japan had reached an index of 170, the US 160, Italy and France 140, Germany 120, and Great Britain 110. No European country has reached the 'high point' of the first configuration (1979).

59. Japan has had a trade surplus since 1981 ($22 billion in 1983 and $35 billion in 1984). In the last four years it has been able to lend $130 billion to the rest of the world (most of it to the USA).

60. Fédération Européenne de Recherches Economiques, *L'Evolution du rapport salarial en Europe*, 1984.

61. CEPII, *Economie mondiale* ....

62. As we have seen, in 1980, the inflow of capital into the South fell below the level of debt-service. The difference between debt-service and total new debt (long and short term) in non-oil developing countries reached $13.7 billion in 1981, $50 billion in 1982 and $12 billion in 1983.

63. The expression is borrowed from Teresa Braga who, after a debate on 'Bloody Taylorization' took me to visit an Agreste Nordestin village. For a general account of the human effects of the monetarist shock – and of its effects on health and children in particular – see K.N. Raj, 'The Cause and Consequences of World Recession', *World Development*, vol. 12, no. 3, March 1984.

64. On the ambiguous relations between local governments, experts and the IMF, and for an analysis of the disastrous effects of IMF policy in general, see *Archimède et Léonard*, no. 1 (*Carnets de L'Association Internationale des Techniciens, Experts et Chercheurs*, available from 14 place de Rungis, 75013 Paris).

65. CEPII, *Economie mondiale* ... .

66. L'Heriteau, 1983.

67. CEPII, *Economie mondiale* ... .

68. *L'Audace ou l'enlisement.* The same orthodox liberals who insist that the Third World must revalue claim that devaluation would have no positive effect in France ('Because the J curve ...', 'Because the theorem of critical elasticity proves that ...'). It is in fact the other way round. So much for the politicians' competence in economics.

69. Arnaud, 'Le Dollar ...'.

70. Michel Aglietta and A. Orléan, *La Violence de la monnaie*, Paris 1982.

71. A.B. Castro, 'Ajustement et adaptation structurelle: l'expérience brésilienne', *Problèmes de l'Amérique Latine. La Documentation française*, no. 4768, Decmber 1984.

72. As Belluzo and Tavares point out in an unpublished manuscript, wage agreements fix the price of labour over at least a month (or even six months), whereas the financial market changes from day to day.

73. T. Gylfason and O. Risager, 'Does Devaluation Improve the Current Account?', *European Economic Review*, no. 25, 1984.

74. M. Fouquin, 'Corée du Sud. Une Clef pour sortir de la crise', *Le Monde*, 22 December 1984.

75. Aldo Ferrer, 'Dette, souveraineté et démocratie en Amérique Latine', *Problèmes de l'Amérique Latine. La Documentation française*, no. 4768, December 1984.

76. P. Salama, 'Endettement et accentuation de la misère', *Revue Tiers-Monde* 99, July 1984.

77. Castro, 'Ajustement ...'.

78. It must be stressed that it is not only imports of luxuries for the beneficiaries of 'excluding regimes' which fall. In 1981-82, Mexico reduced

its food imports by 61 per cent. Agricultural output itself fell by 10 per cent ... . It should also be noted that Latin American GDP is falling much more slowly than imports. The situation is not as resistant to import-substitution as CEPII fears (cf. *Economie mondiale* ...).

79. M. Fouet, 'Les Avenirs inégalement sombres des pays en voie de développement', *Observations et diagnostiques économiques* 7, April 1984.

80. Cf note 44 above.

81. In 1982, the share of manufacturing industry in Chile's GDP fell to 1960 levels (22 per cent), in Argentina, it fell from 32 to 25 per cent.

82. R. Pringle, 'How Developing Countries are Coping with their Debt', *The Banker*, December 1982. The article begins by stressing that the NICs' strategy of deficit-financed growth was quite applicable in the 1970s and had some positive effects.

83. Ominami, *Les Transformations* ...

84. In France, it is possible that Crédit Agricole will be taken to court by the peasants and co-operatives it induced to bankruptcy by giving them unreasonable loans. Similarly, a consumer who is being harassed by a door-to-door salesman has the right to break a credit agreement within a set period of time should the article he has purchased prove to be unsuitable.

85. R. Knieper, 'Transfert de techniques juridiques aux questions de l'endettement des pays du Tiers-Monde', *Revue Tiers-Monde*, 99, July 1984.

86. André Gunder Frank, 'Quand les solutions apparentes deviennent de réels problèmes', *Revue Tiers-Monde* 99, July 1984; C. Jedlicki, 'De l'impossibilité du remboursement de la dette à l'indispensable remboursement des banques', ibid.

87. According to *Kredietbank's Weekly Bulletin* of 16 and 23 November 1984, the debt already stood at $700 billion in 1984.

88. H. Elsenhans, 'Endettement: échec d'une industrialisation du Tiers-Monde', *Revue Tiers-Monde* 99, July 1984.

89. J. Coussy, 'Aspects internationaux de la crise', forthcoming in *Cahiers de l'ISMEA*.

90. F. Chesnais, 'Quelques remarques sur le contexte mondial de la dette des pays en développement et la nature du capital prêté', *Revue Tiers-Monde*, 99, July 1984.

91. Lipietz, *The Enchanted World*.

92. It has been estimated that French bank losses on non-recoverable debts represent 3 per cent of the real interest rate, which stands at between 6 and 7 per cent.

93. S. Mounier and C. Passadeos, 'Gestion de l'insécurité financière et comportement des banques', *Revue Tiers-Monde* 99, July 1984.

94. According to P. Morel, 'Vers un marché de la dette?', *Le Monde diplomatique*, March 1985, the discount rate on Peru's debts has now reached 50 per cent.

95. Cf. note 87 above.

96. This is the title of a dossier by Paul Fabra, *Le Monde*, 13 September 1983. Fabra stresses the 'contradictions of the mentor of the debtor nations'. In fact, the IMF 1983 report argues both for extreme internal

austerity and for a loose international monetary policy that would fuel world inflation (according to Fabra).

97. J. Coussy, 'Introduction', *Economie et société*, vol. 19, no. 6, June 1984.

Conclusion

1.   OECD, *The Impact of Newly Industrializing Countries on Production and Trade in Manufactures*, Paris 1979.
2.   Coussy, 'Aspects internationaux ...'.

Index

225